365 QUESTIONS FOR A
Woman's Soul

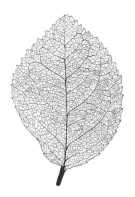

365 QUESTIONS FOR A
Woman's Soul

• • •

with answers from
God's heart

Tyndale House Publishers, Inc.
Carol Stream, Illinois

LIVING EXPRESSIONS™ COLLECTION

Living Expressions invites you to explore God's Word and express your creativity in ways that are refreshing to the spirit and restorative to the soul.

Visit Tyndale online at www.tyndale.com.

TYNDALE, Tyndale's quill logo, and *LeatherLike* are registered trademarks of Tyndale House Publishers, Inc. *Living Expressions* and the Living Expressions logo are trademarks of Tyndale House Publishers, Inc.

365 Questions for a Woman's Soul: With Answers from God's Heart

General editor: Katherine J. Butler

Contributing editors: Ronald A. Beers and Amy Mason

Designed by Ron Kaufmann

Scripture quotations are taken from the *Holy Bible*, New Living Translation, copyright © 1996, 2004, 2015 by Tyndale House Foundation. Used by permission of Tyndale House Publishers, Inc., Carol Stream, Illinois 60188. All rights reserved.

For information about special discounts for bulk purchases, please contact Tyndale House Publishers at csresponse@tyndale.com, or call 1-800-323-9400.

ISBN 978-1-4964-1808-1

Printed in China

24	23	22	21	20	19	18
7	6	5	4	3	2	1

Contents

Introduction

A S WOMEN, we often have a multitude of questions swirling around in our minds. We ask questions of others. (*Where can I meet you? How do you do this? What do you need help with?*) We question ourselves. (*How could I forget to do that? Why did I say that? Why am I feeling this way?*) And sometimes we have deeper questions lingering in our souls. (*Why do so many people have to suffer? If God created me, then why don't I feel beautiful? Why is it so hard to forgive? Why doesn't my husband love me the way I think he should? Why doesn't God seem to care what happens to me?*) This daily devotional asks the deep questions for which a woman's soul longs to find answers.

Sometimes we wonder if asking questions about God, his Word, and his world shows signs of unbelief or doubt in our hearts. And maybe we wonder if there is any point in asking questions of God at all. But when we look at Scripture, we see men and women of great spiritual character asking God questions. When the angel of the Lord appeared to Gideon the prophet, Gideon questioned why God had allowed bad things to happen to his people (Judges 6:12-15). David, whom God called "a man after his own heart" (1 Samuel 13:14), constantly questioned God about why he allowed evil and suffering to occur (Psalm 77). The prophet Habakkuk asked God if he was listening to his pleas and prayers (Habakkuk 1:2). Even Jesus himself questioned his Father at the cross, wondering why God had forsaken him (Matthew 27:46).

Questions are a part of life. And until we reach heaven, we will not see the full picture of God's work on this earth and how it all fits together for good. Some of the questions in this book can be clearly answered if we know where to look in God's Word. Others don't have tidy answers, but by wrestling with them in light of the full counsel of Scripture, we can gain perspective, wisdom, and a better understanding of who God is. Each daily reading begins with a soul-searching question and then provides relevant Bible passages showing us how God has already addressed our questions—either with clear answers or insights we might not have expected. Following the Scripture is a short devotional thought, and then we've included prayer prompts to help you start a conversation with God as you reflect on his Word. We hope these prayer promptings will lead to deeper soul connections with God as you read through this book.

Each day as you read, remember that God welcomes your honest and sincere questions. He promises that if we ask for wisdom, he will gladly give it and will not scold us for asking (James 1:5-6). We pray that no matter what uncertainties come up throughout your life, you would develop the habit of bringing your concerns to God, opening his Word, and allowing your questions to deepen your faith and your knowledge of him.

abandonment

How can I trust that God will never abandon me?

❦

The LORD will not reject his people;
he will not abandon his special possession.
✛ PSALM 94:14

Even if my father and mother abandon me,
the LORD will hold me close.
✛ PSALM 27:10

I will ask the Father, and he will give you another Advocate,
who will never leave you.
✛ JOHN 14:16

Those who know your name trust in you, for you,
O LORD, do not abandon those who search for you.
✛ PSALM 9:10

The LORD will work out his plans for my life—for your faithful love,
O LORD, endures forever. Don't abandon me, for you made me.
✛ PSALM 138:8

AS WOMEN, one of our greatest fears can be the termination of a cherished relationship. Whether abandonment comes through rejection, death, or divorce, we fear being left alone. One of the hardest consequences of being abandoned is the threat to our self-worth. How comforting it is to know that God will never leave us. We know this because he promises it repeatedly in his Word. Take heart that the one who loves you the most will never abandon you.

Prayer Prompts
Lord, I feel tempted to doubt your presence when . . .
When I feel alone, your Word assures me . . .

abilities 🍃

How can I make the most of my abilities?

—————————— ❧ ——————————

[The Lord] takes no pleasure in the strength of a horse or in human might.
+ PSALM 147:10

It is not by force nor by strength, but by my Spirit,
says the Lord of Heaven's Armies.
+ ZECHARIAH 4:6

It is not that we think we are qualified to do anything on our own.
Our qualification comes from God.
+ 2 CORINTHIANS 3:5

All glory to God, who is able, through his mighty power at work within us,
to accomplish infinitely more than we might ask or think.
+ EPHESIANS 3:20

GOD GIVES US special abilities to advance his Kingdom here on earth. Perhaps he has given you leadership ability, made you unusually compassionate, or given you a heart that delights in encouraging others. Your abilities are unique because he chose to give them specifically to you. Abilities give you the potential to do good, while faith gives you the power. Neither potential nor power alone is sufficient; they must work in harmony. If you don't know what your special gifts are, ask him! He promises to answer. Pray for opportunities to use your abilities, and trust God to bring them into your life. All you need to do is wake up each day with a willing heart, be faithful to obey his promptings, and watch God do more than you could ever ask or imagine through your willingness.

Prayer Prompts

Lord, I feel like the special abilities you have given me are . . .
When I feel tempted to trust in my own abilities, your Word reminds me . . .

# abundance

I see God pouring out his love and blessing on others. How can I be sure there is enough for me?

———————— ❧ ————————

May you have the power to understand, as all God's people should, how wide, how long, how high, and how deep his love is. May you experience the love of Christ, though it is too great to understand fully. Then you will be made complete with all the fullness of life and power that comes from God.
+ EPHESIANS 3:18-19

God's law was given so that all people could see how sinful they were. But as people sinned more and more, God's wonderful grace became more abundant.
+ ROMANS 5:20

All humanity finds shelter in the shadow of your wings. You feed them from the abundance of your own house, letting them drink from your river of delights.
+ PSALM 36:7-8

THE GREATER our needs are, the harder it is for us to be generous. When we experience the limits of our time and possessions, our hearts begin to tighten under the pressure. However, that is not the case with God. Because God has no limits, there is more than enough in his economy. The next time you find yourself doubting whether God has enough left over to bless you, take note of all the ways he already has. His blessings may not come in the form of material riches, but perhaps he is blessing you with something much better. He has promised that his love is wide and deep and full, and that it overflows upon you. Open your heart to him and let his love fill you. He is ready to offer you a purposeful, abundant life!

Prayer Prompts

Lord, here are the ways you have blessed me abundantly lately: . . .
Your Word says that you also show your abundant love by . . .

acceptance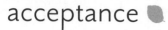

Can God really accept me,
even after all I've done?

❦

*God showed his great love for us by sending Christ
to die for us while we were still sinners.*
+ ROMANS 5:8

*This is a trustworthy saying, and everyone should accept it: "Christ Jesus
came into the world to save sinners"—and I am the worst of them all.*
+ 1 TIMOTHY 1:15

*God showed how much he loved us by sending his one and only
Son into the world so that we might have eternal life through him.
This is real love—not that we loved God, but that he loved us
and sent his Son as a sacrifice to take away our sins.*
+ 1 JOHN 4:9-10

GOD'S ACCEPTANCE is based not on what a person does but on faith in Jesus Christ. Even the most saintly human being is found lacking in comparison to God's holiness. Nothing we do could ever compensate for the sins that have separated us from God, who is perfect. Fortunately, God's forgiveness flows from his love for us, which is why he gave his Son, Jesus, to redeem us before we were even born or had committed our first sins. God's acceptance has been waiting for you your whole life. When you receive his forgiveness, he welcomes you into his presence. What a wonderful moment it is when you realize how fully God accepts you, freeing you from the burden of trying to earn God's love.

Prayer Prompts

*Lord, sometimes it is hard for me to receive your acceptance because . . .
Your Word tells me this is why you accept me: . . .*

❧ accepting forgiveness

How can I get past regrets about things I've done and accept God's forgiveness?

— ❧ —

The kind of sorrow God wants us to experience leads us away from sin and results in salvation. There's no regret for that kind of sorrow.
+ 2 CORINTHIANS 7:10

I—yes, I alone—will blot out your sins for my own sake and will never think of them again.
+ ISAIAH 43:25

Finally, I confessed all my sins to you and stopped trying to hide my guilt. I said to myself, "I will confess my rebellion to the LORD." And you forgave me! All my guilt is gone.
+ PSALM 32:5

IF REGRETS cause us to struggle with feelings of guilt, shame, and self-condemnation, then it's possible we haven't really accepted God's forgiveness for our sin. We may believe God has forgiven us, but if our hearts haven't accepted it, we aren't living in freedom. God promises that if we are faithful to confess our sins with a repentant heart and ask for his forgiveness, we will be considered clean before him. This incredible gift from God is sometimes difficult to accept. God doesn't want you to punish yourself or live in shame from past mistakes. Receive his grace, hold your head high, and trust his promise that he keeps no record of the things you still regret.

Prayer Prompts

Lord, I just can't seem to get past my regret that . . .
Your Word encourages me to move forward by . . .

accusations 🍃

How can I protect myself against Satan's accusations?

—————————— ❧ ——————————

Who dares accuse us whom God has chosen for his own? No one—for God himself has given us right standing with himself. Who then will condemn us? No one—for Christ Jesus died for us and was raised to life for us, and he is sitting in the place of honor at God's right hand, pleading for us.
+ ROMANS 8:33-34

It has come at last—salvation and power and the Kingdom of our God, and the authority of his Christ. For the accuser of our brothers and sisters has been thrown down to earth—the one who accuses them before our God day and night.
+ REVELATION 12:10

The serpent was the shrewdest of all the wild animals the LORD God had made. One day he asked the woman, "Did God really say you must not eat the fruit from any of the trees in the garden?"
+ GENESIS 3:1

SATAN'S ACCUSATIONS are often subtle. He doesn't try to persuade us that God isn't real but rather that we are unworthy to be in relationship with him. Sometimes Satan's voice tells us we are unlovable, undesirable, or simply undeserving of God's forgiveness. Yet the good news is that because of Jesus' life and death, God chooses to shower his love and mercy upon us anyway. We are protected from Satan's accusations when we know the difference between his lies and God's truth. God's voice is always kind, patient, gracious, and loving. So whenever you feel condemnation, remind yourself that Christ loves you, has died for you, and will ultimately defeat the accuser once and for all.

Prayer Prompts

Lord, Satan often accuses me of . . .
Your Word tells me I am worthy because . . .

 # adaptability

How can I learn to adapt when life changes so quickly?

———————— ❧ ————————

It was by faith that Abraham obeyed when God called him to leave home and go to another land that God would give him as his inheritance. He went without knowing where he was going.
+ HEBREWS 11:8

Dear brothers and sisters, when troubles of any kind come your way, consider it an opportunity for great joy. For you know that when your faith is tested, your endurance has a chance to grow. So let it grow, for when your endurance is fully developed, you will be perfect and complete, needing nothing.
+ JAMES 1:2-4

This is my command—be strong and courageous! Do not be afraid or discouraged. For the LORD your God is with you wherever you go.
+ JOSHUA 1:9

THE ABILITY to adapt goes hand in hand with trusting God. When we know that God loves us and we trust that he has the best plan for our lives, it feels easier to adapt willingly if the road of life takes a sudden sharp turn. We don't need to know all the details of God's plan for us in order to adjust to it. We just need to know that he is with us. So if you are struggling to adapt to a new turn in the road, remember that God will be with you, waiting for you around the bend. Move forward in faith and obedience to God, realizing that because he knows the way, you don't have to.

Prayer Prompts

Lord, I am having a hard time adapting to change in my life caused by . . .
Your Word tells me I can trust you in the midst of this change because . . .

9

admiration 🍃

How can I be a woman whom others admire?

— ❧ —

*His disciples began arguing about which of them was the greatest.
But Jesus . . . said to them, "Anyone who welcomes a little child like this
on my behalf welcomes me, and anyone who welcomes me also welcomes
my Father who sent me. Whoever is the least among you is the greatest."*
+ LUKE 9:46-48

*Obviously, I'm not trying to win the approval of people, but of God.
If pleasing people were my goal, I would not be Christ's servant.*
+ GALATIANS 1:10

*Seek the Kingdom of God above all else, and live righteously,
and he will give you everything you need.*
+ MATTHEW 6:33

IT IS PART of the human condition to long for admiration. The disciples argued over which of them was considered the greatest even while they were sitting at the same table as the Son of God! They were so concerned over what others thought about them that they missed out on spending time with Jesus. Have you made the same mistake? Seek God first and let go of trying to win over people. His love has the power to scatter your insecurities, self-doubts, and feelings of unworthiness. This kind of love is the only thing that can free you from being a slave to human opinion. Whenever you notice yourself striving or performing, declare this truth—*I am known and loved by my Creator*. The more you meditate on his love, the less you will care about what others think.

Prayer Prompts

Lord, I want others to admire me because it makes me feel . . .
Instead of seeking the approval of others, your Word tells me to . . .

# adoption

How is adoption a picture of
my relationship with God?

—— ❧ ——

To all who believed him and accepted him,
he gave the right to become children of God.
✦ JOHN 1:12

When the right time came, God sent his Son, born of a woman, subject to
the law. God sent him to buy freedom for us who were slaves to the law,
so that he could adopt us as his very own children.
✦ GALATIANS 4:4-5

Even before he made the world, God loved us and chose us in Christ to
be holy and without fault in his eyes. God decided in advance to adopt
us into his own family by bringing us to himself through Jesus Christ.
This is what he wanted to do, and it gave him great pleasure.
✦ EPHESIANS 1:4-5

THE PROCESS of adoption is a beautiful picture of God's love for us. Adoptive parents make a choice to give a child a new life, giving him or her a place of belonging forever. And when we trust in Jesus for our salvation, God does the same for us. He chose to give us a life we couldn't otherwise achieve. He gives us a permanent place in his family and gives us all of the rights and privileges of belonging to the family. As daughters of God, we are privileged to receive all of his blessings, both in this life and the next. Are you living as a daughter of God Most High? Whenever you feel lonely, unworthy, or as though you are an outcast, remember that God chose you to be his very own child.

Prayer Prompts

Lord, sometimes it's hard for me to accept that I am your daughter because . . .
Your Word assures me that I am part of your family when it says . . .

adventure

How can I view life as an adventure
rather than a burden to bear?

_Teach these new disciples to obey all the commands I have given you.
And be sure of this: I am with you always, even to the end of the age._
+ MATTHEW 28:20

_All glory to God, who is able, through his mighty power at work within us,
to accomplish infinitely more than we might ask or think._
+ EPHESIANS 3:20

_Thank God! He has made us his captives and continues to lead us along in
Christ's triumphal procession. Now he uses us to spread the knowledge of
Christ everywhere, like a sweet perfume._
+ 2 CORINTHIANS 2:14

OUR GOD is not a boring God. He spoke the universe into existence; he parted the sea for Moses; he summoned a fish to swallow Jonah for three days; he brought Shadrach, Meshach, and Abednego out of a fiery furnace. The list goes on. Living a life of adventure depends entirely on our perspective. Do we believe God created us for more than just muddling through a mundane life? What if we woke up each morning looking for opportunities to hear God's voice and to watch how God is unfolding his glorious plan in our lives? No matter what our responsibilities are as women—as employees, volunteers, wives, or moms—every day is an opportunity for adventure. God has a beautiful journey planned for your life, and all you need to do is to seek him and say yes when he calls you.

Prayer Prompts

Lord, this is how I feel about my life right now: . . .
Your Word tells me that I can expect exciting things for my life because . . .

 adversity

Is God listening when I cry to him in times of trouble?

In my distress I cried out to the LORD; yes, I prayed to my God for help.
He heard me from his sanctuary; my cry to him reached his ears.
+ PSALM 18:6

Give all your worries and cares to God, for he cares about you.
+ 1 PETER 5:7

When troubles of any kind come your way, consider it an opportunity
for great joy. For you know that when your faith is tested,
your endurance has a chance to grow.
+ JAMES 1:2-3

Call on me when you are in trouble, and I will rescue you,
and you will give me glory.
+ PSALM 50:15

T HE BIBLE doesn't speculate about whether or not trouble will come; it promises that trouble *will* come. Our problems don't mean that God has turned his back on us or shut his ears to our prayers. God has listening ears and a caring heart, and his Word assures us that nothing can ever separate us from his love. Adversity will come, but it brings with it opportunities to strengthen our faith. If there were no troubles, we wouldn't need to trust God. You may feel that your need is impossible to meet, that you're too weak to go on, or that it's too late for solutions. Yet these are the times when God's power can be most evident in your life. Wait for the moment of God's rescue, and you will experience his presence in new and life-changing ways.

Prayer Prompts

Lord, I tend to doubt you when . . .
Your Word assures me that in every trial you are . . .

advice 🍃

Why is it so important to seek wise advice from others?

------------------------------ ✂ ------------------------------

The instruction of the wise is like a life-giving fountain;
those who accept it avoid the snares of death.
+ PROVERBS 13:14

Wise words are like deep waters; wisdom flows from
the wise like a bubbling brook.
+ PROVERBS 18:4

Fools think their own way is right, but the wise listen to others.
+ PROVERBS 12:15

True wisdom and power are found in God;
counsel and understanding are his.
+ JOB 12:13

GOD CAN USE a conversation with a godly friend or even the advice of a trained counselor to bring about turning points in our lives. He often allows others' words to reach us at the moment when we are most ready to receive them. No one is wise enough to anticipate all the possibilities of a situation or to grasp all the issues related to a problem. Resisting advice is a sign of being unteachable and prideful. And often the one area where we refuse advice is the exact area where we most need it. Ask God to help you let go of your pride so that you can be open to receiving godly counsel. Remember that God uses a variety of ways to speak to us, and his words may often come from the mouth of a trusted friend.

Prayer Prompts

Lord, one area in my life where it might be good for me to get advice is . . .
Your Word promises me that good advice will help me because . . .

 # affirmation

How do I know that God truly values my life?
How does he affirm me?

❧

God created human beings in his own image.
In the image of God he created them; male and female he created them.
+ GENESIS 1:27

Long ago the LORD said to Israel:
"I have loved you, my people, with an everlasting love.
With unfailing love I have drawn you to myself."
+ JEREMIAH 31:3

This is how God loved the world: He gave his one and only
Son, so that everyone who believes in him will not perish but
have eternal life. God sent his Son into the world not
to judge the world, but to save the world through him.
+ JOHN 3:16-17

GOD CHOSE to create us in his image simply because he longs to have a relationship with us. Even when we are unaware of it, God loves us, pursues us, and is in the process of transforming us into the people we were created to be. As you read his Word, think about what he has done recently to show you how much you matter to him. Did he save you from something? Speak truth into your life? Give you a gift you didn't deserve? God is affirming you and cheering you on throughout each moment of your life. Allow your soul to find peace as you seek affirmation from him alone.

Prayer Prompts
Lord, I long to feel affirmed by you in this area: . . .
Right now, I can find affirmation in your Word because it says . . .

aging

How can I age gracefully?

———— ❦ ————

*Yes, you have been with me from birth; from my mother's womb you
have cared for me. No wonder I am always praising you!*
+ PSALM 71:6

*I will be your God throughout your lifetime—until your hair
is white with age. I made you, and I will care for you.*
+ ISAIAH 46:4

Store my commands in your heart. If you do this, . . . your life will be satisfying.
+ PROVERBS 3:1-2

*The godly will flourish like palm trees. . . . For they are transplanted to
the LORD's own house. They flourish in the courts of our God. Even in old
age they will still produce fruit; they will remain vital and green.*
+ PSALM 92:12-14

MANY WOMEN associate aging with weight gain, wrinkles, and
gray hair. But what if women of faith stood against culture
and decided to view aging differently? What if we looked at aging as
an opportunity to see God's care and faithfulness to us throughout the
seasons of our lives? The older we get, the more our perspective can
expand. God promises many benefits to those who decide to engage
with him through faith and obedience. Don't be discouraged by the
passing of time and the changes you may see in your body. Choose
instead to reflect on God's promises to walk faithfully with you
through every season of life.

Prayer Prompts
Lord, this is how I feel about aging: . . .
Your Word says I can flourish as I grow older by . . .

 # agreement

How can I find agreement with others without compromising my convictions?

———— ❧ ————

Daniel was determined not to defile himself. . . . He asked . . .
for permission not to eat these unacceptable foods. . . . "Please test
us for ten days on a diet of vegetables and water," Daniel said. . . .
The attendant agreed to Daniel's suggestion. . . . At the end of the ten days,
Daniel and his three friends looked healthier and better nourished than
the young men who had been eating the food assigned by the king.
+ DANIEL 1:8, 12, 14-15

Always be humble and gentle. Be patient with each other, making allowance
for each other's faults because of your love. Make every effort to keep
yourselves united in the Spirit, binding yourselves together with peace.
+ EPHESIANS 4:2-3

Be on guard. Stand firm in the faith. Be courageous. Be strong.
+ 1 CORINTHIANS 16:13

WHEN WE are trying to reach an agreement with someone, there is a time to compromise and a time to hold firm. When others try to get us to go against God's Word, we must be courageous and stand strong. The test of acceptable compromise is simple: Can two people reach a mutually satisfactory agreement without sacrificing their morals? As women, we're often conditioned to try to agree with others, but that's not always feasible. Yet we can still agree to respect and love each other despite differences in opinions. Work for harmony and agreement wherever possible, and where it is not, pray that God would help you to hold firmly to his Word and love those you disagree with.

Prayer Prompts

Lord, I want to reach agreement with this person: . . .
In the midst of this situation, your Word calls me to . . .

amazement 🪶

How can I recapture a sense of amazement about God?

———— ✣ ————

I have heard all about you, Lord. I am filled with awe by your amazing works.
+ HABAKKUK 3:2

You are the God of great wonders!
You demonstrate your awesome power among the nations.
+ PSALM 77:14

The heavens proclaim the glory of God. The skies display his craftsmanship.
Day after day they continue to speak; night after night they make him known.
+ PSALM 19:1-2

He has given me a new song to sing, a hymn of praise to our God. Many will
see what he has done and be amazed. They will put their trust in the Lord.
+ PSALM 40:3

OUR LIVES are so busy that it can be tempting to sleepwalk through life. When we check out or detach, we miss the amazing things God is doing right now. We need to pay attention—to others' stories and to the world around us. God is doing incredible work everywhere. Don't forget the quiet miracles that take place each day: the birth of a baby, a beautiful sunset, close friends, a feeling of joy in the midst of overwhelming circumstances. Being in awe of God over these "small" miracles prepares your heart to experience even more remarkable things he has done. Listen to how God has amazed others, and add those events to your own list. The more you look for evidence of God's work, the more amazed you will be. How can you search for a little miracle today?

Prayer Prompts

Lord, something amazing you did lately was . . .
Although it seems nothing amazing is happening in my life, your Word says . . .

angels

Are angels real?

❧

Praise him, all his angels! Praise him, all the armies of heaven. . . .
Let every created thing give praise to the LORD,
for he issued his command, and they came into being.
✛ PSALM 148:2, 5

Angels are only servants—
spirits sent to care for people who will inherit salvation.
✛ HEBREWS 1:14

He will order his angels to protect you wherever you go.
✛ PSALM 91:11

ANGELS, LIKE HUMANS, are real beings created by God. Just as God creates each person as a unique individual, he created angels as unique beings. For example, some angels in the Bible, like Michael and Gabriel, are mentioned by name and were given specific tasks, such as protecting people or delivering messages from God. God uses his angels to counsel, guide, protect, minister to, rescue, fight for, and care for his people. Whether he assigns one angel to a specific individual or uses his host of angels is his choice and your blessing. Thank God for the unseen ways in which angels may have touched you. Chances are that angels have played a greater role in your life than you realize.

Prayer Prompts

Lord, I wonder if an angel was protecting me when . . .
Whenever I feel afraid, I can remember that your Word says your angels will . . .

anger

How can I better control my anger?

———— ❧ ————

A gentle answer deflects anger, but harsh words make tempers flare.
+ PROVERBS 15:1

Control your temper, for anger labels you a fool.
+ ECCLESIASTES 7:9

"Don't sin by letting anger control you." Don't let the sun go down while you are still angry, for anger gives a foothold to the devil.
+ EPHESIANS 4:26-27

People with understanding control their anger;
a hot temper shows great foolishness.
+ PROVERBS 14:29

Now is the time to get rid of anger, rage, malicious behavior, slander, and dirty language. . . . Put on your new nature, and be renewed as you learn to know your Creator and become like him.
+ COLOSSIANS 3:8, 10

OF ALL EMOTIONS, anger is probably the most difficult to control. Anger itself is not wrong; even God experiences righteous anger. It becomes a problem when we allow it to lead us to sin against others and God. God promises that our anger, when left unchecked, will have consequences. For example, when we lash out at someone, we damage that relationship and destroy trust. However, even when we make bad decisions, he promises to be kind, merciful, and always ready to receive us with love. When you don't know what to do with your anger, allow God's Word to give you perspective, encourage you toward godliness, and remind you of his endless grace for you.

Prayer Prompts

Lord, when I am angry I often respond like this: . . .
Your Word calls me instead to control my anger by . . .

Does God always answer prayer?

❦

Three different times I begged the Lord to take it away. Each time he said,
. . . "My power works best in weakness." So now I am glad to boast about
my weaknesses, so that the power of Christ can work through me.
+ 2 CORINTHIANS 12:8-9

You faithfully answer our prayers with awesome deeds, O God our savior.
+ PSALM 65:5

The earnest prayer of a righteous person has great
power and produces wonderful results.
+ JAMES 5:16

What mighty praise, O God, belongs to you . . . for you answer our prayers.
+ PSALM 65:1-2

GOD LISTENS CAREFULLY to every prayer, but his answer may be yes, no, or wait. Doesn't any loving parent give all three of these responses to her child at different times? If God answered yes to every request, we would not learn or have the opportunity to grow in faith. If he answered no each time, our spirits would feel defeated and we might begin to think God was vindictive. If he answered wait to every prayer, we would be frustrated. God always answers, but he does so based on what he knows is best for us. When we don't get the answer we want, we shouldn't misinterpret it as silence from God but rather as a signal to point us in a specific direction. Our spiritual maturity will grow as we seek to understand how God's answer is what is best for us. So whatever you have been praying for, don't give up. God can be trusted with your prayers.

Prayer Prompts

Lord, I long for an answer to my prayer that . . .
I know you are faithful to answer because your Word says . . .

anxiety

What can I do when anxiety overwhelms me?

❧

Give all your worries and cares to God, for he cares about you.
+ 1 PETER 5:7

"I know the plans I have for you," says the Lord.
"They are plans for good and not for disaster, to give you a future and a hope."
+ JEREMIAH 29:11

Don't worry about anything; instead, pray about everything.
Tell God what you need, and thank him for all he has done.
Then you will experience God's peace, which exceeds anything
we can understand. His peace will guard your hearts and
minds as you live in Christ Jesus.
+ PHILIPPIANS 4:6-7

ANXIETY STEMS from the concern that God will "get it wrong." It is a result of letting our fears fester and allowing the "what ifs" to cause doubt in our hearts. As women, we have plenty of "what ifs" crossing our minds throughout the day. So what is the secret weapon for battling against anxiety? Anxiety loses its power over us when we choose to reflect on and trust in God's promises to care for us. God tells us throughout his Word that he is good, he loves us, and he wants the very best for our lives. When we begin to accept that the almighty God is caring for us, we become women who are strong, secure, peaceful, and courageous.

Prayer Prompts

Lord, it's hard to trust you with this area in my life: . . .
Your Word assures me you can be trusted because . . .

 # appearance

What can I do when I feel
disappointed by my appearance?

———————— ❧ ————————

God has made everything beautiful for its own time.
+ ECCLESIASTES 3:11

We are God's masterpiece. He has created us anew in Christ Jesus,
so we can do the good things he planned for us long ago.
+ EPHESIANS 2:10

Then God looked over all he had made, and he saw that it was very good!
+ GENESIS 1:31

Yet for a little while you made them a little lower than
the angels and crowned them with glory and honor.
+ HEBREWS 2:7

GOD KNOWS the times when we do not feel beautiful. He sees when we walk away from the mirror feeling disheartened. We can talk to him about our disappointment with our appearance, but we need to remember that he does not make mistakes with his creation. When God made us, he used the words *good, beautiful,* and *masterpiece* to describe us. He says we are crowned with glory and honor simply because we are created in his image. The next time you feel disappointment over your appearance, look to God's Word to remind you of how your Creator sees you.

Prayer Prompts
Lord, if I am honest, I don't like that you made me this way: . . .
Your Word says that when you look at me, you see . . .

appreciation 🌿

Why is it important to appreciate the little things in life?

——————— ✷ ———————

It is good to give thanks to the LORD, to sing praises to the Most High.
It is good to proclaim your unfailing love in the morning,
your faithfulness in the evening.
+ PSALM 92:1-2

Every time I think of you, I give thanks to my God.
Whenever I pray, I make my requests for all of you with joy.
+ PHILIPPIANS 1:3-4

Be thankful in all circumstances,
for this is God's will for you who belong to Christ Jesus.
+ 1 THESSALONIANS 5:18

Give thanks to the LORD, for he is good! His faithful love endures forever.
+ 1 CHRONICLES 16:34

ONE OF THE BEST WAYS to experience God is to notice and appreciate the little things around us. Turning our focus outward helps us see many things to be thankful for. Rather than saying, "I wish," we can try saying, "I'm thankful." We cultivate appreciative hearts by giving thanks both regularly and spontaneously. This kind of attitude helps to keep life's disappointments from blinding us to what God is doing in the here and now. Every moment is an opportunity to see God's provision and presence.

Prayer Prompts

Lord, something small I am thankful for today is . . .
Your Word also reminds me to thank you because you are . . .

# approval

How can I balance my desire for others' approval and God's approval?

꧁ ꧂

We speak as messengers approved by God to be entrusted with the Good News. Our purpose is to please God, not people. He alone examines the motives of our hearts.
+ 1 THESSALONIANS 2:4

The Kingdom of God is not a matter of what we eat or drink, but of living a life of goodness and peace and joy in the Holy Spirit. If you serve Christ with this attitude, you will please God, and others will approve of you, too.
+ ROMANS 14:17-18

I'm not trying to win the approval of people, but of God. If pleasing people were my goal, I would not be Christ's servant.
+ GALATIANS 1:10

MANY WOMEN have a deep need to feel liked and approved of by others. This isn't necessarily a bad thing, but this desire becomes distorted when we allow others' approval to define us. If not having someone's good opinion leaves us feeling rejected, alone, and worthless, we know our priorities are unbalanced. Sadly, some people's approval is impossible to gain. When we're struggling with not receiving someone's approval, we can go back to what God's Word promises. Our lives matter greatly to him, and our highest goal ought to be pleasing him rather than those around us. When you fail to receive the approval of others, remember that almighty God loves you and desires a relationship with you—not because of what you do but simply because of who you are.

Prayer Prompts

Lord, I really want the approval of this person: . . .
Your Word promises me that only your approval matters because . . .

arguments

What is the best way to respond to arguments?

*Don't repay evil for evil. Don't retaliate with insults when
people insult you. Instead, pay them back with a blessing.
That is what God has called you to do, and he will grant you
his blessing. . . . Search for peace, and work to maintain it.*
+ 1 PETER 3:9, 11

*You have heard the law that says, "Love your neighbor" and hate your enemy.
But I say, love your enemies! Pray for those who persecute you! In that way,
you will be acting as true children of your Father in heaven.*
+ MATTHEW 5:43-45

*God blesses those who work for peace,
for they will be called the children of God.*
+ MATTHEW 5:9

BECAUSE we are all sinful people, arguments are bound to happen. Sometimes disagreements lead to greater understanding,
intimacy, and depth of relationship. Other times they result in angry
words, lingering bitterness, and broken relationships. Therefore,
the way we choose to resolve an argument is extremely important.
If you have a challenging relationship in your life right now, take
time to reflect on God's promises to bless those who work for peace.
It is never easy to be the person who takes the high road, but God
tells you that when you do, you will experience his love, peace, and
goodness in your life.

Prayer Prompts

Lord, I am tired of arguing with . . .
Your Word assures me that if I work for peace, then . . .

 # assurance

Where can I find assurance amid the uncertainties of life?

❧

Blessed are those who trust in the LORD and have made the LORD their
hope and confidence. They are like trees planted along a riverbank,
with roots that reach deep into the water. Such trees are not bothered
by the heat or worried by long months of drought.
+ JEREMIAH 17:7-8

Oh, the joys of those who trust the LORD,
who have no confidence in the proud or in those who worship idols.
+ PSALM 40:4

Those who die in the LORD will live; their bodies will rise again!
Those who sleep in the earth will rise up and sing for joy!
+ ISAIAH 26:19

The one who formed you says, "Do not be afraid, for I have ransomed you.
I have called you by name; you are mine. When you go through deep waters,
I will be with you. When you go through rivers of difficulty, you will not drown."
+ ISAIAH 43:1-2

ONE THING we can always be certain of is God's love for us.
Receiving assurance through other relationships feels good
and is important, but God is the only one in whom we can trust
completely without fear of disappointment. We can be assured that
what he says is true and what he does is reliable. Searching for assurance in a world filled with uncertainty will always leave you feeling
insecure. Assurance in this life comes from experiencing God's love
for you, which gives you security for today and for eternity.

Prayer Prompts

Lord, sometimes I look to these things for assurance: . . .
Your Word tells me I can find assurance in you because . . .

attitude 🍃

How can I have a positive attitude during hard times?

⸎

Always be full of joy in the Lord. I say it again—rejoice! . . .
Don't worry about anything; instead, pray about everything.
Tell God what you need, and thank him for all he has done.
+ PHILIPPIANS 4:4, 6

Always be joyful. Never stop praying. Be thankful in all circumstances,
for this is God's will for you who belong to Christ Jesus.
+ 1 THESSALONIANS 5:16-18

Don't copy the behavior and customs of this world, but let
God transform you into a new person by changing the way
you think. Then you will learn to know God's will for you,
which is good and pleasing and perfect.
+ ROMANS 12:2

WE MAY NOT be able to control what happens to us, but we can control how we react to our circumstances. How we think about something impacts our actions, our hearts, and our souls. That is why it is so important to bring every problem to God in prayer. The next time you find yourself focusing on the negative, immediately ask God to renew your mind. This is the first step in allowing him to transform you into a godly person by changing the way you think. That's why the Bible doesn't just suggest being joyful or generous—it commands it! God knows this is what is best for you. Trust that he will give you the strength you need to get through difficult times with a thankful and hopeful heart.

Prayer Prompts

Lord, recently I've had a bad attitude about . . .
Your Word says that the way to change my attitude is to . . .

 # balance

How do I balance caring for others and caring for myself?

❦

Give according to what you have, not what you don't have. Of course, I don't mean your giving should make life easy for others and hard for yourselves. I only mean that there should be some equality. Right now you have plenty and can help those who are in need. Later, they will have plenty and can share with you when you need it. In this way, things will be equal.
✛ 2 CORINTHIANS 8:12-14

Jesus said, "Let's go off by ourselves to a quiet place and rest awhile." He said this because there were so many people coming and going that Jesus and his apostles didn't even have time to eat.
✛ MARK 6:31

MANY WOMEN desire to find a perfect balance between caring for others and caring for themselves. However, life usually isn't balanced; rather, it flows in seasons. Some seasons will be spent taking care of others, like when we have young children or are helping an elderly relative or a friend who is ill. Other seasons will allow more time for self-care. No matter what season we are in, we can look to Jesus as our example. He spent the majority of his time caring for those close to him. However, he also regularly set aside time to rest with God. Even with all the needs around him, he knew when it was time to get away. How attentive are you to the state of your soul as you care for others? When you begin to feel overwhelmed and worn out, schedule time to rest with God. Allow him to care for you so that your care for others will flow from a refreshed soul.

Prayer Prompts

Lord, I am in a season where I am caring for . . .
Your Word says this about balance: . . .

beauty

How can I develop a beautiful soul?

—— ✤ ——

Women who claim to be devoted to God should make themselves attractive by the good things they do.
✝ 1 TIMOTHY 2:10

Don't be concerned about the outward beauty of fancy hairstyles, expensive jewelry, or beautiful clothes. You should clothe yourselves instead with the beauty that comes from within, the unfading beauty of a gentle and quiet spirit, which is so precious to God.
✝ 1 PETER 3:3-4

Oh, the joys of those who do not follow the advice of the wicked, or stand around with sinners, or join in with mockers. But they delight in the law of the Lord, meditating on it day and night. They are like trees planted along the riverbank, bearing fruit each season.
✝ PSALM 1:1-3

THE WORLD tempts women to believe that beauty comes from having the right hairstyle, jewelry, or clothes. But we know this kind of beauty will fade and be quickly forgotten. Do you want to develop beauty that will last—beauty that goes far deeper than physical appearance? You may wonder if this is even possible. It is! This kind of beauty shines out from inside of you and never fades because it flows from your heart. Your heart becomes lovely as you spend more time with God. Moses spent forty days with him on a mountaintop. When he came down, his face was radiant—not because of anything he did, but simply because he had spent time in God's presence. This is the kind of beauty God will give you. Remember, there is nothing more radiant than someone who has spent time in God's company.

Prayer Prompts

Lord, I feel most beautiful when . . .
Your Word tells me that true beauty comes from . . .

# behavior

If God cares most about what is on the inside, why does godly behavior matter?

❧

Yes, just as you can identify a tree by its fruit,
so you can identify people by their actions.
+ MATTHEW 7:20

Let your good deeds shine out for all to see,
so that everyone will praise your heavenly Father.
+ MATTHEW 5:16

Blessed are all who hear the word of God and put it into practice.
+ LUKE 11:28

Don't participate in the darkness of wild parties and drunkenness, or
in sexual promiscuity and immoral living, or in quarreling and jealousy.
+ ROMANS 13:13

WE LIVE from the inside out. What we believe, desire, and think about comes out through our behavior. Faith alone is enough for salvation, but our actions are the evidence that our faith is genuine. If you have made a confession of faith in Jesus and still have not seen any difference in your behavior, it may be time to pause and reflect with God about what is in your heart. Maybe you're scared to change out of fear that others will judge or reject you. Perhaps you are having a hard time breaking old habits because you aren't quite convinced that God's way is really best. Whatever the reason, God desires an authentic relationship with you. He isn't interested in changing your behavior so you can act more "Christian." He is interested in changing your heart so that your actions reflect a woman who seeks, loves, and trusts him.

Prayer Prompts

My behavior shows this about the condition of my heart: . . .
Lord, I want to talk with you about this specific behavior: . . .

being teachable 🍃

Why is it important to be open to learning new things?

~ ❧ ~

Teach me your ways, O Lord, that I may live according to your truth!
+ PSALM 86:11

Intelligent people are always ready to learn.
Their ears are open for knowledge.
+ PROVERBS 18:15

Cry out for insight, and ask for understanding. Search for them as you would
for silver; seek them like hidden treasures. Then you will understand what
it means to fear the Lord, and you will gain knowledge of God.
+ PROVERBS 2:3-5

Though the Lord gave you adversity for food and suffering for drink, he will
still be with you to teach you. You will see your teacher with your own eyes.
+ ISAIAH 30:20

HOW OPEN are you to learning something new? Scripture calls us to be lifelong learners, with the Lord as our primary teacher and guide. And God's Word promises us wisdom and insight. In fact, it even promises that we can begin to know the very mind of God! Life is an adventure, and God always has something new for us to learn if we start with his Word and apply it to daily living. What if we woke up every day ready to grow with God and absorb his wisdom? Even in days of pain and adversity, God wants to teach us. He longs for us to be open to learning from him. Embrace the role of student and eager apprentice today, remembering that someday "you will see your teacher with your own eyes."

Prayer Prompts

Lord, sometimes I just don't want to learn something new because . . .
Your Word reminds me that the benefits of being teachable are . . .

 # belonging

What can I do when I feel like I don't belong anywhere?

❧

Yet I still belong to you; you hold my right hand.
You guide me with your counsel, leading me to a glorious destiny.
+ PSALM 73:23-24

You are included among those . . .
who have been called to belong to Jesus Christ.
+ ROMANS 1:6

I will walk among you; I will be your God, and you will be my people.
+ LEVITICUS 26:12

Listen to the LORD who created you. . . . The one who formed you says, "Do not
be afraid, for I have ransomed you. I have called you by name; you are mine."
+ ISAIAH 43:1

MANY OF US have experienced the ache of feeling like we don't belong. Maybe we long to feel part of a group of friends, be more connected at church, or even become more comfortable in our own homes. When we have faith in Jesus, he promises that we are completely welcomed into his family, which includes all who follow him. Some of the many benefits of being part of his family are complete acceptance, a clear sense of purpose, victory over sin, an inheritance of real value, and the eternal security of knowing we will always be included. You may struggle to find a sense of belonging in this life, but you can rest in the truth that no matter what happens, nothing and no one can take your place as God's daughter.

Prayer Prompts

Lord, I long to feel like I belong to . . .
Your Word tells me I already belong to your family, which means . . .

betrayal

What can I do when I feel the pain of betrayal?

"The mountains may move and the hills disappear, but even then my faithful love for you will remain. My covenant of blessing will never be broken," says the LORD, who has mercy on you.
+ ISAIAH 54:10

Love your enemies! Pray for those who persecute you! In that way, you will be acting as true children of your Father in heaven.
+ MATTHEW 5:44-45

Don't repay evil for evil. Don't retaliate with insults when people insult you. Instead, pay them back with a blessing. That is what God has called you to do, and he will grant you his blessing.
+ 1 PETER 3:9

It was time for supper, and the devil had already prompted Judas, son of Simon Iscariot, to betray Jesus.
+ JOHN 13:2

BETRAYAL has the power to make us feel unwanted, unloved, and even defective. Its sting can last a lifetime if we allow it to. Taking the high road after being betrayed is not an easy path—but it is one that leads toward God's blessings. God promises that when we choose to bless others rather than retaliate, he will bless and reward us in return. When betrayal has caused you to focus on your flaws and doubt all your good qualities, remember that God will never reject you. Come to him with your pain, remembering that Jesus knows exactly what it feels like to be rejected by someone close. Ask for his help to respond well, trusting that he will keep his promises to bless, defend, and comfort you.

Prayer Prompts

Lord, I feel pain from betrayal by this person: . . .
Your Word tells me that my response to being hurt should be . . .

Bible

How can reading the Bible impact my heart?

❧

The instructions of the LORD are perfect, reviving the soul.
The decrees of the LORD are trustworthy, making wise the simple.
The commandments of the LORD are right, bringing joy to the heart.
The commands of the LORD are clear, giving insight for living.
✦ PSALM 19:7-8

All Scripture is inspired by God and is useful to teach us what is
true and to make us realize what is wrong in our lives. It corrects us
when we are wrong and teaches us to do what is right. God uses it to
prepare and equip his people to do every good work.
✦ 2 TIMOTHY 3:16-17

The word of God is alive and powerful. It is sharper than the sharpest two-
edged sword, cutting between soul and spirit, between joint and marrow.
It exposes our innermost thoughts and desires.
✦ HEBREWS 4:12

THE BIBLE isn't just a book written by godly people thousands
of years ago—it is the recorded voice of God and is one way he
communicates with us. How amazing that the God of the universe
would actually want to communicate with us! The Word of God has
the power to shape our hearts, minds, and souls. Reading his Word
every day keeps us in the presence of the one who created us for a
purpose, knows us best, and can guide us along the best pathway for
our lives. No matter what season of life you are in, God has something to say to you through his Word.

Prayer Prompts

Lord, when I read your Word, I often feel . . .
Your Word assures me that the benefits of reading it are . . .

blame 🌿

How can I stop blaming myself or others when things go wrong?

❦

*He will keep you strong to the end so that you will be free
from all blame on the day when our Lord Jesus Christ returns.*
+ 1 CORINTHIANS 1:8

*He has reconciled you to himself through the death of Christ in his
physical body. As a result, he has brought you into his own presence, and
you are holy and blameless as you stand before him without a single fault.*
+ COLOSSIANS 1:22

Great is his faithfulness; his mercies begin afresh each morning.
+ LAMENTATIONS 3:23

*Because the Sovereign LORD helps me, I will not be disgraced.
Therefore, I have set my face like a stone, determined to do his will.
And I know that I will not be put to shame.*
+ ISAIAH 50:7

IT'S SO EASY for us to blame ourselves or others when things go wrong. Assigning blame can dominate our thoughts, turn our perspective negative, and lead our hearts toward discouragement, anger, and bitterness. We need to stop the blame game, letting go of the "what ifs" and "if onlys". If you have brought disappointment upon yourself, ask for forgiveness and move on. If someone else has caused you pain, ask the Lord to help you forgive them. God doesn't want you to dwell on what could have been; he wants you to focus on what can be. He is the God of hope who gives you the gift of a new day, full of fresh starts.

Prayer Prompts

Lord, when things go wrong, my instinct is to blame . . .
Your Word assures me that I don't need to assign blame because . . .

blessing others
What does it look like to bless another person?

❧

*Then the L*ORD *said to Moses, "Tell Aaron and his sons to bless the*
*people of Israel with this special blessing: 'May the L*ORD *bless you*
*and protect you. May the L*ORD *smile on you and be gracious to you.*
*May the L*ORD *show you his favor and give you his peace.'"*
+ NUMBERS 6:22-26

This same God who takes care of me will supply all your needs
from his glorious riches, which have been given to us in Christ Jesus.
Now all glory to God our Father forever and ever! Amen.
+ PHILIPPIANS 4:19-20

Jacob went over and kissed him. And when Isaac caught the smell of his clothes,
he was finally convinced, and he blessed his son.
+ GENESIS 27:27

Bless those who persecute you. Don't curse them; pray that God will bless them.
+ ROMANS 12:14

IN SCRIPTURE, blessing someone else is a profoundly personal and powerful act. When we bless others, we are proclaiming that we want good things for their lives. Blessing another always involves God because when we will the good of another person, we realize only God is capable of bringing that about. To bless someone is to ask God, on behalf of the other person, to support the good we want for them. That helps us understand how Jesus' teaching to bless our enemies was such a revolutionary idea. Who might God be asking you to speak a blessing over? Is it a friend—or perhaps an enemy? Look to Scripture to gain the words to speak a blessing over someone near you.

Prayer Prompts

Lord, I want to speak a blessing over . . .
Your Word inspires me to bless him or her with words like these: . . .

body

How does caring for my body also care for my soul?

———— ✺ ————

Don't you realize that your body is the temple of the Holy Spirit, who lives in you and was given to you by God? You do not belong to yourself, for God bought you with a high price. So you must honor God with your body.
+ 1 CORINTHIANS 6:19-20

Thank you for making me so wonderfully complex!
Your workmanship is marvelous—how well I know it. . . .
How precious are your thoughts about me, O God.
They cannot be numbered!
+ PSALM 139:14, 17

Times of refreshment will come from the presence of the Lord.
+ ACTS 3:20

A S WOMEN with a lot of responsibilities, most of us race through life trying to meet one demand after another. This kind of treadmill existence will inevitably wear us down. The heart, mind, body, and soul are all connected. When we care for the body, we are also caring for the soul. Sometimes we feel guilty when we take the time to exercise, spend money on healthy food, or sleep in. However, when we fail to care for ourselves physically, we become sick, fatigued, impatient, angry, and too exhausted to engage with others and God. It's more than okay to value the only body that God has given you—in fact, it's necessary. Set aside time to care for your body for the sake of your soul.

Prayer Prompts

Lord, I think you are calling me to better care for my body by . . .
Your Word gives me permission to care for my body because . . .

 boredom

What can I do when I feel like being a Christian is boring?

━━━━━━━━━ ❧ ━━━━━━━━━

Our great desire is that you will keep on loving others as long as life lasts, in order to make certain that what you hope for will come true. Then you will not become spiritually dull and indifferent. Instead, you will follow the example of those who are going to inherit God's promises because of their faith and endurance.
✝ HEBREWS 6:11-12

The word of God is alive and powerful.
✝ HEBREWS 4:12

God has given each of you a gift from his great variety of spiritual gifts. Use them well to serve one another.
✝ 1 PETER 4:10

BEING A CHRISTIAN can seem boring if we view it as a life of "Don't do this" or "You can't do that." But those who grasp what the Christian life is really about find it full and exciting. When we realize that the almighty God wants to work through us to accomplish his work in the world, we will be excited at the possibilities of what he might accomplish. If you have found yourself becoming bored in your spiritual life, ask God to help you see opportunities to serve and love others. Focus on using and developing your God-given gifts and on the eternal rewards God promises to believers. If you wake up every day ready to read his Word, listen for his voice, and surrender your plan for his, you will find a life full of excitement and adventure.

Prayer Prompts

Lord, I wonder if my spiritual life feels boring because . . .
When I feel bored, your Word encourages me to . . .

boundaries

I know I need to set some boundaries for myself, but how can I do that?

———————— ❧ ————————

*We will boast only about what has happened within
the boundaries of the work God has given us.*
+ 2 CORINTHIANS 10:13

*The instructions of the LORD are perfect, reviving the soul.
The decrees of the LORD are trustworthy, making wise the simple.
The commandments of the LORD are right, bringing joy to the heart.
The commands of the LORD are clear, giving insight for living.*
+ PSALM 19:7-8

*The LORD says, "I will guide you along the best pathway for your life.
I will advise you and watch over you. Do not be like a senseless horse
or mule that needs a bit and bridle to keep it under control."*
+ PSALM 32:8-9

For everything there is a season, a time for every activity under heaven.
+ ECCLESIASTES 3:1

GOD GIVES US clear boundaries for living the Christian life. These are not meant to keep us from having fun but to protect us. Without moral boundaries, chaos reigns, and we get burned out and suffer. We also benefit from setting relational boundaries to maintain some margin in our lives. To avoid burnout in a busy season, make a list of what you must do and what you'd like to do. Then start scratching off the must-dos until you have enough time to enjoy your family and find peace. Freeing yourself from the trap of incessant activity requires asking for help and learning to say no—even to worthwhile activities.

Prayer Prompts

Lord, I think I need some boundaries in the area of . . .
Your Word affirms that your boundaries are healthy because . . .

 # brokenness

My heart is breaking. I'm overwhelmed, and my life is a mess. Is there any hope?

———————— ❦ ————————

The sacrifice you desire is a broken spirit.
You will not reject a broken and repentant heart, O God.
+ PSALM 51:17

He heals the brokenhearted and bandages their wounds.
+ PSALM 147:3

God blesses those who are poor and realize their need for him,
for the Kingdom of Heaven is theirs.
+ MATTHEW 5:3

The LORD is close to the brokenhearted;
he rescues those whose spirits are crushed.
+ PSALM 34:18

SOMETIMES brokenness is the result of overwhelming circumstances. Other times it is a consequence of our sin. No matter the cause, one thing is certain—brokenness allows us to realize that God's help is the only way out of our mess. It signifies the breaking of our pride and self-sufficiency. You may feel your situation is too messy for God to handle, but remember that he is not afraid of it. God promises not only to be close to you in your heartache but also to use it for your good. If you have been broken, come to God as a little child, recognizing your neediness and utter dependence on him. It's when you feel broken that you're in the perfect position for God to work in your life. Take comfort in his promise to heal the brokenhearted.

Prayer Prompts

Lord, my heart is breaking because . . .
Your Word promises that when I am brokenhearted, you will . . .

busyness

How does God feel about my busy lifestyle?

All our busy rushing ends in nothing.
+ PSALM 39:6

_Plant your seed in the morning and keep busy all afternoon, for you don't
know if profit will come from one activity or another—or maybe both._
+ ECCLESIASTES 11:6

_Be careful how you live. Don't live like fools, but like those
who are wise. Make the most of every opportunity in these
evil days. Don't act thoughtlessly, but understand what the
Lord wants you to do. . . . Be filled with the Holy Spirit._
+ EPHESIANS 5:15-18

Teach us to realize the brevity of life, so that we may grow in wisdom.
+ PSALM 90:12

THE LORD honors those who work hard and make the most of
every opportunity. And sometimes doing a job well requires a
lot of work and busyness. Busyness becomes dangerous only if our
activities replace real accomplishment or if we are neglecting God
or the people in our care. The key to overcoming empty busyness is
to be fully productive for God. We do this by understanding his call
and purpose for our lives and prioritizing our activities around them.
Ask yourself what you are busying yourself with and if it will further
God's Kingdom or your own. Let go of what doesn't need to get done
today to instead accomplish what God is calling you to. Remember,
God will empower you to make the most of the time he's given you.

Prayer Prompts

Lord, sometimes my busyness makes me feel . . .
Your Word calls me instead to live this way: . . .

 # call of God

How do I know when God is calling me to do something?

❧

Let God transform you into a new person by changing the
way you think. Then you will learn to know God's will for you,
which is good and pleasing and perfect.
+ ROMANS 12:2

The LORD called out, "Samuel!" . . .
And Samuel replied, "Speak, your servant is listening."
+ 1 SAMUEL 3:4, 10

Your word is a lamp to guide my feet and a light for my path.
+ PSALM 119:105

THE FIRST STEP to understanding our calling is getting to know God intimately through his Word. As God communicates to us through the Bible and as we pray, he will show us what he wants us to do and where he wants us to go. God calls us in two different ways: generally and specifically. God's general call is to be in relationship with him, obey his Word, do what is right, and show genuine love for others. But God also has a specific call for each person, a special role he wants us to play, based on the unique gifts he has given us. If you don't know what your specific call is, keep obeying and seeking God each day. Over time, his plan for your life will unfold. If God calls you to a specific task, seize the moment and follow God's call. Don't let the window of opportunity close and miss all God has in store for you.

Prayer Prompts

Lord, I can obey your general call today by . . .
Your Word promises you will lead me to my specific call if I . . .

care

Why would God care about me?
Sometimes I feel as if nobody cares.

———————— ❧ ————————

You have been with me from birth; from my mother's womb you have cared for me. No wonder I am always praising you!
+ PSALM 71:6

I will be glad and rejoice in your unfailing love, for you have seen my troubles, and you care about the anguish of my soul.
+ PSALM 31:7

If God cares so wonderfully for wildflowers that are here today and thrown into the fire tomorrow, he will certainly care for you.
+ MATTHEW 6:30

Give all your worries and cares to God, for he cares about you.
+ 1 PETER 5:7

GOD'S CARE for us is deeply personal. His love for us began before we were born, continues throughout our lives, and extends throughout eternity. He created us to have a relationship with him, and he gives us the opportunity to live with him forever. In addition, God's care for us is unique. Only he knows how to love us in ways that will make us feel watched over and supported. In fact, he urges us to bring our needs and worries to him because he cares so much about what happens to us. It is natural to feel lonely when others desert or abandon you, but when you can fully comprehend God's deeply personal care for you, his love breaks through your feelings of loneliness and tends to your deepest needs and worries.

Prayer Prompts

Lord, sometimes I doubt your care for me because . . .
Your Word assures me you care for me in these specific ways: . . .

🌱 caring for ourselves

Is it selfish to take some time to care for myself?

— ❧ —

The generous will prosper;
those who refresh others will themselves be refreshed.
+ PROVERBS 11:25

Despite Jesus' instructions, the report of his power spread even faster, and
vast crowds came to hear him preach and to be healed of their diseases.
But Jesus often withdrew to the wilderness for prayer.
+ LUKE 5:15-16

[Those who trust in the LORD] are like trees planted along a
riverbank, with roots that reach deep into the water. Such trees are
not bothered by the heat or worried by long months of drought.
Their leaves stay green, and they never stop producing fruit.
+ JEREMIAH 17:8

As WOMEN, we often put our own needs on the back burner to instead take care of the needs around us. It is impossible to serve effectively from a depleted soul; eventually we will burn out. Caring for ourselves means carving out enough time to care for our soul as well as our body. This is not self-centeredness because caring for ourselves helps create space in our heart for God and others. Even Jesus had to get away from the crowds in order to experience rest and refreshment. Since God created each person uniquely, what restores your soul may be different from what someone else needs. Give yourself permission to practice self-care so that there is room in your heart for God and others.

Prayer Prompts

Lord, these practices, people, and activities most refresh my soul: . . .
Your Word reminds me that caring for my soul is important because . . .

caution 🔴

How cautious should I be when I make decisions?

――――――――― ❧ ―――――――――

Those who trust their own insight are foolish,
but anyone who walks in wisdom is safe.
+ PROVERBS 28:26

Fools think their own way is right, but the wise listen to others.
+ PROVERBS 12:15

The wise are cautious and avoid danger;
fools plunge ahead with reckless confidence.
+ PROVERBS 14:16

Fools base their thoughts on foolish assumptions,
so their conclusions will be wicked madness.
+ ECCLESIASTES 10:13

THERE IS a difference between being a risk taker and being a fool. The Bible warns us not to take risks that ignore or contradict sound principles. Consulting God—and wise friends who are committed to God—before taking big steps in life is a wise use of caution and provides a high chance of success. Fools rarely take advice from others, never try to follow God's ways, and make plans that are mostly for personal gain or fame. God is looking for wise and obedient risk takers, not foolish people who plunge ahead without first seeking his guidance. If you are facing a decision, take time to pray for wisdom and guidance from God. It brings him great joy when you view him as your most important adviser.

Prayer Prompts

Lord, this is how I usually make decisions when I'm feeling cautious: . . .
Your Word tells me that the difference between fools and the wise is . . .

 # celebration

Why is it important to celebrate?

———————— ❧ ————————

*On this day in early spring, in the month of Abib, you have been set free.
You must celebrate this event.... You must explain to your children,
"I am celebrating what the LORD did for me when I left Egypt."*
+ EXODUS 13:4-5, 8

*Let all who take refuge in you rejoice; let them sing joyful praises forever. Spread
your protection over them, that all who love your name may be filled with joy.*
+ PSALM 5:11

*Let us be glad and rejoice....
For the time has come for the wedding feast of the Lamb.*
+ REVELATION 19:7

*Enter his gates with thanksgiving; go into his courts with praise. Give
thanks to him and praise his name. For the LORD is good. His unfailing love
continues forever, and his faithfulness continues to each generation.*
+ PSALM 100:4-5

W**E CELEBRATE** anniversaries, birthdays, victories, promotions,
marriages, and new babies. We also celebrate occasions such as
the Lord's Supper and baptism. The ultimate reason to celebrate is that
God has rescued us from the consequences of sin and shown us the
wonders of eternity. Celebration is a powerful tool to take our focus
off our troubles and put it on God's blessings—and ultimately on God
himself. Those who love him truly have the most to rejoice about! If
you don't feel much joy in life right now, ask God to awaken you to the
things worth celebrating in daily life. These enjoyable experiences are
a tiny taste of the joyous moments you will experience in eternity.

Prayer Prompts

Lord, today I want to celebrate ...
Your Word encourages me to live a life of celebration because ...

change

How can I experience real,
lasting change in my life with God?

———— ❧ ————

Create in me a clean heart, O God. Renew a loyal spirit within me.
+ PSALM 51:10

Anyone who belongs to Christ has become a new person.
The old life is gone; a new life has begun!
+ 2 CORINTHIANS 5:17

Let the Spirit renew your thoughts and attitudes.
Put on your new nature, created to be like God—truly righteous and holy.
+ EPHESIANS 4:23-24

Put on your new nature, and be renewed as you learn to
know your Creator and become like him.
+ COLOSSIANS 3:10

IT TAKES a long time to complete a great work of art. The project
goes through many stages between inspiration and completion.
We are God's works of art in process. Although salvation occurs in a
moment, the process of transformation into godliness takes a lifetime.
For real and dynamic change to occur, God has to give us a new heart
and a new way of thinking. His Spirit will help us focus on what is true,
good, and right. Eventually you will begin to see the new you, a person
who displays God's good, holy, and true Spirit. While these changes
may appear slow to you, God's work is relentless and certain. Be patient
with yourself and trust God to do his work in you at just the right pace.

Prayer Prompts

Lord, looking back over the past, I can see you have changed me in this way: . . .
Your Word encourages me to pursue growth by . . .

 # chaos

The world seems to be in complete chaos. How can I find order and peace in my spirit?

❦

The LORD is God, and he created the heavens and earth and put everything in place. He made the world to be lived in, not to be a place of empty chaos. "I am the LORD," he says, "and there is no other."
✛ ISAIAH 45:18

As I stood there in silence—not even speaking of good things—the turmoil within me grew worse. . . . And so, Lord, where do I put my hope? My only hope is in you.
✛ PSALM 39:2, 7

He will live with them, and they will be his people. God himself will be with them. He will wipe every tear from their eyes, and there will be no more death or sorrow or crying or pain. All these things are gone forever.
✛ REVELATION 21:3-4

WE LIVE in a broken and scary world. When we focus on all the horrible things going on around the globe, we give them the power to steal our peace. The best thing we can do to find peace in the chaos is to choose to focus on knowing God and having hope in his promises. And he has promised that hope is possible because the story isn't over yet. Someday, when Jesus returns, all chaos, evil, and grief will disappear. So the next time fear and confusion grip your heart, take a deep breath and remember who is in control.

Prayer Prompts

Lord, I feel fearful and confused when I see this happening in the world: . . . Your Word leads me toward peace because you have promised . . .

character 🌿

What is the key to becoming a woman with godly character?

——————————— ❧ ———————————

The Holy Spirit produces this kind of fruit in our lives: love, joy, peace, patience, kindness, goodness, faithfulness, gentleness, and self-control.
+ GALATIANS 5:22-23

God is working in you, giving you the desire and the power to do what pleases him.
+ PHILIPPIANS 2:13

Yes, I am the vine; you are the branches. Those who remain in me, and I in them, will produce much fruit. For apart from me you can do nothing.
+ JOHN 15:5

Keep on doing what is right, and trust your lives to the God who created you, for he will never fail you.
+ 1 PETER 4:19

God blesses those whose hearts are pure, for they will see God.
+ MATTHEW 5:8

WE WORK HARD all our lives to become excellent at what we do. We try to excel in work, marriage, mothering, friendships, ministries, and hobbies. Doesn't it make sense to also work hard at becoming morally excellent so we can be known for character qualities like integrity, kindness, love, and faithfulness? The only way to grow in godly character is by spending time with our Lord. God promises that as we continually seek relationship with him and try to do what he asks, we will become more and more like Jesus through the help of the Spirit.

Prayer Prompts

Lord, I would like to be known for this godly characteristic: . . .
Your Word tells me if I want to grow in this area, I must . . .

 children

How do I raise children who grow to know and love God?

— ❧ —

Commit yourselves wholeheartedly to these words of mine. . . . Teach them to your children. Talk about them when you are at home and when you are on the road, when you are going to bed and when you are getting up.
+ DEUTERONOMY 11:18-19

You have been taught the holy Scriptures from childhood, and they have given you the wisdom to receive the salvation that comes by trusting in Christ Jesus.
+ 2 TIMOTHY 3:15

My Spirit will not leave them, and neither will these words I have given you. They will be on your lips and on the lips of your children and your children's children forever.
+ ISAIAH 59:21

RAISING CHILDREN to know and love the Lord is no easy task. The best thing we as mothers can do is help our children know God personally instead of simply knowing things *about* God. Instead of dragging our children along on our own spiritual journey, we can walk alongside them in theirs and help cultivate their own personal relationship with God. We do this by reading the Word with them, praying with them, and sitting with them in times of celebration and despair. We can ask questions like "Where did you notice God today?" "When do you feel closest to God?" "What do you think God is teaching you?" Teach and train your children's hearts to be open to God's love and care so they will know and love a God who sees them as special—special enough to lovingly pursue a personal relationship with them.

Prayer Prompts

Lord, a spiritual question I would like to ask my child today is . . .
Your Word helps me guide my children on their spiritual journeys by . . .

choices 🍃

How can I be certain the choices I make are in line with God's ways?

——————— ❧ ———————

Love the LORD your God, walk in all his ways, obey his commands, hold firmly to him, and serve him with all your heart and all your soul.
+ JOSHUA 22:5

I have hidden your word in my heart, that I might not sin against you.
+ PSALM 119:11

There is safety in having many advisers.
+ PROVERBS 11:14

[The LORD] guides me along right paths, bringing honor to his name.
+ PSALM 23:3

If you need wisdom, ask our generous God, and he will give it to you. He will not rebuke you for asking.
+ JAMES 1:5

EVERY DAY presents new choices. When faced with a decision, ask yourself, *Will this lead me closer to God or further away from him?* This question will always point you toward God's ways instead of your own. The best way to make good choices—and to avoid making decisions that benefit you at the expense of others—is to read God's Word, seek his guidance in prayer, and seek the advice of godly counselors. The "right" choice may not always be clear. However, you can always ask God for clarity and for the strength to put him and others ahead of everything else.

Prayer Prompts

Lord, please help me make the right choice about . . .
Your Word tells me that before I decide, it would be wise to . . .

 # church

Is going to church really so important to my relationship with God?

❧

The one thing I ask of the LORD—the thing I seek most—
is to live in the house of the LORD all the days of my life.
+ PSALM 27:4

What joy for those who can live in your house, always singing your praises.
+ PSALM 84:4

Just as our bodies have many parts and each part has a
special function, so it is with Christ's body. We are many
parts of one body, and we all belong to each other.
+ ROMANS 12:4-5

Let us not neglect our meeting together, as some people do, but encourage one
another, especially now that the day of his return is drawing near.
+ HEBREWS 10:25

THE CHURCH is home to all of God's family. Home is meant to be a place of safety and belonging. It is a place to teach and counsel one another in wisdom, to encourage each other, and to worship together. God's home cannot run as he intended without each of his children present. The enemy wants us to believe that we are insignificant in the church, that our presence doesn't matter. He whispers excuses in our ears to keep us from attending. But the truth is that we each have a special place in God's family. Have you ever thought that maybe the church needs you just as much as you need the church? Step out in faith and watch how God will use your special gifts and abilities to impact the lives of others.

Prayer Prompts

Lord, this is how I currently feel about my church: . . .
When I don't feel like going to church, your Word reminds me . . .

circumstances 🍃

How can I experience God in the midst of troubling circumstances?

— ⚓ —

Even though the fig trees have no blossoms, and there are no grapes on the vines; even though the olive crop fails, and the fields lie empty and barren; even though the flocks die in the fields, and the cattle barns are empty, yet I will rejoice in the LORD! I will be joyful in the God of my salvation!
+ HABAKKUK 3:17-18

Be thankful in all circumstances, for this is God's will for you who belong to Christ Jesus.
+ 1 THESSALONIANS 5:18

Those who are righteous will be long remembered. They do not fear bad news; they confidently trust the LORD to care for them. They are confident and fearless and can face their foes triumphantly.
+ PSALM 112:6-8

ONE WAY to rise above life's difficult circumstances is to give God thanks. Even if we can't find anything to be thankful for in our present situation, we can thank him for his constant presence and comfort. Whether we are currently living in sunshine or storms, God never changes, and neither does his love for us. God is always eager to come alongside us to teach us something from both the good and the bad of our circumstances. So refuse to worry today. Turn every concern into confident prayer. Come to God with your needs and with thanksgiving for what he has done for you, and trust that he will bring good fruit out of the difficult times.

Prayer Prompts
Lord, the circumstance troubling me now is . . .
Your Word tells me I can experience you in the midst of difficulties by . . .

 comfort

How can I experience God's comfort in difficult times?

———— ❧ ————

In my distress I prayed to the LORD, and
the LORD answered me and set me free.
+ PSALM 118:5

I meditate on your age-old regulations; O LORD, they comfort me.
+ PSALM 119:52

Every word of God proves true.
He is a shield to all who come to him for protection.
+ PROVERBS 30:5

The LORD is good, a strong refuge when trouble comes.
He is close to those who trust in him.
+ NAHUM 1:7

Don't be afraid, for I am with you. Don't be discouraged,
for I am your God. I will strengthen you and help you.
+ ISAIAH 41:10

DO YOU LONG to experience comfort in life? Scripture promises us that God is faithful to comfort us when we need it. Sometimes we miss out because we expect him to comfort us by solving our problems. However, God calms and reassures us in a variety of ways. His comfort may come through his love, his Word, his presence, or his people. As you read his Word, reflect on how God may be comforting you right now. Go to him in your times of need and watch him encourage you in ways you might never have expected.

Prayer Prompts

Lord, the area of my life where I long to feel your comfort is . . .
Your Word shows me you might be comforting me in these unexpected ways: . . .

commitment 🍃

How can I know if I am truly committed to God?

_____ ❧ _____

Fear the LORD and serve him wholeheartedly.
+ JOSHUA 24:14

*Jesus called out to them, "Come, follow me, and I will show you how
to fish for people!" And they left their nets at once and followed him.*
+ MATTHEW 4:19-20

*Give yourselves completely to God, for you were dead,
but now you have new life. So use your whole body as
an instrument to do what is right for the glory of God.*
+ ROMANS 6:13

Commit everything you do to the LORD. Trust him, and he will help you.
+ PSALM 37:5

BEING COMMITTED to God means being dedicated to living our
lives like Jesus and for Jesus. Commitment is more than intellec-
tual agreement; it involves giving our whole selves—body, soul, emotions, and mind—to God for his use. Do we strive to love others as
Jesus did? Do we pray for others the way Jesus did? Think about your
commitment. Which activities take priority in your life? What do you
love most? When we make Jesus the central, dominating commitment
of our lives, we properly place all our activities in order. Commitment
to God can be costly, but God promises great blessings for those who
are faithful in their commitment to him.

Prayer Prompts

*Lord, if I am honest, sometimes these commitments take priority over you: . . .
Your Word tells me that to be fully committed to you, I must . . .*

🌿 communication

Does God really talk to people?
How can I know if he's speaking to me?

—————— ❧ ——————

Devote yourselves to prayer with an alert mind and a thankful heart.
+ COLOSSIANS 4:2

*"Go out and stand before me on the mountain," the LORD told
him. And as Elijah stood there, the LORD passed by, and a mighty
windstorm hit the mountain. It was such a terrible blast that the rocks
were torn loose, but the LORD was not in the wind. After the wind
there was an earthquake, but the LORD was not in the earthquake.
And after the earthquake there was a fire, but the LORD was not in
the fire. And after the fire there was the sound of a gentle whisper. . . .
And a voice said, "What are you doing here, Elijah?"*
+ 1 KINGS 19:11-13

Come close to God, and God will come close to you.
+ JAMES 4:8

THE BIBLE is one continual story of God communicating with his people. While we might prefer to hear an audible voice from God, he more often communicates with us in other ways. He might speak through his Word, his people, or his creation, or in the quietness of our own hearts. If we are too busy rushing through life at a frantic pace, we will miss hearing God. How can you slow down in order to better listen to God today? Set aside some time to sit quietly in his presence, asking if he has anything to say to you.

Prayer Prompts

Lord, I desire to hear you speak to me about . . .
Your Word tells me that I will hear your voice if I . . .

community

How can I have a good impact on my community?

———————— ✖ ————————

Be careful to live properly among your unbelieving neighbors. Then even if they accuse you of doing wrong, they will see your honorable behavior, and they will give honor to God when he judges the world.
+ 1 PETER 2:12

If someone asks about your hope as a believer, always be ready to explain it. But do this in a gentle and respectful way. Keep your conscience clear. Then if people speak against you, they will be ashamed when they see what a good life you live because you belong to Christ.
+ 1 PETER 3:15-16

You are the light of the world. . . . No one lights a lamp and then puts it under a basket. Instead, a lamp is placed on a stand, where it gives light to everyone in the house. In the same way, let your good deeds shine out for all to see, so that everyone will praise your heavenly Father.
+ MATTHEW 5:14-16

GOD'S INFLUENCE in our lives is very attractive to others. The more we are women who reflect God's loving character, the more people will be drawn to us. Practically, this may mean just being friendly neighbors, volunteering to serve the needy in our communities, being responsible citizens, making peace with difficult people, or treating others with fairness and respect. Through these simple actions we can be attractive examples of God's love to people in our communities. With God's power, your character can become a beacon of light that brightens the whole community with God's transforming ways.

Prayer Prompts

Lord, the people in my community I feel called to impact are . . .
Your Word says I can best do this by . . .

58

 # comparison

How do I resist the temptation to
compare myself to others?

———— ❧ ————

Pay careful attention to your own work, for then you will get the satisfaction
of a job well done, and you won't need to compare yourself to anyone else.
For we are each responsible for our own conduct.
+ GALATIANS 6:4-5

We are God's masterpiece. He has created us anew in Christ Jesus,
so we can do the good things he planned for us long ago.
+ EPHESIANS 2:10

Think about the things of heaven, not the things of earth.
+ COLOSSIANS 3:2

As WOMEN, we learn early on to rank ourselves with those around us, whether by appearance, intelligence, or personality. But if we only knew how much God loves us, we wouldn't feel the need to compare ourselves to anyone else. We are so valuable to him. He loves us just as we are. Therefore, it is foolish to look to others for who we "should" or "shouldn't" be. Whenever you start comparing yourself to someone else, look to God instead. He is your Creator, the one who gave you all your unique character traits and talents. Stay focused on him, for only he can make you fully satisfied, happy, and complete. Don't allow comparison to distract you from the unique, wonderful journey he has in store for you.

Prayer Prompts

Lord, the area where I am most tempted to compare my life with others is . . .
Your Word says I can resist this urge to compare by remembering that . . .

compassion

How should my faith affect my compassion for others?

❦

He will rescue the poor when they cry to him; he will help the oppressed, who have no one to defend them. He feels pity for the weak and the needy, and he will rescue them. He will redeem them from oppression and violence, for their lives are precious to him.
+ PSALM 72:12-14

You must be compassionate, just as your Father is compassionate.
+ LUKE 6:36

God is our merciful Father and the source of all comfort. He comforts us in all our troubles so that we can comfort others. When they are troubled, we will be able to give them the same comfort God has given us.
+ 2 CORINTHIANS 1:3-4

OUR WORLD is full of people who desperately need to experience the compassion of Jesus in their lives. Since Christ is always loving, tender, and full of sympathy toward us, how can we not respond to others the same way? Compassion involves opening our hearts to those around us who are hurting and then doing something about their struggle. It is both an emotion (feeling concern for someone) and an action (doing something to meet the person's need). Instead of trying to avoid the pain of the world, compassion compels us to step into it intentionally. Your level of compassion is a litmus test of your commitment and desire to love others as Christ loves you. If you find it hard to feel compassion for others, remember how Christ has shown compassion to you.

Prayer Prompts

*Lord, your Word reminds me that you show me compassion by . . .
Therefore, I can show compassion toward . . .*

 # complacency

How can I overcome my complacency?

❧

I know all the things you do, that you are neither hot nor cold.
I wish that you were one or the other! But since you are like lukewarm water,
neither hot nor cold, I will spit you out of my mouth!
  + REVELATION 3:15-16

Simpletons turn away from me—to death.
Fools are destroyed by their own complacency.
  + PROVERBS 1:32

Stay alert! Watch out for your great enemy, the devil.
He prowls around like a roaring lion, looking for someone to
devour. Stand firm against him, and be strong in your faith.
  + 1 PETER 5:8-9

Teach us to realize the brevity of life, so that we may grow in wisdom.
  + PSALM 90:12

COMPLACENCY is not motionlessness. It is choosing to be self-satisfied and unaware, which actually moves us away from God. We need to remain active and alert in our faith, and realize there is a battle going on over our souls. The enemy would like nothing better than to sway us in moments of indecision. Make a choice to move toward God today even if the movement feels insignificant. Read his Word, talk with him about your day, or simply remind yourself that he is with you. Do not simply try to avoid doing wrong; be proactive in doing what is right. Most importantly, be passionate about your relationship with God. Ask him to give you an eternal perspective so you can be wise with the one life you have been given.

Prayer Prompts

Lord, this is one small way I can move toward you today: . . .
Your Word encourages me to continually stay active in my faith by . . .

complaining 💬

Why is it important that I break my habit of complaining?

—— ❧ ——

Do everything without complaining and arguing.
+ PHILIPPIANS 2:14

Let everything you say be good and helpful, so that your words will be an encouragement to those who hear them.
+ EPHESIANS 4:29

You must give an account on judgment day for every idle word you speak.
+ MATTHEW 12:36

The tongue can bring death or life.
+ PROVERBS 18:21

WHEN TALKING with our friends or coworkers, it's easy to gripe about everything from our jobs to our romantic relationships to our kids and even our churches. It is tempting to believe our complaining is just innocent banter or a way to get something off our chests. But complaining has a greater impact on our hearts and lives than we realize. It saps our joy and leaves us feeling bitter, discouraged, and ungrateful. Our words have the power to change the way we view our circumstances and even our relationship with God. That is why God's Word emphasizes the incredible influence our tongues hold. We can actively fight against complaining by becoming aware of what comes out of our mouths and then, with the power of the Holy Spirit, changing irritable words into those that are thankful, cheerful, and encouraging to others. The attitude of your heart changes as you intentionally seek to change your words.

Prayer Prompts

Lord, I am most tempted to complain about . . .
Your Word warns me to be careful with my words because . . .

 # compliment

Why is it important to know the difference between a true compliment and flattery?

&

May the words of my mouth and the meditation of my heart be pleasing to you, O Lord, my rock and my redeemer.
+ PSALM 19:14

In the end, people appreciate honest criticism far more than flattery.
+ PROVERBS 28:23

Christ died for us so that . . . we can live with him forever. So encourage each other and build each other up, just as you are already doing.
+ 1 THESSALONIANS 5:10-11

THE BIBLE makes it clear that the motives of our heart are important to the Lord. We need to know the difference between a compliment and flattery because it's all about the motivation behind the words. A sincere compliment is about the other person, designed to build up him or her. Flattery is all about us; we're saying something nice just to get something in return. Sincere compliments are also true, whereas flattery tends to be exaggerated. Before offering another a compliment, ask yourself, *Are my motives calculating or sincere? Self-serving or other focused?* Ask the Lord to help you be aware of the motives behind your words so that you may sincerely build others up in love.

Prayer Prompts

Lord, sometimes my motives for complimenting someone are . . .
This is what your Word says about complimenting another: . . .

condemnation

What can I do when others look down on me because of my faith?

———— ❧ ————

The LORD is my light and my salvation—so why should I be afraid?
The LORD is my fortress, protecting me from danger, so why should I tremble?
+ PSALM 27:1

See how very much our Father loves us,
for he calls us his children, and that is what we are!
+ 1 JOHN 3:1

Can anything ever separate us from Christ's love? Does it mean he no
longer loves us if we have trouble or calamity, or are persecuted, or
hungry, or destitute, or in danger, or threatened with death? . . . No,
despite all these things, overwhelming victory is ours through Christ,
who loved us.
+ ROMANS 8:35, 37

THE BEST THING we can do when others look down on us for our faith is to remind ourselves of this truth: We are known and loved by God. Meditating on and receiving God's love is the foundation for how we live, make decisions, and relate to others. If we go through life with confidence that we are loved by God, we remain secure and joyful—even when others condemn us for what we believe. Our ultimate purpose is to please the one who made us and redeemed us, no matter what others may think. The next time you feel condemned for your faith, remember who your Father is. He is able to free you from the bondage of human opinion and criticism because of his deep love for you.

Prayer Prompts

Lord, when others look down on me for my faith, I often respond by . . .
But when I feel condemned by others, I will remember that your Word says . . .

 # confession

Does confession strengthen
my relationship with God?

— ❧ —

*When I refused to confess my sin, my body wasted away, and
I groaned all day long. . . . Finally, I confessed all my sins to you and
stopped trying to hide my guilt. I said to myself, "I will confess my
rebellion to the LORD." And you forgave me! All my guilt is gone.*
+ PSALM 32:3, 5

*People who conceal their sins will not prosper, but if they
confess and turn from them, they will receive mercy.*
+ PROVERBS 28:13

*Oh, what joy for those whose disobedience is forgiven,
whose sin is put out of sight!*
+ PSALM 32:1

*The man and his wife heard the LORD God walking about in
the garden. So they hid from the LORD God among the trees.*
+ GENESIS 3:8

IT IS HUMAN NATURE to hide when we have done something wrong.
After Adam and Eve sinned in the Garden, they hid in the bushes
and covered themselves with leaves. Their guilt and shame placed a
relational barrier between them and God. If sin separates us from God,
confession is the bridge that reconnects us. It allows us to come back to
God so we can receive his mercy and forgiveness. Confession is essential
because it reminds us of our need for Jesus and the Cross. Bring the dark
places in your heart into God's light, and he will replace your guilt with
the joy of unconditional love and acceptance.

Prayer Prompts
Lord, I need to confess to you that . . .
Your Word promises that if I confess my sin, you are faithful to . . .

confidence

How can I become a confident woman?

─────────── ❦ ───────────

*God has given us both his promise and his oath. These two
things are unchangeable because it is impossible for God to lie.
Therefore, we who have fled to him for refuge can have great
confidence as we hold to the hope that lies before us.*
+ HEBREWS 6:18

*If the old way, which has been replaced, was glorious,
how much more glorious is the new, which remains forever!
Since this new way gives us such confidence, we can be very bold.*
+ 2 CORINTHIANS 3:11-12

*Because of Christ and our faith in him, we can now
come boldly and confidently into God's presence.*
+ EPHESIANS 3:12

WE ALL WANT to be women who exude confidence. Sometimes our confidence comes from feeling good about our
outfits, our bodies, or the people we surround ourselves with. But
these things leave us feeling assured only for a moment. Real and
lasting confidence comes from knowing and trusting that God is
on our side. What would it be like to live each day truly believing we
are loved and cared for by the God of the universe? Most likely, this
belief would change what we say, how we act, and the way we carry
ourselves. Be confident in God's promises to watch over you, to give
you what you need for each day, and to welcome you into his presence when you come face to face with him in heaven.

Prayer Prompts

Lord, I lack confidence in the areas of . . .
Your Word assures me I can walk with confidence because . . .

 # confrontation

How do I know when to confront someone and when to let an offense go?

— ❧ —

If another believer sins, rebuke that person; then if there is repentance, forgive.
+ LUKE 17:3

If another believer sins against you, go privately and point out the offense. If the other person listens and confesses it, you have won that person back. But if you are unsuccessful, take one or two others with you and go back again.
+ MATTHEW 18:15-16

God has not given us a spirit of fear and timidity, but of power, love, and self-discipline.
+ 2 TIMOTHY 1:7

Patiently correct, rebuke, and encourage your people with good teaching.
+ 2 TIMOTHY 4:2

MANY WOMEN tend to think of confrontation as something to avoid because it can feel awkward and tense. These feelings make confrontation seem negative, but the Bible tells us differently. Confrontation can actually be good and helpful. When approached with a desire to help rather than hurt, confrontation becomes a valuable tool to bring resolution to a problem or to bring someone back to Christ. Godly confrontation can help begin the process of transforming difficult situations into positive results. Everyone gets off track once in a while, so we all need grace. Before confronting someone who has wronged you, ask yourself, *Is my desire for this person to become more holy or to be put in his or her place?* Then ask the Lord to give you patience, grace, and the right words as you lovingly confront.

Prayer Prompts

Lord, confrontation makes me feel . . .
Before I confront another, I need to follow this guidance from your Word: . . .

confusion 🍃

How should I respond when I'm confused about what God wants me to do?

❧

Listen to my voice in the morning, LORD.
Each morning I bring my requests to you and wait expectantly.
✝ PSALM 5:3

Your word is a lamp to guide my feet and a light for my path.
✝ PSALM 119:105

Show me the right path, O LORD; point out the road for me to
follow. Lead me by your truth and teach me, for you are the
God who saves me. All day long I put my hope in you.
✝ PSALM 25:4-5

The most important commandment is this: . . . "Love the LORD your God
with all your heart, all your soul, all your mind, and all your strength."
The second is equally important: "Love your neighbor as yourself."
No other commandment is greater than these.
✝ MARK 12:29-31

EVERYONE experiences times when they are uncertain about which road to take. But confusion happens when we don't even know what we are looking for at the end of the road. God has given us his Word to be our compass for life. It guides us by giving us one goal—to be women who love God and love others. Whenever you feel confused about what path to take, make this goal your destination. Continue to read his Word, pray for his wisdom, and wait. If he still hasn't made the decision clear, continue to love him and love others until he tells you which path to take.

Prayer Prompts

Lord, I'm confused about . . .
Your Word tells me I can have clarity by . . .

 conscience

How does my conscience work?

———————— ❧ ————————

Cling to your faith in Christ, and keep your conscience clear.
For some people have deliberately violated their consciences;
as a result, their faith has been shipwrecked.
+ 1 TIMOTHY 1:19

They knew God, but they wouldn't worship him as God or even give him
thanks. And they began to think up foolish ideas of what God was like.
As a result, their minds became dark and confused.
+ ROMANS 1:21

My child, listen to what I say. . . . Then you will understand what is
right, just, and fair, and you will find the right way to go.
+ PROVERBS 2:1, 9

OUR CONSCIENCE is the innate part of our soul that helps us discern whether or not we are in line with God's will. It is God's gift for keeping us sensitive to his moral code. If we don't listen to and obey our conscience, we will become less sensitive to its promptings. It will function effectively only when we stay close to God, spend time in his Word, and make an effort to understand ourselves and our own tendencies toward sin. If you find yourself unmoved by evil, it may be an indication that your soul is desperately in need of time with the Lord. Ask God to sharpen your conscience as you seek him and read his Word.

Prayer Prompts

Lord, I sometimes ignore my conscience when . . .
Your Word tells me I can have a clear conscience by . . .

contentment 🌰

What is the key to contentment in life?

———————————— ❧ ————————————

Satisfy us each morning with your unfailing love,
so we may sing for joy to the end of our lives.
+ PSALM 90:14

I have learned how to be content with whatever I have. I know how to live on
almost nothing or with everything. I have learned the secret of living in every
situation, whether it is with a full stomach or empty, with plenty or little.
For I can do everything through Christ, who gives me strength.
+ PHILIPPIANS 4:11-13

Each time [God] said, "My grace is all you need."
+ 2 CORINTHIANS 12:9

CONTENTMENT is among life's most elusive qualities. The answer
to the question "How much is enough?" always seems to be
"Just a little bit more." Our deepest contentment and joy come not
from pursuing happiness, pleasure, or material possessions but from
pursuing intimacy with God. When we depend on material wealth,
it means we're trying to build our own security, which always leaves
us craving more. The more we crave, the less satisfied we will be. But
God has promised that he is sufficient. The Bible teaches that human
beings are most fully satisfied when they experience God's unfailing
love. Do you believe this? Let go of finding fulfillment in "things," and
instead receive true peace and contentment, which only come from
being in relationship with God.

Prayer Prompts

Lord, sometimes I believe I will finally be content if only I have . . .
Your Word assures me that real contentment comes from . . .

 # control

Is God really in control, or do a lot of things just happen by chance?

————— ❧ —————

The LORD will work out his plans for my life.
+ PSALM 138:8

I am Joseph, your brother, whom you sold into slavery in Egypt.
But don't be upset, and don't be angry with yourselves for selling me
to this place. It was God who sent me here ahead of you to preserve
your lives. . . . It was God who sent me here, not you!
+ GENESIS 45:4-5, 8

You see me when I travel and when I rest at home. You know everything I do.
+ PSALM 139:3

FROM OUR HUMAN PERSPECTIVE, the world and our individual lives often seem random and unpredictable. However, the truth is that God is still in control. Joseph's story in Genesis shows how God used even the unjust treatment of Joseph by his own brothers to fulfill a bigger plan. People's sinful ways do not ruin God's sovereign plans. In the end, we will discover that our lives are like tapestries; right now we can see only sections of the back, with all its knots and loose ends. Someday we will see the front in its beautiful entirety— the picture of world history and our personal history from God's perspective. Ask God to help you trust that he is working through your unexpected and unwelcome circumstances. This attitude will help you embrace both the good and the bad, knowing that through them, God is weaving a beautiful picture with your life.

Prayer Prompts

Lord, I'm still trying to understand this part of my life that seems random: . . .
I know you are in control because your Word says . . .

conversation

How can I live in conversation with God?

———————— ✺ ————————

You will show me the way of life, granting me the joy of your presence and the pleasures of living with you forever.
+ PSALM 16:11

Devote yourselves to prayer with an alert mind and a thankful heart.
+ COLOSSIANS 4:2

Never stop praying.
+ 1 THESSALONIANS 5:17

Are any of you suffering hardships? You should pray.
Are any of you happy? You should sing praises.
+ JAMES 5:13

GOD IS BY OUR SIDE, just as a friend can be. Yet how often are we aware of his company? We can practice his presence by inviting him into all our moments, even the mundane and messy. This can be as simple as transforming our "self-talk" into continual conversation with him. If we have a person on our mind, we can ask God how to pray for him or her. If we are worried about something, we can tell God our fears. Intimate conversation can happen even during dishwashing, driving, or yard work. Over time this will become more natural. As you invite God into your thoughts, you also become more aware of his presence and his voice. Prayer doesn't take time away from your life; it is your lifeline to God! Weave small prayers throughout your day and learn the joy of living in God's company.

Prayer Prompts

Lord, this is on my heart today: . . .
Your Word encourages me to pray about it this way: . . .

 coping

How can I cope when pain becomes overwhelming?

✦

Don't be afraid, for I am with you. Don't be discouraged,
for I am your God. I will strengthen you and help you.
I will hold you up with my victorious right hand.
+ ISAIAH 41:10

I have told you all this so that you may have peace in me.
Here on earth you will have many trials and sorrows.
But take heart, because I have overcome the world.
+ JOHN 16:33

The LORD is good, a strong refuge when trouble comes.
He is close to those who trust in him.
+ NAHUM 1:7

GOD IS THE FATHER of compassion and comfort. Just as a mother longs to hold her child who is in pain, so he longs to hold us in the midst of our struggles. We can use our time of suffering to draw near to him. We can open his Word, cry out to him in our distress, and remind ourselves of his presence with us. Times of distress tempt us to forget his promises, so we need to remember to hold on to the hope that Jesus gave. He told us we will have sorrows on this earth, but we can face them with courage because he has overcome the world! No matter what your circumstances are, you don't need to panic, for God will not let you go. Choose to trust in him and experience the comfort of his everlasting promises and his abiding presence.

Prayer Prompts

Lord, I often cope with pain by . . .
When I am in pain, I will be encouraged because your Word says . . .

courage

Where can I find courage to
face the things I am afraid of?

———————— ❧ ————————

Be strong and courageous! Do not be afraid and do not panic before
them. For the LORD your God will personally go ahead of you.
He will neither fail you nor abandon you.
+ DEUTERONOMY 31:6

Who is God except the LORD? Who but our God is a solid rock? God arms me
with strength, and he makes my way perfect. He makes me as surefooted
as a deer, enabling me to stand on mountain heights.
+ PSALM 18:31-33

The LORD is my strength and shield. I trust him with all my heart.
He helps me, and my heart is filled with joy.
+ PSALM 28:7

MARK TWAIN once said, "Courage isn't the absence of fear. It is acting in spite of it." Fear is a normal part of life, and sometimes we have no choice but to step into a situation that terrifies us. However, we can choose how to move forward—timidly or courageously. Even if we aren't feeling very brave, we can trust that God is greater than any enemy or problem we are facing. Throughout his Word, God promises that he will give his people strength and courage and that he will never leave them. His words still hold true for you today. Grow in courage, trusting God's promise to be with you wherever you go.

Prayer Prompts

Lord, I am scared of . . .
Your Word assures me that I can face this with courage because . . .

 # creation

How should my faith affect the way I care for creation?

———— ❧ ————

God said, "Let us make human beings in our image, to be like us. They will reign over the fish in the sea, the birds in the sky, the livestock, all the wild animals on the earth, and the small animals that scurry along the ground."
+ GENESIS 1:26

When you are attacking a town and the war drags on, you must not cut down the trees. . . . Are the trees your enemies, that you should attack them?
+ DEUTERONOMY 20:19

God looked over all he had made, and he saw that it was very good! And evening passed and morning came, marking the sixth day.
+ GENESIS 1:31

CARING for creation stands in opposition to today's consumerism as well as our own selfish desires to live an easy, convenient life. However, God sees all of his creation as good, and he instructs us to be good stewards over it. Caring for the earth challenges us to live within our God-given boundaries by not taking more than we need. It requires us to selflessly love our neighbor as well as future generations by making the earth a better place. It gives us the opportunity to care for something that was meant to glorify God and point people to him. What an amazing way to participate with God in his work! Ask God to open your heart to love and care for creation the way he does.

Prayer Prompts

Lord, I confess I have neglected or hurt your creation by . . .
Your Word motivates me to think about creation this way: . . .

creativity 🍃

Does God value my creativity?

———————— ❧ ————————

The heavens proclaim the glory of God. The skies display his craftsmanship.
Day after day they continue to speak; night after night they make him known.
+ PSALM 19:1-2

Beautiful words stir my heart. I will recite a lovely poem
about the king, for my tongue is like the pen of a skillful poet.
+ PSALM 45:1

There will be an abundance of flowers and singing and joy!
The deserts will become as green as the mountains of
Lebanon, as lovely as Mount Carmel or the plain of Sharon.
There the LORD will display his glory, the splendor of our God.
+ ISAIAH 35:2

You are worthy, O Lord our God, to receive glory and honor and power. For
you created all things, and they exist because you created what you pleased.
+ REVELATION 4:11

ALL NATURE sings and displays beauty that surpasses the finest
music, poetry, and creative genius of all human artists put
together. God the Creator is a God of design, color, beauty, and order.
The great art of the world only copies his creation. The finest model
of craftsmanship and artistic skill is found in the universe he made.
Our own creativity is the overflow of hearts and minds filled with
the good things of God. As you create, remind yourself that you're
expressing how you were made in the image of God. If you're looking for a little inspiration or motivation, read in God's Word about
his creative wonders.

Prayer Prompts

Lord, I enjoy expressing my creativity by . . .
I see how much you value creativity when I read in your Word that . . .

If I'm obeying God, why am I facing a crisis?

———————— ❧ ————————

Jesus said to his disciples, "Let's cross to the other side of the lake."
So they got into a boat and started out. . . . Jesus settled down for a nap.
But soon a fierce storm came down on the lake. The boat was filling with
water, and they were in real danger. The disciples went and woke him up,
shouting, "Master, Master, we're going to drown!" When Jesus woke up,
he rebuked the wind and the raging waves. Suddenly the storm stopped
and all was calm. Then he asked them, "Where is your faith?"
+ LUKE 8:22-25

Call on me when you are in trouble, and I will rescue you,
and you will give me glory.
+ PSALM 50:15

I will answer them before they even call to me. While they are still talking
about their needs, I will go ahead and answer their prayers!
+ ISAIAH 65:24

THE DISCIPLES were devoted followers of Jesus. They may have thought that being his disciples would exclude them from the trials of life, but that wasn't the case. However, when a dangerous storm threatened their lives, they knew where to turn for help. The truth is, doing the will of God does not exclude us from this world's trials. When we experience trouble, we need to call out to Jesus for his care and protection. Like a mother who can hear her child's cry over the din of a crowd, Jesus hears you. When you call out to God, it is his presence with you that breaks through your fears and calms your heart, even when the storms of life continue to rage around you.

Prayer Prompts

Lord, I don't know why I am facing this crisis: . . .
Your Word promises me that even in the midst of the storm, you will . . .

criticism 🍂

What is a wise way to approach criticism—
both giving and receiving it?

———————— ❧ ————————

Fools think their own way is right, but the wise listen to others.
A fool is quick-tempered, but a wise person stays calm when insulted.
An honest witness tells the truth; a false witness tells lies.
Some people make cutting remarks, but the words of the wise bring healing.
+ PROVERBS 12:15-18

Timely advice is lovely, like golden apples in a silver basket.
To one who listens, valid criticism is like a gold earring or other gold jewelry.
+ PROVERBS 25:11-12

Don't speak evil against each other, dear brothers and sisters. If you criticize
and judge each other, then you are criticizing and judging God's law.
+ JAMES 4:11

If you listen to constructive criticism, you will be at home among the wise.
+ PROVERBS 15:31

IT'S SO EASY to be overly critical—of ourselves and especially of others. There is a time and place for healthy criticism, but too often we find fault with others simply because they are doing something that bothers us. However, our words are only helpful if they bring healing and encouragement. God's Word instructs us how to give and receive criticism in a way that honors him. Whether you are on the giving or receiving end of criticism, allow God's truth to convict you and encourage you toward speech that is gracious, truthful, and loving, and a blessing to others.

Prayer Prompts

Lord, my most recent interaction with criticism left me feeling . . .
Your Word reminds me that before I criticize others, I need to . . .

 # culture

How can I be a part of today's culture and still avoid its negative impact?

———— ✂ ————

Don't copy the behavior and customs of this world, but let God transform you into a new person by changing the way you think. Then you will learn to know God's will for you, which is good and pleasing and perfect.
+ ROMANS 12:2

You are the light of the world—like a city on a hilltop that cannot be hidden. No one lights a lamp and then puts it under a basket. Instead, a lamp is placed on a stand, where it gives light to everyone in the house. In the same way, let your good deeds shine out for all to see.
+ MATTHEW 5:14-16

Feed the hungry, and help those in trouble. Then your light will shine out from the darkness, and the darkness around you will be as bright as noon.
+ ISAIAH 58:10

GOD'S MESSAGE has always been countercultural. If we are truly following Jesus rather than the culture, we will at some point be misunderstood, mocked, and possibly even persecuted. When we decide to stand against certain worldviews, pray for our enemies, or give away our money instead of spending it on ourselves, it will not make any sense by the world's standards. However, God promises many benefits to those who bravely choose to go against culture to follow Jesus instead. No matter how our society responds to your beliefs or your faith, choose to stand strong. Reflecting on God's Word will give you strength, perspective, and encouragement to influence your culture instead of allowing your culture to influence you.

Prayer Prompts
Lord, I find myself being influenced by culture in this way: . . .
Your Word calls me to be countercultural by . . .

danger 🍃

What is the greatest danger to my faith?

━━━━━━━━ ❧ ━━━━━━━━

*Dear children, keep away from anything that
might take God's place in your hearts.*
✝ 1 JOHN 5:21

*Stay alert! Watch out for your great enemy, the devil.
He prowls around like a roaring lion, looking for someone to devour.*
✝ 1 PETER 5:8

*The wise are cautious and avoid danger;
fools plunge ahead with reckless confidence.*
✝ PROVERBS 14:16

THE PURPOSE of a guardrail on a dangerous curve is not to
inhibit our freedom to drive but to save our lives! Similarly,
God's Word is the guardrail we need to travel through life—not to
restrict us but to help us avoid danger and keep our lives from going
out of control. One of the greatest dangers we face is the temptation
to do wrong. God's Word warns us that we must guard our hearts
because they are the source of our actions. Guarding our hearts
means being extra careful what we allow ourselves to see, hear, and
think about. Satan is constantly on the attack, trying to steer us away
from God and toward sin. Keep careful watch over what you let into
your heart; guard it from danger, and stay focused on the road God
has asked you to travel.

Prayer Prompts

Lord, something I should guard my heart from is . . .
Your Word warns me that guarding my heart is important because . . .

 # death

Is fearing or thinking about death a bad thing?

———————— ✀ ————————

*Since you have been raised to new life with Christ,
set your sights on the realities of heaven. . . .
Think about the things of heaven, not the things of earth.*
+ COLOSSIANS 3:1-2

*Don't be afraid of those who want to kill your body;
they cannot touch your soul.*
+ MATTHEW 10:28

*Jesus told her, "I am the resurrection and the life.
Anyone who believes in me will live, even after dying."*
+ JOHN 11:25

*He will swallow up death forever! The Sovereign LORD will wipe
away all tears. He will remove forever all insults and mockery against
his land and people. The LORD has spoken! In that day the people will
proclaim, "This is our God! We trusted in him, and he saved us!"*
+ ISAIAH 25:8-9

IT'S NATURAL to be afraid of something we have never experienced before. However, if we find ourselves feeling an inordinate fear of death or spending an unreasonable amount of time thinking about it, it may be an indication that we misunderstand heaven and lack trust in God's promises. God calls us to set our minds on the things of heaven, not on death. Take time to learn what the Bible says about heaven. Read God's promises about what eternity is like for those who love Jesus. The more you know and trust God, the less fearsome death will be.

Prayer Prompts

Lord, when I think about death, I feel . . .
Your Word promises I can look forward to this kind of life after death: . . .

decisions

Does each little decision I make really matter all that much?

My steps have stayed on your path; I have not wavered from following you.
+ PSALM 17:5

If you are faithful in little things, you will be faithful in large ones.
+ LUKE 16:10

Commit your actions to the LORD, and your plans will succeed.
+ PROVERBS 16:3

Oh, that we might know the LORD! Let us press on to know him.
He will respond to us as surely as the arrival of dawn or
the coming of rains in early spring.
+ HOSEA 6:3

Seek his will in all you do, and he will show you which path to take.
+ PROVERBS 3:6

THE RIGHT DECISION is simply being faithful in little things. Perhaps that means refraining from bending the truth, being honest on our taxes, or saying yes when God prompts us to spend time with him. God's Word is clear that his will for us today is to obey him, serve others, read his Word, and do what is right. If you stay in the center of his will today, you are more likely to be in the center of his will twenty years from now. If you ask God about the small decisions of life, you will know what to do when bigger decisions come along.

Prayer Prompts

Lord, sometimes I feel tempted to disobey in these small ways: . . .
Your Word teaches me that each decision I make matters because . . .

 # defeat

What can I learn from defeat?

—— ❧ ——

*I used to wander off until you disciplined me; but now I
closely follow your word. . . . My suffering was good for me,
for it taught me to pay attention to your decrees.*
+ PSALM 119:67, 71

*We think you ought to know, dear brothers and sisters, about the trouble we
went through in the province of Asia. We were crushed and overwhelmed
beyond our ability to endure, and we thought we would never live through
it. In fact, we expected to die. But as a result, we stopped relying on ourselves
and learned to rely only on God, who raises the dead. And he did rescue
us from mortal danger, and he will rescue us again. We have placed our
confidence in him, and he will continue to rescue us.*
+ 2 CORINTHIANS 1:8-10

*Humble yourselves under the mighty power of God,
and at the right time he will lift you up in honor.*
+ 1 PETER 5:6

DEFEAT AND FAILURE can feel crushing. When we experience them after we've put forth a lot of effort, it's difficult to accept that our work hasn't paid off. However, defeat is a reality that each of us will face. God promises that good things can come even in failure. Defeat teaches us to overcome adversity and persevere through trouble. It strengthens our character, keeping us humble and dependent on God. If you are in a season where you feel defeated, don't lose heart. Be open to God and allow him to use this time to grow you into the kind of woman who is humbly reliant on him.

Prayer Prompts

Lord, I usually respond to defeat by . . .
Your Word tells me that defeat is an opportunity to experience . . .

dependence 🍃

What does it mean to depend on God?

❦

I know the LORD is always with me. I will not be shaken, for he is right beside me.
+ PSALM 16:8

[Jesus said,] "I am with you always, even to the end of the age."
+ MATTHEW 28:20

Humble yourselves before the Lord, and he will lift you up in honor.
+ JAMES 4:10

Do not be afraid, for I am with you.
+ ISAIAH 43:5

*I said to the LORD, "You are my Master!
Every good thing I have comes from you."*
+ PSALM 16:2

*O our God, we thank you and praise your glorious name! But who am I, and
who are my people, that we could give anything to you? Everything we have
has come from you, and we give you only what you first gave us!*
+ 1 CHRONICLES 29:13-14

ONE OF THE MYSTERIES of the Christian faith is that the more we humble ourselves and depend on God, the stronger we become in character and integrity. Depending on God means recognizing him as the source of our strength, our success, and all good things in our lives. If you are in a place where it feels hard or scary to depend on God, remember that everything you have ultimately came from his hand of mercy. Because he created you, he knows you inside and out, and he can be trusted to guide your life.

Prayer Prompts

Lord, I am depending on your strength to get me through . . .
Your Word assures me you are dependable when it says . . .

 depression

Where is God in my times of depression?

❧

He lifted me out of the pit of despair, out of the mud and the mire.
He set my feet on solid ground and steadied me as I walked along.
+ PSALM 40:2

He will listen to the prayers of the destitute. He will not reject their pleas.
+ PSALM 102:17

The Holy Spirit helps us in our weakness. For example, we
don't know what God wants us to pray for. But the Holy Spirit
prays for us with groanings that cannot be expressed in words.
+ ROMANS 8:26

O LORD, you are my lamp. The LORD lights up my darkness.
+ 2 SAMUEL 22:29

The eternal God is your refuge, and his everlasting arms are under you.
+ DEUTERONOMY 33:27

SOMETIMES what we need most during seasons of immense sadness is just to know we are not alone. If there is one thread of hope to hold on to in times of despair, it is that God is not absent, and he's not afraid of our sadness. In fact, he promises to be with us in it. He listens to our prayers even when they feel empty to us. He gives us the support and strength we need to get through each day, and he sends his Spirit to pray for us when we cannot find the words ourselves. If you feel like you are sinking, be encouraged that no matter how low you get, there is no depth to which you can descend where God is not present with you.

Prayer Prompts

Lord, I just feel so . . .
Your Word gives me hope of your presence because it says . . .

desirability

How can I know God really desires a close relationship with me?

❧

My heart has heard you say, "Come and talk with me."
And my heart responds, "LORD, I am coming."
+ PSALM 27:8

His unfailing love for us is powerful; the LORD's
faithfulness endures forever. Praise the LORD!
+ PSALM 117:2

See how very much our Father loves us, for he calls us his children.
+ 1 JOHN 3:1

When the cool evening breezes were blowing, the man and his wife heard
the LORD God walking about in the garden. So they hid from the LORD God
among the trees. Then the LORD God called to the man, "Where are you?"
+ GENESIS 3:8-9

WE DON'T NEED to do anything to make God want a close relationship with us. He knows everything about us, even our deepest secrets, and yet his love for us has never changed. When we doubt if God wants to spend time with us, we can take a look at his Word. It is a beautiful story about God pursuing his people, beginning with the very first humans on earth. Just as God enjoyed walking in the Garden with Adam and Eve in the cool evenings, he longs to walk with you, too. He is continually whispering to your heart, "Come talk with me." Do you hear him? Relax with God and remember that because he is your heavenly Father, you don't need to try so hard. He is proud of you, his daughter, and he delights in you just the way you are.

Prayer Prompts

Lord, sometimes I doubt that you desire a close relationship with me because . . .
Your Word promises me that I am desirable to you because . . .

 # desires

How can I know if my own desires match what God wants for me?

———— ❦ ————

He grants the desires of those who fear him;
he hears their cries for help and rescues them.
+ PSALM 145:19

Trust in the LORD and do good. . . . Take delight in the LORD,
and he will give you your heart's desires.
+ PSALM 37:3-4

The world offers only a craving for physical pleasure, a craving for
everything we see, and pride in our achievements and possessions.
These are not from the Father, but are from this world. And this
world is fading away, along with everything that people crave.
But anyone who does what pleases God will live forever.
+ 1 JOHN 2:16-17

OUR DESIRES can feel overwhelming and confusing. Sometimes it is hard to trust whether they are right or wrong. Two questions that can help us are these: Do the longings of my heart lead me away from the Lord or toward him? If my desires came to fruition, would they bring glory to God or to me? God promises that as long as we strive to know him, trust him, and pray for his will, he will guide the desires of our hearts. When our greatest wish is a close relationship with God, that will influence everything else we hope for. We can breathe a sigh of relief knowing that God is in control—even over our desires—and he will help us long for the things that please him.

Prayer Prompts

Lord, the deepest desire of my heart is . . .
Your Word says this about discerning whether my desires match yours: . . .

dignity 🍃

How can I become a woman of dignity?

— ❧ —

God created human beings in his own image.
+ GENESIS 1:27

*You made [people] only a little lower than God
and crowned them with glory and honor.*
+ PSALM 8:5

*Choose a good reputation over great riches;
being held in high esteem is better than silver or gold.*
+ PROVERBS 22:1

*A virtuous and capable wife . . . is clothed with strength and
dignity, and she laughs without fear of the future.*
+ PROVERBS 31:10, 25

*Pray this way for kings and all who are in authority so that we can live
peaceful and quiet lives marked by godliness and dignity.*
+ 1 TIMOTHY 2:2

D IGNITY is the quality of worth and significance that every human
being has because we are created in the image of God. Dignity
has two angles: recognizing our own worth before God and recognizing that same worth in others. Unfortunately, it is human nature to rank
others from important to insignificant. But a proper view of dignity
motivates us to see others as God sees them—worthy of our love and
respect no matter how they live or what they do. If you struggle with
self-worth, remind yourself that you can walk with dignity because of
how highly you are esteemed by God. When you see yourself and
others as reflections of God's image, you can't help but recognize dignity.

Prayer Prompts

Lord, sometimes I feel that I've lost my dignity when . . .
Your Word assures me I am a woman of dignity because . . .

disappointment

How can I handle life's disappointments?

———— ❧ ————

Always continue to fear the LORD. You will be rewarded for this;
your hope will not be disappointed.
+ PROVERBS 23:17-18

"My thoughts are nothing like your thoughts," says the LORD.
"And my ways are far beyond anything you could imagine."
+ ISAIAH 55:8

This hope will not lead to disappointment.
For we know how dearly God loves us, because he has
given us the Holy Spirit to fill our hearts with his love.
+ ROMANS 5:5

GOD SEES the disappointments that linger in our hearts—the small letdowns as well as the large regrets that haunt us. Expecting life to go a certain way sets us up for disappointment. What would life be like if we let go of our expectations and instead were open to God's will for us? When we are in seasons of setback and regret, we can place our hope in God and his plans for us. We can always have hope because God loves to surprise his children with his goodness—especially during times of disappointment. Be open when God leads you to unexpected places. His ways may not always be yours, but you can trust in his promise that his way is always better. He is able to use any setback, regret, or failure for your ultimate good.

Prayer Prompts

Lord, I can't seem to get over the disappointment in my life caused by . . .
Your Word says I can have hope in the midst of disappointment because . . .

disapproval 🗨

How can I care about my friends even when I don't approve of the way they live?

─────────── ❧ ───────────

When Jesus came by, he looked up at Zacchaeus and called him by name. "Zacchaeus!" he said. "Quick, come down! I must be a guest in your home today." Zacchaeus quickly climbed down and took Jesus to his house in great excitement and joy. But the people were displeased. "He has gone to be the guest of a notorious sinner," they grumbled. . . . Jesus responded, ". . . The Son of Man came to seek and save those who are lost."
+ LUKE 19:5-7, 9-10

When the teachers of religious law who were Pharisees saw him eating with tax collectors and other sinners, they asked his disciples, "Why does he eat with such scum?" When Jesus heard this, he told them, "Healthy people don't need a doctor—sick people do. I have come to call not those who think they are righteous, but those who know they are sinners."
+ MARK 2:16-17

JESUS was not one to enjoy the company of only good, God-fearing people. Even though he was the Son of God, he didn't see himself as too holy to spend time with men and women who made immoral choices. Jesus focused on finding those who were farthest from him and ministering to their needs. Following Jesus' example means looking past people's behavior to their souls. It takes special effort to love those we may disapprove of, but they are the people who are most in need of a godly friend. Your faith shouldn't separate you from the ungodly; rather, it ought to motivate you to connect with them in order to show them God's love.

Prayer Prompts

Lord, I am having a hard time being a friend to . . .
Your Word reminds me to follow Jesus' example by . . .

# disaster

Why does God allow disasters to happen? Why doesn't he prevent them?

❧

Your Father in heaven . . . sends rain on the just and the unjust alike.
+ MATTHEW 5:45

We know that God causes everything to work together for the good of those who love God and are called according to his purpose for them.
+ ROMANS 8:28

The LORD himself, the King of Israel, will live among you!
At last your troubles will be over, and you will never again fear disaster.
+ ZEPHANIAH 3:15

God is our refuge and strength, always ready to help in times of trouble. So we will not fear when earthquakes come and the mountains crumble into the sea.
+ PSALM 46:1-2

FOR REASONS only God knows, he allows disasters to happen—not only to the ungodly but also to those who follow him. He may allow crises in our lives in order to get our attention and draw us back to himself. Sometimes a disaster can be the consequence of our own sin or the ripple effect of someone else's. Sometimes it is man-made, like war, and other times it comes through nature in the form of a violent storm, a flood, a fire, or a drought. No matter what disasters you face, have faith that God still loves you and has your best interests at heart. If you have experienced disaster, hold on to the truth that God himself is with you in your crisis and promises to bring something good out of it.

Prayer Prompts

Lord, these disasters in my life and around the world are on my heart: . . .
When disaster comes my way, your Word encourages me to remember . . .

discernment 🍃

What is discernment, and why is it important?

———————————— ❧ ————————————

*Your own ears will hear [the Lord]. Right behind you a voice will say,
"This is the way you should go," whether to the right or to the left.*
+ ISAIAH 30:21

*The LORD says, "I will guide you along the best pathway for your life.
I will advise you and watch over you."*
+ PSALM 32:8

*Let those who are wise understand these things. Let those with discernment
listen carefully. The paths of the LORD are true and right, and righteous
people live by walking in them. But in those paths sinners stumble and fall.*
+ HOSEA 14:9

*My child, listen to what I say. . . . Tune your ears to wisdom . . .
ask for understanding . . . and you will gain knowledge of God.*
+ PROVERBS 2:1-3, 5

DISCERNMENT is sensitivity to God's direction. God promises that he will guide us, counsel us, lead us to truth, and help us to hear his voice—but this happens only when we live life connected to him. This involves practical choices like praying, reading Scripture, being open to God's direction and his interruptions to our schedules, and recognizing how our desires and motives can hinder us from hearing him. Would you like to be so in tune with God's voice that you recognize it when he speaks to you? Then make spending time with him your top priority. Invite him into all your plans and decisions, big and small.

Prayer Prompts

*Lord, I want to talk with you about this decision I need to make: . . .
I know you help me become a discerning woman because your Word says . . .*

discouragement

Is discouragement ever from God?

❧

Be strong and courageous, and do the work. Don't be afraid or discouraged,
for the LORD God, my God, is with you. He will not fail you or forsake you.
+ 1 CHRONICLES 28:20

But God, who encourages those who are discouraged,
encouraged us by the arrival of Titus.
+ 2 CORINTHIANS 7:6

Why am I discouraged? Why is my heart so sad? I will put my
hope in God! I will praise him again—my Savior and my God!
Now I am deeply discouraged, but I will remember you.
+ PSALM 42:5-6

Don't ever be afraid or discouraged. . . .
Be strong and courageous, for the LORD is going to do this.
+ JOSHUA 10:25

Don't be dejected and sad, for the joy of the LORD is your strength!
+ NEHEMIAH 8:10

FEELINGS of discouragement are never from God. They are a
tactic Satan uses to steal our joy and make us doubt the God we
serve. When we notice discouraging thoughts, we need to remember
God's promises to us. His Word proclaims that he is always with us,
he will never fail us, and he will give us the strength to get through
each day. With these promises in mind, what do we really have to be
discouraged about? No matter what disappointments linger from
your past or what impossible tasks hover over your future, remember
that the God you serve is your greatest supporter and encourager.

Prayer Prompts

Lord, I think Satan is trying to make me feel discouraged by . . .
Your Word encourages me this way: . . .

distractions

What can I do when I get distracted during prayer?

— ❧ —

Devote yourselves to prayer with an alert mind and a thankful heart.
+ COLOSSIANS 4:2

*O Lord, you have examined my heart and know everything
about me. . . . Search me, O God, and know my heart; test me
and know my anxious thoughts. Point out anything in me that
offends you, and lead me along the path of everlasting life.*
+ PSALM 139:1, 23-24

Pray in the Spirit at all times and on every occasion.
+ EPHESIANS 6:18

SOMETIMES prayer feels frustrating because we can have trouble
focusing. However, God wants us to pray about *everything*—
even our distractions. When something else comes to mind while
we are praying, we can stop and talk to God about it. We shouldn't
be afraid to pray about what is on our minds even if it seems trivial,
insignificant, or embarrassing. If you feel free to share anything with
your closest friend, how much more freedom might you have to
share with God, your Creator, who loves you unconditionally? Allow
yourself to trust that God is eager to have a conversation about whatever is on your heart.

Prayer Prompts

Lord, when I try to pray, I am often distracted by thoughts about . . .
I know you care even about my distractions because your Word says . . .

 # doubting God

Is it a sin to doubt God?

———— ✤ ————

When doubts filled my mind, your comfort gave me renewed hope and cheer.
+ PSALM 94:19

John the Baptist, who was in prison, heard about all the things the Messiah was doing. So he sent his disciples to ask Jesus, "Are you the Messiah we've been expecting, or should we keep looking for someone else?"
+ MATTHEW 11:2-3

Jesus immediately reached out and grabbed [Peter].
"You have so little faith," Jesus said. "Why did you doubt me?"
+ MATTHEW 14:31

God has said, "I will never fail you. I will never abandon you."
+ HEBREWS 13:5

"What do you mean, 'If I can'?" Jesus asked. "Anything is possible if a person believes." The father instantly cried out, "I do believe, but help me overcome my unbelief!"
+ MARK 9:23-24

DAVID, John the Baptist, Peter, and many other biblical leaders struggled with doubts about God and his ability to help them. This doesn't mean they had less faith than others, but it does mean their faith was challenged. Doubt can become sin if it leads us away from God into skepticism, cynicism, or hard-heartedness. But doubt can be beneficial when our honest searching leads us to a better understanding of God and deepens our faith in him. Allow your doubts to move you closer to God, not further away from him. Recognize and acknowledge your doubts before God and ask him to help you in your unbelief.

Prayer Prompts

Lord, I believe, but help me in this area of doubt: . . .
When I doubt, your Word assures me I can trust you because . . .

dreams 🍃

Does God still speak through dreams today?

———————— ❧ ————————

Long ago God spoke many times and in many ways to our ancestors through the prophets. And now in these final days, he has spoken to us through his Son.
+ HEBREWS 1:1-2

When it was time to leave, they returned to their own country by another route, for God had warned them in a dream not to return to Herod.
+ MATTHEW 2:12

I will pour out my Spirit upon all people. Your sons and daughters will prophesy. Your old men will dream dreams, and your young men will see visions.
+ JOEL 2:28

Then Pharaoh said to Joseph, "I had a dream last night, and no one here can tell me what it means. But I have heard that when you hear about a dream you can interpret it." "It is beyond my power to do this," Joseph replied. "But God can tell you what it means and set you at ease."
+ GENESIS 41:15-16

GOD SPEAKS to us in a variety of ways: through his Word, through the godly wisdom of others, through nature, through our consciences, and sometimes through dreams and visions. If God speaks to you in a dream, his message will always be consistent with what he has already told you in his Word. He will never contradict his own commandments or ask you to do something immoral or illegal. If a dream moves you to serve God and others with greater passion, do so; it may be God speaking to you in a new way!

Prayer Prompts

Lord, I wonder if you are speaking to me through a dream I had about . . . Your Word says this about dreams: . . .

 # drifting

How can I avoid drifting away from God?

— ❧ —

Keep watch and pray, so that you will not give in to temptation.
For the spirit is willing, but the body is weak!
+ MATTHEW 26:41

We must listen very carefully to the truth we have heard,
or we may drift away from it.
+ HEBREWS 2:1

Come close to God, and God will come close to you.
+ JAMES 4:8

Temptation comes from our own desires, which entice us
and drag us away. These desires give birth to sinful actions.
And when sin is allowed to grow, it gives birth to death.
+ JAMES 1:14-15

DRIFTING means taking a step away from God in our spiritual walk, falling back into a sinful lifestyle or habit that slowly causes separation in our relationship with God. Each time we drift away, we grow more comfortable with the sinful habit we have given in to and our hearts become a bit harder, making it more difficult to come back to him. But each time we obey God's Word, each time we offer a prayer, and each time we remind ourselves to be alert to temptation, we will take a step toward God rather than away. Remember, it takes discipline and intentionality to stay close to God. It sounds simple, and in some ways it is. Choose each day to take a small step toward God. Read his Word, pray instead of engaging in something else, sing a song of praise, or simply remind yourself of his presence.

Prayer Prompts

Lord, one way I can take a step toward you today is to . . .
I am reminded to stay close to you when I read in your Word that . . .

ease

Jesus talked a lot about suffering.
Is it okay to live a comfortable, easy life?

———————————— ❧ ————————————

The world offers only a craving for physical pleasure . . . and pride in our achievements and possessions. These are not from the Father, but are from this world. And this world is fading away, along with everything that people crave. But anyone who does what pleases God will live forever.
+ 1 JOHN 2:16-17

People who long to be rich fall into temptation and are trapped by many foolish and harmful desires that plunge them into ruin and destruction.
+ 1 TIMOTHY 6:9

*Remember the words of the Lord Jesus:
"It is more blessed to give than to receive."*
+ ACTS 20:35

SOME WOMEN are happy to rough it on a campground, and others are most content in a five-star hotel. Though our levels of comfort may vary, no one wants to be truly uncomfortable. On some level we expect life to be easy. But God's Word is clear that we will have some suffering in this world. If you are in a season where life is easy, make sure your hope and security lie in God instead of in what this world offers you. Keep an eternal mind-set, remembering to invest what you have received to further the Kingdom of God. To be wise during easy times, do these things: (1) Be generous with others because of how generous God has been with you, and (2) seek God and immerse yourself in his Word. Life will not always be easy, so use God's Word to prepare yourself for whatever hardships the future holds.

Prayer Prompts

Lord, when I think about the season I am in, I feel . . .
No matter what is happening, your Word encourages me to remember that . . .

 # effectiveness

I feel like I'm not doing enough for God where I am. Should I move on?

—— ❧ ——

You died to the power of the law when you died with Christ. And now you are united with the one who was raised from the dead. As a result, we can produce a harvest of good deeds for God.
+ ROMANS 7:4

We know that God causes everything to work together for the good of those who love God and are called according to his purpose for them.
+ ROMANS 8:28

Never stop praying.
+ 1 THESSALONIANS 5:17

If you are faithful in little things, you will be faithful in large ones. But if you are dishonest in little things, you won't be honest with greater responsibilities.
+ LUKE 16:10

GOD WASTES NOTHING but instead uses everything to further his good purposes. He has a reason for placing us in our homes, neighborhoods, jobs, and communities. If we are waiting for God to use us in the future, we may be missing out on chances to be used by him now. We need to watch for opportunities to serve effectively until he leads us to move on somewhere else. If your current role doesn't feel significant, remember that God might be using this time to prepare you for later service. When you faithfully serve God in small ways, being as effective as you can, you show him that you can be trusted with greater responsibilities. Make the most of where God has put you right now.

Prayer Prompts

Lord, one small way I can serve you effectively where I am is . . .
Your Word promises if I am faithful to do this, then . . .

emotions 🍃

How can I best handle my emotions?

---- ✦ ----

Guard your heart above all else, for it determines the course of your life.
+ PROVERBS 4:23

The Holy Spirit produces this kind of fruit in our lives: love, joy, peace, patience, kindness, goodness, faithfulness, gentleness, and self-control.
+ GALATIANS 5:22-23

Don't worry about anything; instead, pray about everything. Tell God what you need, and thank him for all he has done. Then you will experience God's peace, which exceeds anything we can understand. His peace will guard your hearts and minds as you live in Christ Jesus.
+ PHILIPPIANS 4:6-7

E MOTIONS are a good gift from God. They are evidence we are made in God's image, for the Bible shows God experiencing a whole range of emotions. Sometimes our emotions of empathy can lead us to respond to someone with compassion, and anger can motivate us to right an injustice. But like any gift from God, emotions can be misused. The issue isn't the power or intensity of the feeling but what it leads us to do. The best way to handle your emotions is to ask God to help you understand them. The moment you find yourself beginning to spiral out of control, take a deep breath and create space to pray. Ask God to help you notice what people or situations trigger you to lose control. Then discern with him whether your emotions lead you to actions that are productive or destructive. When you come to God, he promises to replace your negative thoughts and attitudes with patience, peace, and self-control.

Prayer Prompts

Lord, this person or situation makes it hard for me to control my emotions: . . .
When I lose control of my feelings, your Word tells me it is wise to . . .

 # empathy

How can I be more empathetic with others?

❧

Be happy with those who are happy, and weep with those who weep.
+ ROMANS 12:15

*I am giving you a new commandment: Love each other.
Just as I have loved you, you should love each other.
Your love for one another will prove to the world that you are my disciples.*
+ JOHN 13:34-35

*If one part suffers, all the parts suffer with it,
and if one part is honored, all the parts are glad.*
+ 1 CORINTHIANS 12:26

*So then, since we have a great High Priest who has entered heaven, Jesus the
Son of God, let us hold firmly to what we believe. This High Priest of ours
understands our weaknesses, for he faced all of the same testings we do.*
+ HEBREWS 4:14-15

EMPATHY is more than feeling bad for someone who is having
a hard time or happy for someone who has success. Empathy
is allowing ourselves to feel the same emotions that other people
feel—almost like crawling inside them to experience their pain or
joy. To empathize with others, we can ask ourselves, *What might
this person be feeling? How would I feel if I were in this person's
shoes?* Empathizing with others softens our hearts toward them and
ultimately leads us to act with compassion. Empathy is close to God's
heart because he sent his Son to earth to empathize with humanity.
Therefore, live as Jesus lived by trying to feel what others feel so that
you can show them the love of Christ.

Prayer Prompts

If I were in the shoes of those I find difficult to love, I would feel . . .
Your Word calls me to empathize and love them by . . .

emptiness 🔴

Why does life seem so empty?

———————— ❧ ————————

She took some of the fruit and ate it. Then she gave some to her husband,
who was with her, and he ate it, too. At that moment their eyes were
opened. . . . So the LORD God banished them from the Garden of Eden.
+ GENESIS 3:6-7, 23

Don't you realize that your body is the temple of the Holy Spirit,
who lives in you and was given to you by God?
+ 1 CORINTHIANS 6:19

Jesus replied, "Anyone who drinks this water will soon become thirsty again.
But those who drink the water I give will never be thirsty again.
It becomes a fresh, bubbling spring within them, giving them eternal life."
+ JOHN 4:13-14

ADAM AND EVE lived in the Garden of Eden, experiencing the joy of God's constant presence and perfect companionship. Imagine what it must have been like for them to suddenly be disconnected from God after they sinned. Most likely, they felt extremely alone and empty. Our emptiness, too, is due to the loss of God's presence. When riches, relationships, or power fail to fill us, we end up feeling the depth of our emptiness even more. However, God promises a way back into his presence, and that is through his Son. Because of Jesus, we live with the certainty that God is always with us because his Spirit resides within us! Whenever you feel empty and alone, remember this: God is always with you. His presence is able to fill the depth of your emptiness.

Prayer Prompts

Lord, I feel most empty when . . .
But your Word says I can find fulfillment by . . .

# encouragement

How can I be encouraged during a difficult season?

God has made everything beautiful for its own time.
He has planted eternity in the human heart.
+ ECCLESIASTES 3:11

May our Lord Jesus Christ himself and God our Father, who loved us and
by his grace gave us eternal comfort and a wonderful hope, comfort you
and strengthen you in every good thing you do and say.
+ 2 THESSALONIANS 2:16-17

I weep with sorrow; encourage me by your word.
+ PSALM 119:28

The heavens proclaim the glory of God.
+ PSALM 19:1

We are looking forward to the new heavens and new earth he has promised.
+ 2 PETER 3:13

HAVE YOU ever experienced a difficult season when you continually asked God, "Why?" or "How long?" Sometimes knowing there is more than what this life has to offer is just the encouragement we need. God has built into us a yearning for a trouble-free, perfect world that can be found only in heaven. Nature, beauty, rest, and enjoyable relationships provide glimpses of heaven in order to encourage us while we're on this earth. When discouragement begins to settle in, engage with God's beauty and awaken your hope for heaven. Remember God's promise to perfectly restore the earth and give you an eternity of never-ending beauty and companionship with God.

Prayer Prompts

Lord, I feel discouraged about . . .
Your Word encourages me by saying . . .

endurance 🍃

How can I be effective in serving Christ over the long haul?

—— ❧ ——

Jesus said, "Come to me, all of you who are weary and carry heavy burdens, and I will give you rest."
+ MATTHEW 11:28

Let's not get tired of doing what is good.
At just the right time we will reap a harvest of blessing if we don't give up.
+ GALATIANS 6:9

Patient endurance is what you need now, so that you will continue to do God's will. Then you will receive all that he has promised.
+ HEBREWS 10:36

Times of refreshment will come from the presence of the Lord.
+ ACTS 3:20

AS WOMEN, we often find ourselves in roles of service. It can be difficult to serve others well over a long period of time, whether in official ministry, in a family, or in a career. Our endurance will be tested many times, and we may be tempted to give up. If you are in a difficult season in service, the Holy Spirit has orchestrated the timing of this devotion just for you. When you find your strength evaporating and your endurance fading, come to God for help first. Create space to care for your own soul so that you can better care for others. Ask God to help you discern when to say yes and when to delegate. God doesn't desire his children to minister until they burn out. He wants to give you times of refreshment, fill you up with his love, and restore your soul.

Prayer Prompts

Lord, these days when I think about serving, I feel . . .
These verses from your Word inspire me to endure: . . .

 enemies

How can I love my enemies?

— ❧ —

[Jesus said,] "You have heard the law that says, 'Love your neighbor' and hate your enemy. But I say, love your enemies! Pray for those who persecute you!"
+ MATTHEW 5:43-44

All of you should be of one mind. Sympathize with each other. Love each other as brothers and sisters. Don't repay evil for evil. Don't retaliate with insults when people insult you. Instead, pay them back with a blessing. That is what God has called you to do, and he will grant you his blessing.
+ 1 PETER 3:8-9

If your enemies are hungry, feed them. If they are thirsty, give them something to drink.... Don't let evil conquer you, but conquer evil by doing good.
+ ROMANS 12:20-21

Everyone has sinned; we all fall short of God's glorious standard.
+ ROMANS 3:23

Jesus said, "Father, forgive them, for they don't know what they are doing."
+ LUKE 23:34

LOVING AN ENEMY means seeing him or her as Jesus does—as a person in need of grace. If someone in our lives feels impossible to love, we can begin by praying, "Lord, how do you want me to pray for this person?" Over time, God will change the posture of our hearts toward this person. Whenever you feel hurt—pray. When you feel betrayed—pray. When you feel heartbroken—pray. Prayer keeps your focus on God and off retaliation. Showing love to one's enemies always feels unreasonable—until you remember that before Jesus saved you, you were an enemy of God.

Prayer Prompts

Lord, please show me how I should pray for this difficult person in my life: . . .
This is how your Word urges me to love and pray for my enemies: . . .

energy 🍃

How can I find the energy to live
each day to the fullest?

—————————— ❧ ——————————

This is the day the LORD has made. We will rejoice and be glad in it.
+ PSALM 118:24

*To enjoy your work and accept your lot in life—this is indeed
a gift from God. God keeps such people so busy enjoying life
that they take no time to brood over the past.*
+ ECCLESIASTES 5:19-20

*Each morning I will sing with joy about your unfailing love.
For you have been my refuge, a place of safety when I am in distress.*
+ PSALM 59:16

Teach us to realize the brevity of life, so that we may grow in wisdom.
+ PSALM 90:12

WHEN WORK, relationships, and commitments press down on
us, it can feel impossible to find the energy to live each day
well. But the truth that we must hold on to is that each day is a gift.
Think about the "lasts" that could happen today. What if today were
the last day of summer? What if today were the last time your child
crawled up onto your lap to snuggle? What if today were the last time
you heard the voice of someone you love? Waking up each morning
with this perspective will strengthen you to live today well. Ask God
to help you cherish each moment of your day—even the ones that
feel messy or insignificant. You will soon find yourself waking up
each morning saying, "This is the day the Lord has made! I will be
rejoice and be glad in it!"

Prayer Prompts
Lord, these things in life are making me weary: . . .
Your Word encourages me to live each day well by . . .

envy

How should I respond when I am envious of others?

꙳

You are jealous of one another and quarrel with each other. Doesn't that prove you are controlled by your sinful nature?
+ 1 CORINTHIANS 3:3

Anger is cruel, and wrath is like a flood, but jealousy is even more dangerous.
+ PROVERBS 27:4

Think about the things of heaven, not the things of earth. For you died to this life, and your real life is hidden with Christ in God. And when Christ, who is your life, is revealed to the whole world, you will share in all his glory.
+ COLOSSIANS 3:2-4

In this new life, it doesn't matter if you are a Jew or a Gentile, circumcised or uncircumcised, barbaric, uncivilized, slave, or free. Christ is all that matters, and he lives in all of us.
+ COLOSSIANS 3:11

GOD ASSURES US that when our thoughts are focused on him and his will, we will no longer feel the need to compete with others because the things of this world won't seem so important anymore. When we are envious of those around us, longing to have a nicer home, a flawless appearance, more status at work, or more possessions, we need to remember God's promises in his Word. He is able to give us satisfying and fulfilling lives when we look to him alone. Fix your thoughts on him, thank him for all you have now and will receive for eternity, and watch how the temptation to envy others fades away.

Prayer Prompts

Lord, I feel envious of others because . . .
When I am tempted to compete, your Word reminds me to focus instead on . . .

equality 🍃

Does God value all people equally?

— ✂ —

God shows no favoritism.
In every nation he accepts those who fear him and do what is right.
+ ACTS 10:34-35

We are made right with God by placing our faith in Jesus Christ.
And this is true for everyone who believes, no matter who we are.
+ ROMANS 3:22

Adam's one sin brings condemnation for everyone, but Christ's one act of
righteousness brings a right relationship with God and new life for everyone.
+ ROMANS 5:18

The heavenly Father to whom you pray has no favorites.
He will judge or reward you according to what you do.
+ 1 PETER 1:17

WE LIVE in a world where gender, ethnicity, political beliefs, and socioeconomic status influence us to rank each other's worth. However, God's Word is clear: He has no favorites. Since all people are created by God in his image, every person has equal value in his eyes. It may be countercultural, but God has made salvation available to everyone. It doesn't matter what color your skin is, what family you were born into, or what sins you've committed—God loves all people. There is not a single person on this earth that God doesn't want a relationship with. If you feel tempted to believe that God loves the next person more than you—or loves you more than the next person—reflect on his Word. He accepts every person who pursues a relationship with him, accepts his forgiveness, and lives to honor him.

Prayer Prompts

Lord, sometimes I feel like you love others more than me because . . .
Your Word assures me that you have no favorites when it says: . . .

 # escape

Sometimes I long to detach from reality. Is this a bad thing?

———— ❧ ————

The LORD is good, a strong refuge when trouble comes.
He is close to those who trust in him.
+ NAHUM 1:7

You are my hiding place; you protect me from trouble.
+ PSALM 32:7

Be strong in the Lord and in his mighty power. Put on all of God's armor so that you will be able to stand firm against all strategies of the devil.
+ EPHESIANS 6:10-11

God has given us everything we need for living a godly life. We have received all of this by coming to know him. . . . And because of his glory and excellence, he has given us great and precious promises . . . that enable you to share his divine nature and escape the world's corruption caused by human desires.
+ 2 PETER 1:3-4

WHEN THE PRESSURES of life become too much, we often want to relieve the stress by escaping for a while. But whether we use travel, work, social media, family, or food to detach from reality, eventually we will need to face our problems. It's important to take some breaks to get away, unless they involve indulging in sin or bad habits. Do something that gives you life and energy so you can love others and God well. Spending time with God is the perfect escape, and it can happen anytime, anywhere. Going outside, spending time in prayer, or meditating on God's Word will reenergize you and give you the strength you need to face any difficult situations.

Prayer Prompts

Lord, I long to escape from . . .
Your Word encourages me to draw near to you instead by . . .

eternity

How does keeping an eternal perspective impact my soul?

———— ❧ ————

No eye has seen, no ear has heard, and no mind has imagined what God has prepared for those who love him.
+ 1 CORINTHIANS 2:9

We don't look at the troubles we can see now; rather, we fix our gaze on things that cannot be seen. For the things we see now will soon be gone, but the things we cannot see will last forever.
+ 2 CORINTHIANS 4:18

[Jesus said,] "I tell you the truth, anyone who believes has eternal life."
+ JOHN 6:47

Look, God's home is now among his people! He will live with them, and they will be his people. God himself will be with them. He will wipe every tear from their eyes.
+ REVELATION 21:3-4

AS WOMEN, we tend to focus on the tasks of today and the problems waiting for us tomorrow. We must take care of our responsibilities, but God also urges us to live with eternity in mind. That is why he has filled his Word with promises about heaven. Thinking about heaven helps us view life differently. We find strength to persevere through trials because we know that this life is not our final destination. The more focused we are on our future with Jesus, the less attached we become to our own plans and to the temporary attractions of this world. If you trust Jesus as your Savior, God promises there is a beautiful future in store for you for all of eternity.

Prayer Prompts

Lord, the tasks and problems on my mind today are . . .
Yet they are minor in comparison to these future blessings: . . .

 # evangelism

How can I share the gospel when people aren't interested in hearing about Christ?

———————————— ✺ ————————————

I planted the seed in your hearts, and Apollos watered it,
but it was God who made it grow.
+ 1 CORINTHIANS 3:6

When they heard Paul speak about the resurrection of the
dead, some laughed in contempt, but others said, "We want
to hear more about this later." That ended Paul's discussion
with them, but some joined him and became believers.
+ ACTS 17:32-34

Jesus came and told his disciples, "I have been given all authority in heaven
and on earth. Therefore, go and make disciples of all the nations, baptizing
them in the name of the Father and the Son and the Holy Spirit.
+ MATTHEW 28:18-19

SOME OF JESUS' last words on earth are about witnessing. He said to his disciples, "You will be my witnesses, telling people about me everywhere—in Jerusalem, throughout Judea, in Samaria, and to the ends of the earth" (Acts 1:8). Not everyone will be interested in hearing the gospel, and we can't *make* someone listen. Jesus simply calls his followers to tell others about him, not force them to believe. Only the Holy Spirit can soften a person's heart. Sometimes your role is to plant a seed. Therefore, always be ready to tell about how you met and grew to love Jesus. Perhaps sharing your own story of becoming a woman of faith will be a pivotal moment that ultimately leads someone to faith in him.

Prayer Prompts

When I think about sharing my faith with those who are disinterested, I feel . . .
Your Word encourages me to share because it promises you will . . .

evil

If God is good,
why does he let people do evil things?

———————— ❧ ————————

*The Lord God placed the man in the Garden of Eden to tend and watch
over it. But the Lord God warned him, "You may freely eat the fruit of every
tree in the garden—except the tree of the knowledge of good and evil."*
+ GENESIS 2:15-17

*Stay alert! Watch out for your great enemy, the devil. He prowls
around like a roaring lion, looking for someone to devour.*
+ 1 PETER 5:8

*We are made right with God by placing our faith in Jesus Christ. . . .
For everyone has sinned; we all fall short of God's glorious standard.*
+ ROMANS 3:22-23

If you love me, obey my commandments.
+ JOHN 14:15

GENUINE LOVE requires the freedom to choose. From the beginning, God desired a loving relationship with us, so he gave us
freedom. But with the ability to make choices comes the possibility
of choosing our own way over God's way. Our way always leads to
sin, because every person since Adam and Eve has been born with
a sinful nature. This breaks God's heart, but he did not want to force
us to love him. And there is no genuine love without choice. Even
though evil is a reality, we must remember it is also temporary.
Eventually, God will destroy Satan, and good will prevail. Until that
day, you can fight evil in your own heart by striving to know and
love God and to follow his ways.

Prayer Prompts
Lord, even though there is evil in the world, I see your goodness by . . .
Your Word says this about staying close to you and keeping away from evil: . . .

 # examination

Why is it important to examine my heart?
How can I do this?

———— ✂ ————

Examine yourselves to see if your faith is genuine. Test yourselves.
+ 2 CORINTHIANS 13:5

Search me, O God, and know my heart; test me and know my
anxious thoughts. Point out anything in me that offends you,
and lead me along the path of everlasting life.
+ PSALM 139:23-24

Throw off your old sinful nature and your former way of life,
which is corrupted by lust and deception. Instead,
let the Spirit renew your thoughts and attitudes.
+ EPHESIANS 4:22-23

THE GOAL of self-examination is not to make us feel bad about ourselves but rather for us to bring authenticity to our lives with God and others. Theologian John Calvin stated, "True wisdom consists in two things: knowledge of God and knowledge of self." If we know a lot about ourselves but do not know much about God, we become self-absorbed. If we know a lot about God but not much about ourselves, we become spiritually proud. Knowing God and knowing ourselves are both vitally important. Growing in awareness of the self involves voluntarily testing and examining your own heart. Ask the Holy Spirit to reveal what is true about you so that you can better understand the truth about your relationships with God and others.

Prayer Prompts

Lord, examining my heart makes me feel . . .
Your Word reminds me that self-examination is important because . . .

exhaustion

How can I function when I'm so exhausted?

———— ❧ ————

Jacob's well was there; and Jesus, tired from the long walk, sat wearily beside the well about noontime.
+ JOHN 4:6

We grow weary in our present bodies, and we long to put on our heavenly bodies like new clothing.
+ 2 CORINTHIANS 5:2

My grace is all you need. My power works best in weakness.
+ 2 CORINTHIANS 12:9

Jesus said, "Come to me, all of you who are weary and carry heavy burdens, and I will give you rest."
+ MATTHEW 11:28

He knows how weak we are; he remembers we are only dust.
+ PSALM 103:14

JESUS LIVED in a human body, so he understands what it means to be tired. He knows we are flesh-and-blood women with physical limitations. When we are exhausted, God cares for us like a tender parent who carries a sleeping child to bed. God is not disappointed in our weariness. In fact, he invites us to bring our exhausted bodies and souls to him so that he can give us rest. Allow your weariness to remind you of your need for God. You can't do life on your own, and that is how God designed it. Take the rest you need and trust that some of God's best work is done through your weakness.

Prayer Prompts

Lord, when I feel exhausted, I fear I am letting others down because . . .
When I am tired, your Word encourages me to . . .

 # expectations

Is it wrong to expect things from God?

❦

Abraham never wavered in believing God's promise. In fact, his faith
grew stronger, and in this he brought glory to God. He was fully
convinced that God is able to do whatever he promises.
+ ROMANS 4:20-21

The Lord isn't really being slow about his promise, as some
people think. No, he is being patient for your sake. He does not
want anyone to be destroyed, but wants everyone to repent.
+ 2 PETER 3:9

He is the Rock; his deeds are perfect. Everything he does is just and fair.
He is a faithful God who does no wrong; how just and upright he is!
+ DEUTERONOMY 32:4

W E OFTEN have expectations of others, whether we are conscious of them or not. Sometimes we expect too much of the people in our lives. Other times we lower our expectations to protect ourselves from the possibility of disappointment. The good news is, we never need to lower our expectations of God. His Word states that if we follow him, we can expect him to work on our behalf, to guide us and faithfully keep all his promises. God may not answer our prayers in the way we desire, but we can always expect him to answer in the best way. So pray boldly and trust that God has great things in store for your future.

Prayer Prompts

Lord, my expectations of you are often . . .
Your Word assures me that what I can expect of you is . . .

experiencing God 🍃

I haven't experienced God in a long time.
How can I feel his presence more?

— ❧ —

God blesses those whose hearts are pure, for they will see God.
+ MATTHEW 5:8

We can be sure that we know [God] if we obey his commandments.
+ 1 JOHN 2:3

The LORD is good to those who depend on him, to those who search for him.
+ LAMENTATIONS 3:25

*God is working in you, giving you the desire and the power
to do what pleases him.*
+ PHILIPPIANS 2:13

*His purpose was for the nations to seek after God and perhaps feel their way
toward him and find him—though he is not far from any one of us.*
+ ACTS 17:27

GOD ISN'T elusive or passive; he is personal and relational. He wants us to search for him and experience him. At times, God may feel far away, maybe even nonexistent. In those times, we must rely on the truth of God's promises rather than on the strength of our feelings. He doesn't hide or avoid us. He will never abandon us. Do you strive to have a pure heart? Do you obey his commandments? Do you depend on him and search for his presence throughout your day? If you can answer yes to these questions, then God promises you will experience more of him. Trust that he is working in your life as you wait, and remember that if you search for him wholeheartedly, you will find him.

Prayer Prompts

Lord, I want to experience you in this way: . . .
Your Word reminds me that I can experience you more when . . .

 # failure

What can I do when I feel like a failure?

— ❧ —

The godly may trip seven times, but they will get up again.
+ PROVERBS 24:16

*The LORD directs the steps of the godly. He delights in every
detail of their lives. Though they stumble, they will never fall,
for the LORD holds them by the hand.*
+ PSALM 37:23-24

I will be your Father, and you will be my sons and daughters.
+ 2 CORINTHIANS 6:18

You are a chosen people. You are royal priests . . . God's very own possession.
+ 1 PETER 2:9

Great is his faithfulness; his mercies begin afresh each morning.
+ LAMENTATIONS 3:23

AS WOMEN, we hate feeling that we've failed—and especially that we have failed others. During these times we must ask ourselves, *Whose voice is accusing me of being a failure? Is it my own, someone else's, or Satan's?* It is vital to our emotional and spiritual health to remember that God doesn't see us as failures. If we have fallen away from God, it is never too late to come back to him. If we have hurt others through our mistakes, we can ask for forgiveness and trust God to help mend those relationships. If we have really messed up, God can still clean up our mess. Nothing is too disastrous for him. Remind yourself of the loving names God does use for you—his daughter, a royal priest, and his very own possession. Tomorrow is a new day, and God is waiting for you there, ready to give you a fresh start.

Prayer Prompts

Lord, I feel like a failure when I listen to the voice of . . .
Even when I fail, your Word says you still call me . . .

fairness 🍂

How should I respond when life doesn't seem fair?

———————— ❧ ————————

[The Lord said,] "You say, 'The Lord isn't doing what's right!' Listen to me,
O people of Israel. Am I the one not doing what's right, or is it you?"
+ EZEKIEL 18:25

Who are you, a mere human being, to argue with God? Should the thing that
was created say to the one who created it, "Why have you made me like this?"
+ ROMANS 9:20

The Lord . . . does not want anyone to be destroyed,
but wants everyone to repent.
+ 2 PETER 3:9

His government and its peace will never end.
He will rule with fairness and justice.
+ ISAIAH 9:7

God's way is perfect.
+ PSALM 18:30

SOMETHING inside of us longs for fairness. However, the fact
is that life really isn't fair. Life seems relatively easy for some,
while others have years full of struggle. God doesn't give us all the
same circumstances, jobs, families, or environment in which to live.
Whether we find ourselves feeling resentful when life feels unfair or
sad for those who are less fortunate, we can look to God's Word to
gain perspective on how he interacts with his creation. We can trust
that God is sovereign over all the world, that he loves each of us the
same, and that he desires the same salvation for us all.

Prayer Prompts

Lord, the situation I'm experiencing feels unfair because . . .
This is how your Word reminds me that you have everything under control: . . .

How does God strengthen my faith, even when I can't see him?

❧

[Jesus] said to Thomas, "Put your finger here, and look at my hands. Put your hand into the wound in my side. Don't be faithless any longer. Believe!" "My Lord and my God!" Thomas exclaimed. Then Jesus told him, "You believe because you have seen me. Blessed are those who believe without seeing me."
+ JOHN 20:27-29

Faith comes from hearing, that is, hearing the Good News about Christ.
+ ROMANS 10:17

The people's minds were hardened, and to this day whenever the old covenant is being read, the same veil covers their minds so they cannot understand the truth. And this veil can be removed only by believing in Christ.
+ 2 CORINTHIANS 3:14

Faith shows the reality of what we hope for; it is the evidence of things we cannot see.
+ HEBREWS 11:1

FAITH IS not simply a matter of positive thinking or human effort. Faith is the result of the Holy Spirit working through the Word of God. Our faith grows as we read stories of God working through his people and as we watch for the great work he does through us. The strongest faith is based not on physical senses but on spiritual conviction. There is a spiritual element to this world that we cannot see, but it is very real. The more you ask God to sharpen your "spiritual vision," the stronger your faith will become—and the more you will sense the results of God's work in your life and in the lives of those around you.

Prayer Prompts

Lord, even though I can't see you, I long to have faith that . . .
Your Word describes real faith as . . .

faithfulness 🍃

How does my faithfulness to God impact others?

———————— ❧ ————————

Each generation tells of your faithfulness to the next.
+ ISAIAH 38:19

The love of the LORD remains forever with those who fear him.
His salvation extends to the children's children of those who are
faithful to his covenant, of those who obey his commandments!
+ PSALM 103:17-18

In the future, your children will ask you, "What does all this mean?"
Then you will tell them, "With the power of his mighty hand,
the LORD brought us out of Egypt, the place of our slavery."
+ EXODUS 13:14

IT IS BOTH the privilege and the obligation of each generation to reveal to the next the faithfulness of God. God's blessings for your faithfulness often overflow to those around you. Likewise, you are the benefactor of other people's faithfulness to God. What kind of heritage do you want to leave for your children and, someday, your grandchildren? What words and actions from your life do you want your children to remember? Here is a good place to start: Each day, decide to obey God in the small things. If you try to obey God every day in each small decision, someday you will look back on a full life devoted to faithfulness and obedience. Remember, you never know who is watching you and which actions will most impact them. A life of faith, hope, and love for God will have far more lasting value than any other kind of inheritance we might leave behind.

Prayer Prompts

Lord, the kind of legacy I want to leave behind is . . .
Your Word tells me that to do this, I should . . .

 # family

How can I raise a family that actually makes a difference in this world?

If you refuse to serve the LORD, then choose today whom you will serve. . . . As for me and my family, we will serve the LORD.

+ JOSHUA 24:15

The most important commandment is this: . . . "You must love the LORD your God with all your heart, all your soul, all your mind, and all your strength." The second is equally important: "Love your neighbor as yourself." No other commandment is greater than these.

+ MARK 12:29-31

How joyful are those who fear the LORD and delight in obeying his commands. Their children will be successful everywhere; an entire generation of godly people will be blessed.

+ PSALM 112:1-2

TOO OFTEN we think about our effectiveness in individualistic terms. How can *I* make an impact as a Christian woman? What can *I* do? But God works through groups of people too, especially families. When a group of people is passionate about serving God, together they can make an enormous impact. How can your family be influential for God? Start by praying, not just for the individuals in your family but also for your family as a whole. Look for opportunities in your neighborhood, schools, and church to serve together. If you are faithful to pray together as a family and have hearts that are willing to serve, God will use your household in great ways! You never know what impact your family could have on someone's life.

Prayer Prompts

Lord, one place my family could serve is . . .
Before we begin to serve, Scripture gives me these words to pray: . . .

farewells 🍃

What will help me say good-bye in a healthy and positive way?

When he had finished speaking, he knelt and prayed with them.
They all cried as they embraced and kissed him good-bye. They were sad
most of all because he had said that they would never see him again.
+ ACTS 20:36-38

I long to see you again, for I remember your tears as we parted.
And I will be filled with joy when we are together again.
+ 2 TIMOTHY 1:4

If I ride the wings of the morning, if I dwell by the farthest oceans,
even there your hand will guide me, and your strength will support me.
+ PSALM 139:9-10

Be sure of this: I am with you always, even to the end of the age.
+ MATTHEW 28:20

PARTING from those we love is always painful. Before we say good-bye, we can make sure we take time to thank them for what they have meant to us and pray together, thanking God for giving us a special relationship. Whether we are the ones leaving or the ones being left behind, we can remember that God is with us. No matter where we or our loved ones have to go—even across the "farthest oceans"—God's hand will guide and give strength for the task ahead. There is great comfort in knowing that God will take care of those to whom we say farewell. He promises that one day, when we are with him in eternity, we will never need to say good-bye again.

Prayer Prompts

Lord, my heart still hurts from saying good-bye to . . .
Your Word encourages me through the pain of farewells to . . .

fear

How can I overcome my battle with fear?

❧

*Be strong and courageous! . . . For the LORD your God will personally go
ahead of you. He will neither fail you nor abandon you.*
+ DEUTERONOMY 31:6

*God is our refuge and strength, always ready to help in times of trouble. So we
will not fear when earthquakes come and the mountains crumble into the sea.*
+ PSALM 46:1-2

*Even when I walk through the darkest valley, I will not be afraid, for you are
close beside me. Your rod and your staff protect and comfort me.*
+ PSALM 23:4

*Do not be afraid . . . for the LORD your God is among you,
and he is a great and awesome God.*
+ DEUTERONOMY 7:21

*I am leaving you with a gift—peace of mind and heart. . . .
So don't be troubled or afraid.*
+ JOHN 14:27

GOD MUST have known the human heart would be prone to fear,
because time and time again his Word reminds us not to be afraid.
What's interesting is that whenever God tells his people not to fear, he
always reminds them of his presence with them. The more we reflect on
his presence, the less power fear will have over our lives. What we fear
the most might be the very thing that produces great faith in us. The
next time you feel anxiety consuming your thoughts, remind yourself
that your great and awesome God is right beside you. Being aware of his
presence will give you strength to stand strong in the face of fear.

Prayer Prompts
Lord, I am afraid of . . .
Your Word encourages me to face the future bravely because . . .

fear of God

What does it mean to fear God?

— ❧ —

Doesn't his majesty terrify you? Doesn't your fear of him overwhelm you?
+ JOB 13:11

Let the whole world fear the LORD, and let everyone stand in awe of him.
+ PSALM 33:8

How joyful are those who fear the LORD—all who follow his ways!
+ PSALM 128:1

Fear of the LORD is the foundation of wisdom.
Knowledge of the Holy One results in good judgment.
+ PROVERBS 9:10

Serve the LORD with reverent fear, and rejoice with trembling.
+ PSALM 2:11

FEARING GOD is not the same as being afraid of God. Being afraid of someone drives us away from that person, while fearing God means being awed by his power and goodness. This draws us closer to him and to the blessings he gives. Fearing God is similar to having respect for a beloved teacher, coach, parent, or mentor who motivates us to do our best and avoid doing anything that would offend him or her. Because God is so great and mighty, and because he holds the power of life and death in his hands, we can have a reverent awe of him. A healthy fear of God recognizes what he could do if he gave us what we deserved, but then is grateful for the mercy and forgiveness he shares instead.

Prayer Prompts

Lord, sometimes I feel a little afraid of you when . . .
Your Word describes what it means to fear you when it says . . .

 # fellowship

Why do I need fellowship with other believers?

— ❧ —

Teach and counsel each other with all the wisdom he gives.
Sing psalms and hymns and spiritual songs to God with thankful hearts.
+ COLOSSIANS 3:16

We are many parts of one body, and we all belong to each other.
+ ROMANS 12:5

When we get together, I want to encourage you in your faith,
but I also want to be encouraged by yours.
+ ROMANS 1:12

If we are living in the light, as God is in the light, then we have fellowship
with each other, and the blood of Jesus, his Son, cleanses us from all sin.
+ 1 JOHN 1:7

CLOSE COMMUNITY with other believers encourages intention-ality, authenticity, generosity, and love. If you have a strong community, you already know what an incredible blessing it is. However, if you are still searching for a place of belonging, you might be feeling lonely, discouraged, and uncomfortable as you try out new relationships. Trust that God will reward your efforts as you pursue fellowship. Real community with other women takes time and some effort, but remember that each interaction could be the beginning of a beautiful friendship. Going through life with others is not always easy, but with the help of the Holy Spirit, it is one of the best ways to grow and be transformed into Christlikeness.

Prayer Prompts

Lord, my friends are drawing me closer to you [or pulling me away] by . . .
Your Word reminds me of these blessings that result from godly fellowship: . . .

finding God 🍃

How can I find God in my everyday life?

———— ❧ ————

If you search for him with all your heart and soul, you will find him.
+ DEUTERONOMY 4:29

*The LORD will stay with you as long as you stay with him! Whenever you
seek him, you will find him. But if you abandon him, he will abandon you.*
+ 2 CHRONICLES 15:2

*"If you look for me wholeheartedly, you will find me.
I will be found by you," says the LORD.*
+ JEREMIAH 29:13-14

*I said, "Plant the good seeds of righteousness, and you will harvest a crop
of love. Plow up the hard ground of your hearts, for now is the time to seek
the LORD, that he may come and shower righteousness upon you."*
+ HOSEA 10:12

ALL OF US as believing women go through seasons when we find
it difficult to see God's activity and presence in our lives. But
we can be comforted by the truth that God never abandons those
who search for him. If we begin each day by deciding to search for
him wholeheartedly, we will find him. How might God be working
in your life at this very moment? Where was he present with you
today that perhaps you failed to recognize? What events or people
did he put in your way to remind you of his love for you? If God feels
far away, remind yourself of his promise to be faithful to those who
look for him with all their hearts.

Prayer Prompts
Lord, this is how I can see your presence in my life recently: . . .
Your Word promises these things to those who continue to search for you: . . .

 # finishing

Where can I find encouragement to finish well?

— ❦ —

*Joshua . . . said to them, "I am now a very old man. You have seen everything
the LORD your God has done for you during my lifetime. . . . So be very
careful to follow everything Moses wrote in the Book of Instruction.
Do not deviate from it, turning either to the right or to the left. . . .
Cling tightly to the LORD your God as you have done until now."*
+ JOSHUA 23:1-3, 6, 8

*I have fought the good fight, I have finished the race,
and I have remained faithful.*
+ 2 TIMOTHY 4:7

*He will give eternal life to those who keep on doing good,
seeking after the glory and honor and immortality that God offers.*
+ ROMANS 2:7

The master said, "Well done, my good and faithful servant."
+ MATTHEW 25:23

FEW THINGS are as powerful as the testimony of one who has been
faithful to the Lord and has experienced a lifetime of watching him
keep his promises. Younger people who listen to these life stories will be
greatly encouraged by hearing about decades of God's faithfulness. If
you are young, ask older believers to tell you about their lives with God
and encourage you to live today well. If you are older, encourage the
younger generations in their faith. No matter what age you are, commit
yourself to living each day well so that when you see your Lord face to
face, you can hear the words "Well done, my good and faithful servant."

Prayer Prompts

*Lord, please bring someone into my life so we can encourage each other by . . .
Your Word encourages me to finish well by . . .*

flexibility

How does being flexible make me available for divine moments with God?

———— ❧ ————

We've given up everything to follow you.
✝ MATTHEW 19:27

If any of you wants to be my follower, you must give up your own way, take up your cross, and follow me. If you try to hang on to your life, you will lose it. But if you give up your life for my sake and for the sake of the Good News, you will save it.
✝ MARK 8:34-35

As soon as they landed, they left everything and followed Jesus.
✝ LUKE 5:11

One day as Jesus was walking along the shore of the Sea of Galilee, he saw Simon and his brother Andrew throwing a net into the water, for they fished for a living. Jesus called out to them, "Come, follow me, and I will show you how to fish for people!" And they left their nets at once and followed him.
✝ MARK 1:16-18

INFLEXIBILITY can make our hearts rigid and overly focused on our own plans and agendas. This kind of tunnel vision keeps us unaware of God's presence. But often he blesses us not because of our ability but because of our availability. How would our lives be different if we walked through each day ready to hear God's voice and were open to his leading? God loves to surprise us with divine moments with him as he guides us through life. Ask God to help you go with the flow, be open to his timing, and allow room in your life for a change of plans.

Prayer Prompts

Lord, help me be more flexible with my plans today by . . .
Your Word reminds me of these benefits of flexibility: . . .

 # following

I'm afraid that if I follow God, he will take me someplace I don't want to go. What can I do about this fear?

Take delight in the LORD, and he will give you your heart's desires.
+ PSALM 37:4

My purpose is to give them a rich and satisfying life.
+ JOHN 10:10

May he grant your heart's desires and make all your plans succeed.
+ PSALM 20:4

"I know the plans I have for you," says the LORD. "They are plans for good and not for disaster, to give you a future and a hope."
+ JEREMIAH 29:11

He fills my life with good things.
+ PSALM 103:5

GOD'S PLANS are *always* good. His desires for us will always fulfill and satisfy. If our minds and hearts are truly in tune with his will, we won't be going anywhere we don't want to go. God will change our hearts and give us peace before he adjusts our future plans. Since God alone knows all things, who can plan your future better than he? Open your heart to God about your fears and desires. Ask him to give you a willing heart to follow him wherever he leads. While this may feel risky, you can be assured that following him will be a great adventure.

Prayer Prompts

Lord, I am afraid that if I follow you, . . .
Your Word reminds me that I can trust you with my future because . . .

foolishness 🍂

How can I keep from making a foolish decision?

—— ∞ ——

Fear of the LORD is the foundation of true knowledge,
but fools despise wisdom and discipline.
+ PROVERBS 1:7

Fools have no interest in understanding;
they only want to air their own opinions.
+ PROVERBS 18:2

Cry out for insight, and ask for understanding. Search for them
as you would for silver.... Then you will understand what is
right, just, and fair, and you will find the right way to go.
+ PROVERBS 2:3, 9

There is safety in having many advisers.
+ PROVERBS 11:14

WHEN WE are tired, overworked, overwhelmed, or disconnected
from God and others, it is wise to put off making big decisions
until we are in a healthier place. If you are on the verge of making a
decision, it may also be wise to ask yourself, *Did I talk to God about*
this and open his Word for wisdom? Did I ask for advice from
godly advisers? Is my heart open to other options? Have I consid-
ered whether or not the timing is good for this decision? If you have
answered yes to these questions, then you have wisely prepared yourself. Sometimes you can do all the right things and your decision still
doesn't turn out the way you had hoped. However, you can have peace
of mind, knowing that you did not make that decision foolishly. Use
wisdom in making your decisions, and trust God with the outcome.

Prayer Prompts

Lord, I am tempted to make foolish decisions when . . .
Your Word encourages me to make wise decisions by . . .

 # forgiveness

Will God forgive me for the things I've done wrong?
Why would he even *want* to forgive me?

— ❧ —

Everyone who calls on the name of the LORD will be saved.
+ JOEL 2:32

Nothing can ever separate us from God's love.
+ ROMANS 8:38

*He forgives all my sins and heals all my diseases. . . . He does not
punish us for all our sins; he does not deal harshly with us, as we
deserve. For his unfailing love toward those who fear him is as great
as the height of the heavens above the earth. He has removed our
sins as far from us as the east is from the west.*
+ PSALM 103:3, 10-12

*"Come now, let's settle this," says the LORD. "Though your
sins are like scarlet, I will make them as white as snow.
Though they are red like crimson, I will make them as white as wool."*
+ ISAIAH 1:18

FORGIVENESS is based not on the magnitude of the sin but on the
magnitude of the forgiver's love. Nothing we have done is so bad
that God's complete and unconditional love can't forgive it. The Bible
does, however, mention one unforgivable sin: holding on to an attitude of defiant hostility toward God that prevents us from accepting
his forgiveness. Only those who don't want his forgiveness are out of
its reach. No matter how seriously you've messed up, it will never be
enough for God to turn his back on you and deny you forgiveness
when you ask him for it.

Prayer Prompts
Lord, please forgive me for . . .
When I ask for forgiveness, your Word promises me that . . .

forgiving others 🍃

Is there something wrong if I am having a hard time forgiving someone who has wronged me?

— ❧ —

Love your enemies! Pray for those who persecute you!
In that way, you will be acting as true children of your Father in heaven.
+ MATTHEW 5:44-45

If you forgive those who sin against you, your heavenly Father will forgive you.
But if you refuse to forgive others, your Father will not forgive your sins.
+ MATTHEW 6:14-15

Peter came to him and asked, "Lord, how often should I forgive
someone who sins against me? Seven times?" "No, not seven times,"
Jesus replied, "but seventy times seven!"
+ MATTHEW 18:21-22

FORGIVING does not mean forgetting. Sometimes the pain of an insult, rejection, or betrayal leaves a deep scar. So how can God ask us to forgive someone who has caused so much damage to our heart? When God asks us to forgive, he isn't asking us to stop feeling pain over the situation. He knows that true forgiveness takes time, which sometimes means forgiving another over and over again. If you are struggling to forgive someone right now, ask God to help you take just a small step today toward loving that person. Start by praying for him or her. This may be one of the hardest things you will ever do, but prayer has the power to change your heart. Remember, God sees your pain. He promises to walk beside you as you choose to go down the long road of forgiveness.

Prayer Prompts

Lord, I just can't seem to forgive this person: . . .
Your Word uses these phrases to encourage me to forgive: . . .

 # freedom

What does "freedom in Christ" mean? How can I be free if I'm supposed to follow God's commands?

———— ❧ ————

Jesus said, . . . "You are truly my disciples if you remain faithful to my teachings. And you will know the truth, and the truth will set you free."
+ JOHN 8:31-32

Sin is no longer your master, for you no longer live under the requirements of the law. Instead, you live under the freedom of God's grace.
+ ROMANS 6:14

The Scriptures declare that we are all prisoners of sin, so we receive God's promise of freedom only by believing in Jesus Christ.
+ GALATIANS 3:22

THE WORLD tells us that freedom is being able to do whatever we want. However, God tells us that we are free *from* sin but not free *to* sin. The early church father Augustine taught that true freedom is not choice or lack of constraint but being what you are meant to be. For example, if you take a train off the railroad tracks, is it really free? Of course not! It may be unrestricted, but it can't move about the way it's intended to. However, a train that stays on the tracks is free to live out its purpose. Freedom in Christ is the same concept. We are children of God, eternally loved, forgiven, and redeemed because of what Jesus did for us. When we try to live apart from that truth, we aren't really living in freedom. God promises that those who trust in him and follow his ways are free from the bondage of sin as they live in the freedom of his wonderful grace.

Prayer Prompts

Lord, sometimes I feel my freedom constricted by . . .
Your Word says that true freedom is . . .

friendship

How can I be a good friend?

— ❧ —

A friend is always loyal, and a brother is born to help in time of need.
+ PROVERBS 17:17

As iron sharpens iron, so a friend sharpens a friend.
+ PROVERBS 27:17

Be happy with those who are happy, and weep with those who weep.
+ ROMANS 12:15

When Job prayed for his friends, the LORD restored his fortunes.
In fact, the LORD gave him twice as much as before!
+ JOB 42:10

THE BIBLE has a lot to say about friendship. Perhaps this is because God knows how important it is to walk through life with a good friend by our side. God's Word describes a good friend as someone who is loving, loyal, helpful, intentional, sympathetic, edifying, and always ready to offer grace. Our friendships with others may go through seasons. At times, being a good friend means gently confronting or challenging each other. Sometimes being a good friend means just sitting in silence with another who is suffering. True friendship strives to love others right where they are. What kind of friend is God calling you to be toward those closest to you? Ask God to give you wisdom and guidance in your friendships. It gives him great pleasure to see you deepen your friendships as you love others well.

Prayer Prompts

Lord, the friend who is on my heart right now is . . .
Your Word encourages me to love her by . . .

🍁 friendship with God

Does God really enjoy spending time with me, even if I have done something wrong?

———————— ✂ ————————

Inside the Tent of Meeting, the LORD would speak to Moses face to face, as one speaks to a friend. . . . The LORD replied to Moses, "I will indeed do what you have asked, for I look favorably on you, and I know you by name."
+ EXODUS 33:11, 17

The LORD is a friend to those who fear him. He teaches them his covenant.
+ PSALM 25:14

Since our friendship with God was restored by the death of his Son while we were still his enemies, we will certainly be saved through the life of his Son.
+ ROMANS 5:10

The LORD your God is living among you. He is a mighty savior. He will take delight in you with gladness.
+ ZEPHANIAH 3:17

THE WORLD has taught us that relationships are based on cause and effect. When we do something nice for someone, she will want to spend time with us. If we are good, our parents will be proud. Or the opposite—if we are bad, people will no longer love us. This is not so with God and us. God delights in us simply because of who he is—the one who created us. When you doubt that God wants a friendship with you, take a look in his Word. No matter what you have done, your friendship can be restored through Jesus. If you trust in God, you can be confident that he calls you his friend.

Prayer Prompts

Lord, sometimes I doubt you want a close relationship with me because . . .
Your Word reminds me that no matter what, I can call you friend because . . .

fruit of the Spirit

What is the fruit of the Spirit?

———— ❧ ————

The Holy Spirit produces this kind of fruit in our lives: love, joy, peace,
patience, kindness, goodness, faithfulness, gentleness, and self-control.
+ GALATIANS 5:22-23

They delight in the law of the LORD, meditating on it day and night.
They are like trees planted along the riverbank, bearing fruit each
season. Their leaves never wither, and they prosper in all they do.
+ PSALM 1:2-3

THE FRUIT OF THE SPIRIT is the result of growth in our relationship with Jesus. Love, joy, peace, patience, kindness, goodness, faithfulness, gentleness, and self-control are evidence of God's work in our lives. The more we mature in our relationship with God, the more growth we will see in these areas. Some fruit grows quickly, while others take a long time to mature. Think of the Holy Spirit as the gardener of our souls. He works to weed out the roots of sin so it won't choke out the fruit. He prunes anything in our lives that doesn't help us grow. He cultivates and nurtures what is life-giving. Your job is to surrender to the Master Gardener, realizing that he knows how to help you grow best. God wants to produce beautiful fruit in all seasons of life so that others will recognize the work of the Master Gardener in you.

Prayer Prompts

Lord, the fruit I want you to grow in my life is . . .
Your Word describes those who bear fruit as being . . .

 # frustration

What can I do when I am so easily frustrated?

—— ❦ ——

O my people, trust in him at all times.
Pour out your heart to him, for God is our refuge.
+ PSALM 62:8

Don't worry about anything; instead, pray about everything.
Tell God what you need, and thank him for all he has done. Then you
will experience God's peace, which exceeds anything we can understand.
His peace will guard your hearts and minds as you live in Christ Jesus.
+ PHILIPPIANS 4:6-7

The LORD gives his people strength. The LORD blesses them with peace.
+ PSALM 29:11

Be still, and know that I am God!
+ PSALM 46:10

FRUSTRATION is like the blinking "check engine" light on the dashboard of our souls, telling us that something inside is not right. When we find ourselves becoming easily irritated, snapping at others, or abruptly losing our tempers, it is time to get alone with the Lord and look at our souls. Sometimes making some space to reconnect with God feels impossible, yet it could be the most important thing we can do for ourselves and for our relationships with others. God is not disappointed by our frustrations but rather invites us to pour out our hearts to him about them. Next time you find yourself becoming frustrated, use it as a reminder to step away from the busyness of life and step into the quiet with God.

Prayer Prompts

Lord, I get easily frustrated when . . .
Your Word says that when I become frustrated, I should remember that . . .

fun 🍂

Can I follow God and still have fun?

———————— ❧ ————————

People should eat and drink and enjoy the fruits of their labor,
for these are gifts from God.
+ ECCLESIASTES 3:13

Go and celebrate with a feast . . . and share gifts of food with people
who have nothing prepared. This is a sacred day. . . . Don't be dejected
and sad, for the joy of the LORD is your strength!
+ NEHEMIAH 8:10

You have been faithful in handling this small amount. . . .
Let's celebrate together!
+ MATTHEW 25:21

The life of the godly is full of light and joy.
+ PROVERBS 13:9

For the despondent, every day brings trouble;
for the happy heart, life is a continual feast.
+ PROVERBS 15:15

FROM THE NUMBER of feasts and festivals God instituted for the Israelites, we can tell that he intended for his people to have times of celebration. Following God doesn't exclude fun. In fact, following God's commandments is the way to get the most out of life as it was originally created to be enjoyed. God wants us to have rich lives, to celebrate with others, and to find joy in our relationship with him. These important aspects of faith lift our spirits and help us see the beauty and meaning in life. So feel the freedom to laugh with God and others, delight in the ordinary, and experience fun in your life—this is God's desire for you!

Prayer Prompts
Lord, something that is really fun for me is . . .
I see in your Word how you delight in my enjoyment: . . .

 future

How can I be confident in my future instead of being afraid of it?

———————— ❧ ————————

I am trusting you, O LORD, saying, "You are my God!"
My future is in your hands.
+ PSALM 31:14-15

[Those who are righteous] do not fear bad news;
they confidently trust the LORD to care for them.
+ PSALM 112:7

Worry weighs a person down; an encouraging word cheers a person up.
+ PROVERBS 12:25

Blessed are those who trust in the LORD and
have made the LORD their hope and confidence.
+ JEREMIAH 17:7

AS WOMEN, we often long for security, and the unknowns of the future can seem frightening. But our fears of loss, suffering, and bad news will only leave us feeling weighed down. We can't allow the "what ifs" of the future to steal the joy God has for us in the present. We miss some good gifts God has placed right in front of us when we focus on the bad that may or may not come. We can be confident in our future because God is good and wants good things for us! Do you expect him to do something wonderful with your life? God wants to teach you to believe his promises and to accept his good gifts. Start by taking one day at a time. Decide to begin each day with a contented heart, and you will experience life as a continual feast. Receive God's peace for tomorrow by trusting him for today.

Prayer Prompts
Lord, what I fear most about the future is . . .
Your Word calls me to live in confidence today because . . .

generosity

How can I learn to be more generous?

You must each decide in your heart how much to give.
And don't give reluctantly or in response to pressure.
"For God loves a person who gives cheerfully."
+ 2 CORINTHIANS 9:7

Remember the words of the Lord Jesus:
"It is more blessed to give than to receive."
+ ACTS 20:35

The generous will prosper; those who refresh others
will themselves be refreshed.
+ PROVERBS 11:25

Give, and you will receive. Your gift will return to you in full—pressed down,
shaken together to make room for more, running over, and poured into
your lap. The amount you give will determine the amount you get back.
+ LUKE 6:38

THE BIBLE has a lot to say about money—not how much or how little we should make, but rather, how we should give it away. The way we spend our money reveals what we care most about. Generosity is not just giving money to help others, but also giving our time, talents, and possessions. Generosity is important because it teaches us to trust God with our resources and put others before ourselves. When we give, we begin to release our grip on the things we hold too tightly. If generosity feels hard for you, perhaps God wants to show you a treasure that has taken priority over him in your heart. Ask him to unleash the gift of generosity in you so you can receive the joy that comes from giving.

Prayer Prompts

Lord, it is hard for me to be generous with . . .
Your Word promises this for those who are generous: . . .

 # gentleness

What does gentleness accomplish?
Won't everyone walk all over me if I am gentle?

The Holy Spirit produces this kind of fruit in our lives: love, joy, peace, patience, kindness, goodness, faithfulness, gentleness, and self-control.
+ GALATIANS 5:22-23

You should clothe yourselves instead with the beauty that comes from within, the unfading beauty of a gentle and quiet spirit, which is so precious to God.
+ 1 PETER 3:4

Pursue righteousness and a godly life, along with faith, love, perseverance, and gentleness.
+ 1 TIMOTHY 6:11

God blesses those who are humble, for they will inherit the whole earth.
+ MATTHEW 5:5

CULTURE tells us that we as women need to stand up for our rights and be assertive, yet God calls us to gentleness. How do we reconcile the two? Gentleness does not mean that we let others walk all over us. We can be gentle and strong at the same time. God is the perfect example of gentleness, and yet he stands firm for what is good and true. Think of Jesus inviting little children to come to him, celebrating them in the midst of the disciples' impatience. God greatly values gentleness. It is a fruit of the Spirit and a byproduct of living a godly life. In God's eyes, gentle people are the most influential in the world because they make an impact without causing conflict. Don't be afraid of being gentle. Ask God to grow this trait in you, and watch how much more you accomplish through gentleness than through force.

Prayer Prompts

Lord, up until now I have viewed gentleness as . . .
But your Word tells me this is the way you value gentleness: . . .

giving up 🍃

How can I keep going when I'm tempted to give up?

— ❧ —

I am certain that God, who began the good work within you, will continue his work until it is finally finished on the day when Christ Jesus returns.
+ PHILIPPIANS 1:6

When troubles of any kind come your way, consider it an opportunity for great joy. For you know that when your faith is tested, your endurance has a chance to grow. So let it grow, for when your endurance is fully developed, you will be perfect and complete, needing nothing.
+ JAMES 1:2-4

I will never forget this awful time, as I grieve over my loss. Yet I still dare to hope when I remember this: The faithful love of the LORD never ends! His mercies never cease. Great is his faithfulness; his mercies begin afresh each morning.
+ LAMENTATIONS 3:20-23

IN THE MIDDLE of a tough situation, giving up sometimes seems like the only option. However, when we feel like throwing in the towel, God provides another way. He offers to help us through his strength and supernatural power. When we stop striving and start praying, a miracle happens within us—we find hope to lift our spirits and faith to keep going. If you feel on the verge of quitting, step out in faith and ask God to help you get through just one more day. If you do this every day, eventually you will realize you've made it through the difficult season. When you're on the other side, you will discover things about God you hadn't previously experienced—and strength you never knew you had.

Prayer Prompts

Lord, I feel tempted to give up in the area of . . .
Your Word encourages me to keep going because . . .

🍁 glory

How can I possibly glorify God in my pain?

❧

*My life is an example to many, because you have been
my strength and protection. That is why I can never stop
praising you; I declare your glory all day long.*
+ PSALM 71:7-8

*When you produce much fruit, you are my true disciples.
This brings great glory to my Father.*
+ JOHN 15:8

*Jesus looked up to heaven and said, "Father, the hour has come. . . . I brought
glory to you here on earth by completing the work you gave me to do.
Now, Father, bring me into the glory we shared before the world began."*
+ JOHN 17:1, 4-5

CHRISTIANS often talk about glorifying God, but what does this
actually mean? Glory involves two aspects. First, to glorify or
give glory means to demonstrate or represent. Second, it means to
reflect or bring something to light. Therefore, to glorify God is to represent Christ and reflect him to others. God uses our circumstances,
good and bad, to help us and others grow. It's easy to be joyful and
faithful when life goes well, but when life gets tough, believers have
a unique opportunity to show how a relationship with God brings
comfort, confidence, and hope. When we glorify God in difficult circumstances, two wonderful things happen: We learn to rely on God's
presence and strength, and others are blessed by seeing our faith
and hope in action. God can use anything to make himself known
in the world, even the most painful part of our lives.

Prayer Prompts
Lord, I want to glorify you in this painful circumstance: . . .
Your Word teaches me to glorify you by . . .

goals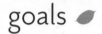

What kinds of goals should I set in order to grow closer to God?

———————— ∞ ————————

I run with purpose in every step.
+ 1 CORINTHIANS 9:26

Look straight ahead, and fix your eyes on what lies before you.
Mark out a straight path for your feet; stay on the safe path.
Don't get sidetracked; keep your feet from following evil.
+ PROVERBS 4:25-27

We can make our plans, but the LORD determines our steps.
+ PROVERBS 16:9

I press on to reach the end of the race and receive the heavenly
prize for which God, through Christ Jesus, is calling us.
+ PHILIPPIANS 3:14

GOALS GIVE us direction. Setting a goal gives us purpose and keeps us from straying away from God regardless of what life throws at us. Jesus sought to please and give glory to his Father in everything he did. That goal shaped the way he lived every day and helped him to serve others in every interaction. If you want to set a goal, ask yourself this question: *How can I take one step closer to God today?* Maybe this means setting aside a certain amount of time to read his Word, praying for the day before you get out of bed, or simply setting an alarm on your phone to remind yourself that God is with you. Start small and work your way up to more challenging goals. Whatever goal you decide to set, remember that even if you don't reach it every single day, you will still be pointed in the right direction.

Prayer Prompts

Lord, one goal I want to set for this week is . . .
As I set my goal, I will remember that your Word says . . .

 # God's blessings

What kinds of blessings can I expect from God?

❧

*You will show me the way of life, granting me the joy of your presence
and the pleasures of living with you forever.*
+ PSALM 16:11

*All praise to God, the Father of our Lord Jesus Christ,
who has blessed us with every spiritual blessing in the
heavenly realms because we are united with Christ.*
+ EPHESIANS 1:3

*How great is the goodness you have stored up for those
who fear you. You lavish it on those who come to you for
protection, blessing them before the watching world.*
+ PSALM 31:19

*This is how God loved the world: He gave his one and only Son, so that
everyone who believes in him will not perish but have eternal life.*
+ JOHN 3:16

GOD'S BLESSINGS are everywhere, but we need spiritual eyes to see them as his gifts and not merely as luck or good fortune. His blessings come to us every day, in every conceivable form. Success and prosperity are not the most common blessings from God, for they tend to take our minds off him. Rather, he blesses us with his presence, the beauty of creation, peace of heart, joy, spiritual gifts, family, friends, comfort, and hope. The greatest blessings God wants to give you are salvation and eternal life. You just need to ask for them.

Prayer Prompts

Lord, today you have blessed me with . . .
Your Word reminds me that I am also blessed because . . .

God's discipline 🍂

What is the purpose of God's discipline?

───────── ❧ ─────────

*Think about it: Just as a parent disciplines a child,
the LORD your God disciplines you for your own good.*
+ DEUTERONOMY 8:5

Joyful are those you discipline, LORD, those you teach with your instructions.
+ PSALM 94:12

*As you endure this divine discipline,
remember that God is treating you as his own children.*
+ HEBREWS 12:7

*No discipline is enjoyable while it is happening—it's painful!
But afterward there will be a peaceful harvest of right living
for those who are trained in this way.*
+ HEBREWS 12:11

SOMETIMES God disciplines us by taking away something we have come to love more than him. Sometimes he allows us to experience the painful consequences of our own sinful choices. Other times, he may bring adversity into our lives as a way to refine us. God doesn't discipline us to control us but to protect us. Sin always damages our relationship with God and others. He knows that if we continue down sinful paths, it will only end in pain. Therefore, God's discipline is an act of love to keep us from destroying relationships, to help us build good character and habits, and to teach us right from wrong. If the weight of God's discipline feels heavy in your life, remind yourself of his loving heart. God's desire is to help you become the person he created you to be so you can experience a life of joy and peace.

Prayer Prompts

*Lord, I see your hand of discipline on this area of my life: . . .
As painful as this is, help me remember that you discipline because . . .*

 God's hand

How can I notice the hand of God working in my life?

❧

Job replied, . . . "Should we accept only good things from the hand of God and never anything bad?"
+ JOB 2:10

Come and see what our God has done, what awesome miracles he performs for people!
+ PSALM 66:5

It is the LORD who provides the sun to light the day and the moon and stars to light the night, and who stirs the sea into roaring waves. His name is the LORD of Heaven's Armies.
+ JEREMIAH 31:35

Whatever is good and perfect is a gift coming down to us from God our Father, who created all the lights in the heavens.
+ JAMES 1:17

GOD MAY WORK through events in our lives or use unexpected people to accomplish his will. Sometimes God is a still, quiet voice in our minds, and at other times he is a force to be reckoned with. The point is that some things about God are unchanging: his love, his law, his promises. Other things about God are wild and mysterious. This means we must be watchful and always expectant about how he may be working in our lives. Often, it isn't until we look back on our lives that we can see God's fingerprints all over them. Whether or not you realize it, God's hand is on you, and he is always working to accomplish his will in your life.

Prayer Prompts

Lord, perhaps you are working through this unexpected situation: . . .
Your Word encourages me to look for you in other areas as well, such as . . .

God's timing

How can I patiently wait for God's timing?

I wait quietly before God, for my victory comes from him. . . .
Let all that I am wait quietly before God, for my hope is in him.
+ PSALM 62:1, 5

Rejoice in our confident hope. Be patient in trouble, and keep on praying.
+ ROMANS 12:12

ALMOST EVERYONE hates to wait. Even trivial delays like red lights or slow cashier lines can make us edgy, and more serious delays can provoke serious anger. We can be especially frustrated when it feels like we are waiting in line for God to do something for us, even though the right answer to our prayers seems obvious. It's hard to accept when God's timing is different from ours, and even harder to accept that his timing is best for us. We want what we think is right, and we want it now. Waiting can feel like a waste of time. But what if there is more happening during seasons of waiting than we are aware of? Waiting places us in the perfect position to grow strong in character, in persistent prayer, and in patient confidence in God's promises for our lives. If you are in a season where God's timing is different from your own, use it as an opportunity to grow. As the old saying goes, "God is rarely early, but he's never late." Remind yourself continually of God's faithfulness. He is actively working in your life to help you become all he made you to be.

Prayer Prompts

Lord, in this time of waiting, I see you growing this area of my faith: . . .
When I feel discouraged by the wait, your Word encourages me by . . .

 good out of bad

How is God able to bring good out of bad situations?

———— ❧ ————

We can rejoice, too, when we run into problems and trials, for we know that they help us develop endurance. And endurance develops strength of character, and character strengthens our confident hope of salvation.
+ ROMANS 5:3-4

We don't look at the troubles we can see now; rather, we fix our gaze on things that cannot be seen. For the things we see now will soon be gone, but the things we cannot see will last forever.
+ 2 CORINTHIANS 4:18

In his kindness God called you to share in his eternal glory. . . . So after you have suffered a little while, he will restore, support, and strengthen you.
+ 1 PETER 5:10

TRIALS have a way of exposing our hearts; they help us know whether God's Word has really sunk in. Most of us know intellectually that trials strengthen our character and help us grow, but when we are in a challenging season, we live out the beliefs that are really in our hearts. If you are walking through a trial right now, look to God's Word for encouragement and comfort. He promises to be present with you—right now in this very moment. He will not abandon you in your trial. You can't change your circumstances, but you can choose to allow them to strengthen your faith instead of destroy it. Be encouraged because God promises to work everything into something good. You will have to endure these trials for only a little while, and afterward you will experience wonderful joy for all eternity.

Prayer Prompts

Lord, I wonder if it's possible for good to come out of this situation: . . .
As I think about trials, your Word encourages me that . . .

gossip

Is gossip really that bad?

———— ❧ ————

Gossip separates the best of friends.
+ **PROVERBS 16:28**

A gossip goes around telling secrets, so don't hang around with chatterers.
+ **PROVERBS 20:19**

Fire goes out without wood, and quarrels disappear when gossip stops.
+ **PROVERBS 26:20**

*The Scriptures say, "If you want to enjoy life and see many happy days,
keep your tongue from speaking evil and your lips from telling lies."*
+ **1 PETER 3:10**

OUR WORDS hold such power—even the ones we say behind one another's backs. Gossip is tempting because it makes us feel like we are part of a secret. And let's be honest: Depending on our circle of friends, gossip can make up a significant portion of our conversation. But gossip is much more dangerous than we realize. God's Word tells us that gossip has the power to separate best friends, take away our good days, and lead us to sin. Likewise, God promises that controlling our tongues will reduce quarrels, help us avoid trouble, and lead to happier lives. In the end, the thrill of gossip isn't worth the damage it causes. Perhaps God is asking you to refrain from gossip by limiting your time around certain friends, changing the subject when gossip comes up, or removing yourself from certain conversations. Take time to think about what God's Word says regarding the tongue while asking yourself if your words are kind, loving, true, and necessary.

Prayer Prompts

Lord, I am tempted to gossip when . . .
Your Word gives these warnings about the power of the tongue: . . .

 # government

How should I pray for my country?

———————— ✀ ————————

Pray this way for kings and all who are in authority so that we can live
peaceful and quiet lives marked by godliness and dignity.
+ 1 TIMOTHY 2:2

May you hear the humble and earnest requests from me
and your people Israel when we pray toward this place.
Yes, hear us from heaven where you live, and when you hear, forgive.
+ 1 KINGS 8:30

When there is moral rot within a nation, its government topples easily.
+ PROVERBS 28:2

If my people who are called by my name will humble themselves
and pray and seek my face and turn from their wicked ways,
I will hear from heaven and will forgive their sins and restore their land.
+ 2 CHRONICLES 7:14

IN MANY COUNTRIES, the word *government* is associated with division, conflict, and pain. God's Word may not have clear instructions on every political issue, but it clearly instructs us to pray. And as believers, we should pray that our nation will be protected by God's mighty hand. We should pray that our leaders will be humble and wise, able to discern right from wrong and advocate for the needy and helpless. God's Word warns that nations who endorse and condone immorality are subject to judgment and will eventually collapse from the inside out. A nation that collectively worships the one true God will stand firm. As you read the news this week, remember to let prayer for your country be your first response.

Prayer Prompts

Lord, I feel that the current state of my country is . . .
Your Word instructs me to pray for my government in this way: . . .

grace

How does grace affect the way I live?

------------ ❧ ------------

God saved you by his grace when you believed. And you can't take credit for this; it is a gift from God. Salvation is not a reward for the good things we have done, so none of us can boast about it.
+ EPHESIANS 2:8-9

The wages of sin is death, but the free gift of God is eternal life through Christ Jesus our Lord.
+ ROMANS 6:23

Sin is no longer your master, for you no longer live under the requirements of the law. Instead, you live under the freedom of God's grace.
+ ROMANS 6:14

GRACE is one of the most tangible expressions of love. It is both a onetime act (the grace of God giving us salvation through faith in Jesus) and a way of life (living in freedom rather than captive to guilt and shame). In either case, grace is simply God's special favor. The fact that grace is God's gift and not the product of our own effort gives us an example of how we are to extend grace to others. Are you known for being someone who is quick to forgive, eager to extend kindness, and generous in showing love—even to those who don't deserve it? If this feels hard for you, look to God's Word to be reminded of how he has shown grace to you. As you increase your understanding of his grace, you can't help but be moved to share that same gift with those around you.

Prayer Prompts

Lord, I want to extend grace to others in my life by . . .
Your Word reminds me that you showed grace to me by . . .

Is there something wrong with me if I'm still feeling sad long after a great loss?

———— ❧ ————

*I will never forget this awful time, as I grieve over my loss.
Yet I still dare to hope when I remember this: The faithful love
of the LORD never ends! His mercies never cease. Great is his
faithfulness; his mercies begin afresh each morning.*
+ LAMENTATIONS 3:20-23

*You keep track of all my sorrows. You have collected all my
tears in your bottle. You have recorded each one in your book.*
+ PSALM 56:8

God blesses those who mourn, for they will be comforted.
+ MATTHEW 5:4

*The LORD is close to the brokenhearted;
he rescues those whose spirits are crushed.*
+ PSALM 34:18

THE GRIEVING process after a significant loss is not swift, nor is it a steady progression. Even after a good week, a good laugh, a theological insight, or a renewal of hope, you most likely will weep again. There is nothing wrong with you; this is part of the process of grieving and healing. The fact that you are still grieving over your loss shows how deeply you allowed yourself to love and be loved. Don't try to move past your grief too quickly. When it is time, God will begin to create space in your heart so you can embrace the next chapter in your life. Until then, allow yourself the time to grieve, and remember that God is with you, comforting you in your pain.

Prayer Prompts
*Lord, I am still grieving the loss of . . .
Your Word gives me hope that . . .*

growth ⬮

How can I know if I am growing spiritually?

———————— ❧ ————————

If you remain in me and my words remain in you,
you may ask for anything you want, and it will be granted!
When you produce much fruit, you are my true disciples.
+ JOHN 15:7-8

All Scripture is inspired by God and is useful to teach us what
is true and to make us realize what is wrong in our lives.
It corrects us when we are wrong and teaches us to do what is right.
+ 2 TIMOTHY 3:16

I am certain that God, who began the good work within you, will continue his
work until it is finally finished on the day when Christ Jesus returns.
+ PHILIPPIANS 1:6

HOW DO we know if we are growing spiritually? It is simple: Are we bearing fruit? Becoming less irritable and discouraged and more joyful, peaceful, and kind? Sometimes our spiritual growth feels like two steps forward and one step back. But remember—that means we're still growing. With this in mind, don't be discouraged when you feel you're at a spiritual standstill or aren't growing fast enough. God promises to continue his good work in you. Your job is to continually pursue relationship with him. The growth you experience in this life is forming who you will be for all eternity. Invest your time in the only thing that will last forever—your relationship with your Savior.

Prayer Prompts

Lord, this is how I feel about my spiritual growth recently: . . .
Your Word reminds me that real growth happens through . . .

 guidance

How can I know that God will guide my life?

— ❧ —

The LORD directs the steps of the godly.
+ PSALM 37:23

Seek his will in all you do, and he will show you which path to take.
+ PROVERBS 3:6

He is our God forever and ever, and he will guide us until we die.
+ PSALM 48:14

*The LORD says, "I will guide you along the best pathway
for your life. I will advise you and watch over you."*
+ PSALM 32:8

*The LORD leads with unfailing love and faithfulness
all who keep his covenant and obey his demands.*
+ PSALM 25:10

MAKING a hard decision can be an excruciating process. Tough decisions bring up tough questions like "How do I know which way God wants me to go?" "Does he have a perfect plan for my life?" and "What happens if I make the wrong decision?" When these questions come up, it is so important to open God's Word for guidance. He promises to counsel us, lead us to truth, and help us hear his voice. Isn't it a gift to know we have a loving God who hasn't left us to figure out life on our own? Don't allow your feelings of insecurity about your life's direction to tempt you to doubt God's care for you. Trust that he has it all under control, and remember that he promises to guide you faithfully.

Prayer Prompts

Lord, I need guidance specifically for . . .
Your Word assures me you will guide my future by . . .

guilt 🍃

Why do I still feel guilty even though I have accepted God's gift of salvation?

———————— ❦ ————————

Now you are free from the power of sin and have become slaves
of God. Now you do those things that lead to holiness and result
in eternal life. For the wages of sin is death, but the free gift of God
is eternal life through Christ Jesus our Lord.
✝ ROMANS 6:22-23

Even if we feel guilty, God is greater than our feelings, and he knows everything.
✝ 1 JOHN 3:20

If we confess our sins to [God], he is faithful and just to forgive us our sins
and to cleanse us from all wickedness. If we claim we have not sinned, we are
calling God a liar and showing that his word has no place in our hearts.
✝ 1 JOHN 1:9-10

HAVE YOU ever confessed your sin to God but still felt guilty?
If so, perhaps the problem isn't that God hasn't forgiven you,
but rather that you haven't forgiven yourself. Part of accepting God's
salvation is also accepting our new identity. No matter what we have
done, if we come to God for forgiveness, he forgives, cleanses, and
makes us holy in his eyes. God does not want us to atone for our
sin by feeling guilty and miserable. Rather, he wants us to trust his
forgiveness and then walk in freedom. Faith is not simply a matter
of believing with our minds; it is a matter of trusting in God's grace
with our hearts. Next time you confess a sin and still feel guilty, proclaim out loud that you are known, loved, and forgiven by God.

Prayer Prompts

Lord, even though I have confessed, I still feel guilty about . . .
Your Word promises me that though I have sinned, I am . . .

 # habits

How can I establish good habits that will result in lasting change?

Physical training is good, but training for godliness is much better, promising benefits in this life and in the life to come.
+ 1 TIMOTHY 4:8

Don't copy the behavior and customs of this world, but let God transform you into a new person by changing the way you think. Then you will learn to know God's will for you, which is good and pleasing and perfect.
+ ROMANS 12:2

Blessed are all who hear the word of God and put it into practice.
+ LUKE 11:28

A HABIT is a routine of behavior repeated regularly and usually unconsciously. Obviously, most of us want our good habits, not our bad ones, to become second nature to us. Whether we realize this or not, everything we do is training our hearts either toward God or away from him. When we regularly watch a TV show, we are training our hearts. When we choose day after day to pray instead of worry, we are training our hearts. Therefore, it is essential that we develop the habit of "exercising" our hearts in the practice of moving ever closer to God. Take time to think about your current habits. Which ones help you grow toward God? Which ones don't? The goal is to create habits that change not only your behavior but also your heart. Those habits will stay with you forever. Only when you recognize the places where you currently live apart from God can you prayerfully develop routines that will daily draw you to him and not away.

Prayer Prompts
Lord, one habit I would like to form is . . .
Those who daily train themselves to move toward you will experience . . .

happiness

How can I live a happier life?

*Make me walk along the path of your commands,
for that is where my happiness is found.*
+ PSALM 119:35

Do what is right and good in the LORD's sight, so all will go well with you.
+ DEUTERONOMY 6:18

*For the despondent, every day brings trouble;
for the happy heart, life is a continual feast.*
+ PROVERBS 15:15

*The hopes of the godly result in happiness, but
the expectations of the wicked come to nothing.*
+ PROVERBS 10:28

MANY OF US strive to make happiness our primary goal. We are tempted to believe that if we can just have the right spouse, the perfect job, a beautiful appearance, or a nicer house, then we will finally be happy. In reality, the surest way to be *unhappy* is to think the next great thing will make you content. With that perspective, happiness is always just out of reach. But God's Word promises some specific, achievable things we can do to be truly happy. A few key actions are to follow Jesus; do everything to honor God, not ourselves; place our hope in God's promises rather than in those the world tries to give us; and delight in reading God's Word. If you can do these things, then God promises you will be genuinely happy because you will know without a doubt who you are and where you are headed for eternity.

Prayer Prompts

Lord, sometimes I think I would be happy if . . .
Your Word promises happiness for those who . . .

🍂 hard-heartedness

How can I know if my heart has become hard?

Pharaoh's heart, however, remained hard.
He still refused to listen, just as the Lord had predicted.
+ EXODUS 7:13

Get rid of all bitterness, rage, anger, harsh words, and slander, as well as
all types of evil behavior. Instead, be kind to each other, tenderhearted,
forgiving one another, just as God through Christ has forgiven you.
+ EPHESIANS 4:31-32

I will give you a new heart, and I will put a new spirit in you. I will take out
your stony, stubborn heart and give you a tender, responsive heart.
+ EZEKIEL 36:26

A HARD HEART rejects love from God and others. It refuses to forgive, see the good in life, or recognize blessings from God. An open heart receives love from God and others. It is gracious and forgiving, and asks for God's help, trusting he will respond at the perfect time. We should ask ourselves, *Is my heart becoming more hard and stubborn or more open to God?* If you have noticed that your heart has gradually hardened, take time to do the following things: (1) Remind yourself that you are known and loved by your Creator. (2) Start forgiving others even when they don't deserve it. (3) Remember God's faithfulness to you in the past. (4) Thank him for what he has done and is doing now, even if you cannot see it. These truths help begin the process of softening your heart. Remember, God is able to change the hardest of hearts; all you need to do is ask.

Prayer Prompts

Lord, one way I feel my heart has hardened is . . .
Your Word says that these things will help soften my heart toward you: . . .

healing 🍃

Will God heal the hurts in my life?

— ❧ —

For you who fear my name, the Sun of Righteousness will rise with healing in his wings. And you will go free, leaping with joy like calves let out to pasture.
+ MALACHI 4:2

My health may fail, and my spirit may grow weak, but God remains the strength of my heart; he is mine forever.
+ PSALM 73:26

He will take our weak mortal bodies and change them into glorious bodies like his own.
+ PHILIPPIANS 3:21

God himself will be with them. He will wipe every tear from their eyes, and there will be no more death or sorrow or crying or pain.
+ REVELATION 21:3-4

WHETHER WE have a physical or mental illness, are battling a spiritual affliction, or feel the ache of a trauma from our past, pain resides deep in each of us. We long for God's healing, and when it doesn't happen right away, we can feel disheartened and doubt his goodness. But God's Word promises two things in our pain: (1) He will heal us—if not in this short life, then for all eternity—and (2) he honors the persistent prayers of his people. He who made our bodies, minds, and hearts can certainly repair and restore them. If you are longing for healing, don't lose heart. Continue praying with persistence, and trust God to give you the strength you need to get through this season. Be encouraged that someday all your pain will be taken away and you will be healed once and for all.

Prayer Prompts

Lord, I long for you to heal me of . . .
This is how your Word encourages me in my pain: . . .

 # health

Does God care about my physical health?
Isn't spiritual health more important to him?

❦

Physical training is good, but training for godliness is much better,
promising benefits in this life and in the life to come.
+ 1 TIMOTHY 4:8

And so, dear brothers and sisters, I plead with you to give your bodies to God
because of all he has done for you. Let them be a living and holy sacrifice—
the kind he will find acceptable. This is truly the way to worship him.
+ ROMANS 12:1

Give yourselves completely to God, for you were dead,
but now you have new life. So use your whole body as
an instrument to do what is right for the glory of God.
+ ROMANS 6:13

THE BODY AND SOUL are intimately connected, and God cares about both. Our Creator knows that spiritual disciplines— worship, prayer, obedience to God's Word—have a profound impact on our lives, and that physical habits—from nutrition to hygiene—influence our spiritual lives. Although our souls are the most important part of us, we are also physical beings. Therefore we are called to care for our bodies and honor God with them, remembering that they are good creations from him. Ask God how to help you keep your physical and spiritual health in a wholesome balance so that you can best worship your Creator.

Prayer Prompts

Lord, a choice I can make for better physical and spiritual health is . . .
Your Word assures me that both are important because . . .

hearing 🍃

How can I know that God hears my prayers?

—————————— ❧ ——————————

*I love the LORD because he hears my voice and my prayer for mercy.
Because he bends down to listen, I will pray as long as I have breath!*
+ PSALM 116:1-2

*We are confident that he hears us whenever we ask for anything that
pleases him. And since we know he hears us when we make our requests,
we also know that he will give us what we ask for.*
+ 1 JOHN 5:14-15

*Morning, noon, and night I cry out in my distress,
and the LORD hears my voice.*
+ PSALM 55:17

WE OFTEN PRAY with the expectation that God will solve all our problems. And when he doesn't, or he doesn't seem to move fast enough, it is tempting to assume he isn't listening. But just because God isn't answering our prayers right now doesn't mean he doesn't hear our cries. Maybe one of the most loving things God can do for us in this season is to sit beside us and give us space to share our hearts. We all go through seasons when it feels like our prayers just hit the ceiling. However, God assures us in his Word that he always listens to us, no matter what. If you doubt that God hears you, remind yourself of his promises. Trust him to love you well by offering his open ears whenever you need to talk.

Prayer Prompts

Lord, I wonder if you heard my prayer about . . .
Your Word assures me I can trust you to listen because . . .

How do I protect my heart?

❦

Guard your heart above all else, for it determines the course of your life.
+ PROVERBS 4:23

Christ will make his home in your hearts as you trust in him.
Your roots will grow down into God's love and keep you strong.
+ EPHESIANS 3:17

My child, listen and be wise: Keep your heart on the right course.
+ PROVERBS 23:19

Create in me a clean heart, O God. Renew a loyal spirit within me.
+ PSALM 51:10

THE BIBLE STATES that the heart is the center of thought and feeling. Every action flows from our hearts; therefore it is important for us to be aware of what we let into them. Practically, this means using caution with what we hear, see, watch on television or other media, and choose to dwell on. When we neglect our hearts, our sin nature quickly moves in to take over. When we fail to protect our hearts, we lose sensitivity to what is good for us and what is harmful. What steps are you taking to guard your heart? Ask God to clean its impurities and help you grow in sensitivity to what kinds of things you allow into it.

Prayer Prompts

Lord, one way I feel you calling me to protect my heart is by . . .
Your Word urges me to protect my heart because . . .

heaven

What will heaven be like?

———— ❧ ————

There is more than enough room in my Father's home. If this were not so,
would I have told you that I am going to prepare a place for you?
+ JOHN 14:2

We are looking forward to the new heavens and new earth he has promised,
a world filled with God's righteousness.
+ 2 PETER 3:13

Look! I am creating new heavens and a new earth,
and no one will even think about the old ones anymore.
+ ISAIAH 65:17

There will be no night there—no need for lamps or sun—for the
Lord God will shine on them. And they will reign forever and ever.
+ REVELATION 22:5

HEAVEN IS not merely an extension of our lives here on earth. It's a restoration of all that is good and an elimination of all that is wrong with this current world. God promises something new to us and yet very original to him—a world with no sin, sorrow, or pain. We will live in the world we've longed for, and it will be everything we have hoped for. God created humans for this earth, so the new earth will have many similarities to this one. However, it will be better and more amazing in every way. You don't have to worry about sitting around on some cloud and strumming a harp. Eternity will be physical, productive, purposeful, and perfect. You will be in God's presence and forever filled with joy.

Prayer Prompts

Lord, what I am most looking forward to in heaven is . . .
When I feel discouraged, I will dwell on this promise about heaven: . . .

help

I find it hard to ask for help.
How can I move past this?

❧

The LORD God said, "It is not good for the man to be alone.
I will make a helper who is just right for him."
+ GENESIS 2:18

The LORD is my strength and shield. I trust him with all my heart.
He helps me, and my heart is filled with joy.
+ PSALM 28:7

This same God who takes care of me will supply all your needs from
his glorious riches, which have been given to us in Christ Jesus.
+ PHILIPPIANS 4:19

EVERYONE has limitations—areas of weakness, feelings of inadequacy, a lack of skill or knowledge. Although our culture may admire the strong, independent spirit, no one can really survive alone. That's why God created us to be in relationship with him and with other people. Part of relationship is giving and receiving help. We need help to get work done. We need help to restore relationships. We need help to develop our skills. We need help to think through problems. We need help to say, "I'm sorry." Just as we might be more than willing to help a friend, God wants to help us too. He is the ultimate helper, for he is wise, strong, and infinitely loving. Not only does our help come from God, but God also uses others to help us. Ask God to teach you how to humble yourself to receive help so that one day you can offer help to another in need.

Prayer Prompts

Lord, I really want help with . . .
Your Word encourages me to ask for help because . . .

helping others 🗨

How can I best help others with their problems?

———— ✀ ————

This is the message you have heard from the beginning:
We should love one another.
+ 1 JOHN 3:11

You have done well to share with me in my present difficulty.
+ PHILIPPIANS 4:14

All praise to God, the Father of our Lord Jesus Christ. God is our
merciful Father and the source of all comfort. He comforts us in all
our troubles so that we can comfort others. When others are troubled,
we will be able to give them the same comfort God has given us.
+ 2 CORINTHIANS 1:3-4

Share each other's burdens, and in this way obey the law of Christ.
+ GALATIANS 6:2

W**HEN OTHERS** are facing problems, we can genuinely love them with our actions, emotions, attitudes, words, and presence. The best way to help others is by being intentional about recognizing their needs and then meeting them! If someone we know is going through a trial, we can ask ourselves, *What does this person really need? A meal? An encouraging word? A listening ear?* When we serve others this way, we are doing exactly what Jesus would have done—blessing them by meeting a need in their lives. Helping others helps them see Jesus. Pay attention to opportunities to serve those around you. Ask God to help you set aside your own needs, desires, and agenda to instead seek out and meet the needs of others.

Prayer Prompts

Lord, one person I can help today is . . .
Your Word encourages me to help them by . . .

 # hiding

What can I do when it feels like God is hiding himself and his plans from me?

Ever since the world was created, people have seen the earth and sky. Through everything God made, they can clearly see his invisible qualities—his eternal power and divine nature. So they have no excuse for not knowing God.
+ ROMANS 1:20

If you search for him with all your heart and soul, you will find him.
+ DEUTERONOMY 4:29

His purpose was for the nations to seek after God and perhaps feel their way toward him and find him—though he is not far from any one of us.
+ ACTS 17:27

Anyone who wants to come to him must believe that God exists and that he rewards those who sincerely seek him.
+ HEBREWS 11:6

SOMETIMES IT FEELS like God is hiding himself and his plans, but in reality, he is everywhere. Sometimes we just look for him in the wrong places. C. S. Lewis said, "We may ignore, but we can nowhere evade the presence of God. The world is crowded with Him. He walks everywhere incognito." We can see glimpses of him through his creation, his Word, and his people. If you feel like there is distance between you and God right now, remind yourself of the truths from his Word. The Bible is a beautiful story about how God loves, pursues, and reveals himself to his people. Take heart because God is nearer than you think.

Prayer Prompts

Lord, I long to see you in this area of my life: . . .
When it seems you are hiding, your Word reminds me that . . .

holiness 🍃

Holiness feels like an impossible standard. Is it even possible to be holy?

---— ❧ ———

I plead with you to give your bodies to God because of all he has done for you. Let them be a living and holy sacrifice—the kind he will find acceptable.
+ ROMANS 12:1

I am writing . . . to you who have been called by God to be his own holy people. He made you holy by means of Christ Jesus, just as he did for all people everywhere who call on the name of our Lord Jesus Christ.
+ 1 CORINTHIANS 1:2

Even before he made the world, God loved us and chose us in Christ to be holy and without fault in his eyes.
+ EPHESIANS 1:4

HOLINESS IS both a journey and a final destination. To be completely holy is to be sinless, pure, and perfect before God. Of course, no one is perfect here on earth; perfection is our final destination when we stand before God in heaven. But holiness also means being different, "set apart" by God for a specific purpose. We are to be different from the rest of the world, and our lives are journeys toward becoming a little more like Jesus with each passing day. Talk to God when you don't feel holy. Ask him to change your heart so your thoughts, actions, and motives become more like his. Strive to be holy during your earthly journey, remembering that one day you will stand before God in perfect holiness.

Prayer Prompts

Lord, one area of my life where I long to become holy is . . .
These phrases from your Word assure me it is possible to pursue a holy life: . . .

Holy Spirit

How does the Holy Spirit help me?

❧

Let the Holy Spirit guide your lives. Then you won't be doing what your sinful nature craves. . . . The Spirit gives us desires that are the opposite of what the sinful nature desires.
+ GALATIANS 5:16-17

The Holy Spirit helps us in our weakness. For example, we don't know what God wants us to pray for. But the Holy Spirit prays for us with groanings that cannot be expressed in words.
+ ROMANS 8:26

The Spirit is God's guarantee that he will give us the inheritance he promised and that he has purchased us to be his own people. He did this so we would praise and glorify him.
+ EPHESIANS 1:14

[Jesus said,] "When the Father sends the Advocate as my representative—that is, the Holy Spirit—he will teach you everything and will remind you of everything I have told you."
+ JOHN 14:26

WHEN JESUS ascended into heaven, he promised to leave all believers with a gift: the Holy Spirit as their advocate, helper, source of strength, defender, teacher, and constant companion. Unlike those who lived during Old Testament times, the followers of Christ now had the Holy Spirit indwelling them—and as believers in Christ today, we do too. To really understand the work of the Spirit, we need to read God's Word. Reflect on God's promises about the Holy Spirit, invite him to work in your life, and praise God for his gracious gift.

Prayer Prompts

Lord, I notice the help of the Holy Spirit in my life when . . .
Your Word encourages me to look for the Spirit's help in these ways too: . . .

honesty

How honest does God want me to be?
How does he feel about little white lies?

—— ❧ ——

All who cheat with dishonest weights and measures are detestable to the LORD your God.
+ DEUTERONOMY 25:16

The LORD detests double standards; he is not pleased by dishonest scales.
+ PROVERBS 20:23

If you are faithful in little things, you will be faithful in large ones. But if you are dishonest in little things, you won't be honest with greater responsibilities.
+ LUKE 16:10

Who may climb the mountain of the LORD? Who may stand in his holy place? Only those whose hands and hearts are pure, who do not worship idols and never tell lies. They will receive the LORD's blessing and have a right relationship with God their savior.
+ PSALM 24:3-5

HONESTY ISN'T only about keeping ourselves from lying. It is about living a truly authentic life—even in the smallest of ways. This means refraining from exaggeration, manipulation, spinning our retelling of events to make ourselves look better, and stretching the truth. It also means keeping promises, speaking the truth in love, and striving to live with integrity. God assures us that those who live in complete honesty have a wonderful future ahead. However, he promises negative consequences for those who fail to be honest. When are you tempted to waver from honesty? Ask God to show you where your speech and actions can be more filled with authenticity and integrity.

Prayer Prompts

Lord, I am tempted to bend the truth when . . .
Your Word calls me to be a woman of honesty by . . .

hope in God

What does it mean to be a woman who hopes in God?

— ❧ —

Let us hold tightly without wavering to the hope we affirm, for God can be trusted to keep his promise.
+ HEBREWS 10:23

[Jesus said,] "I have told you all this so that you may have peace in me. Here on earth you will have many trials and sorrows. But take heart, because I have overcome the world."
+ JOHN 16:33

Joyful are those who have the God of Israel as their helper, whose hope is in the LORD their God.
+ PSALM 146:5

Why am I discouraged? Why is my heart so sad? I will put my hope in God! I will praise him again—my Savior and my God!
+ PSALM 42:11

WE ALL HAVE a universal expectation for good in our lives, even in the midst of adversity. The need to believe that things will get better is what the concept of *hope* is all about. When we long for life to get better, where do we place our hope? In our own abilities, good fortune, or luck? Or does our hope come from trusting God? Only when we trust God with our future can hope begin to grow. Hope in God gives us confident joy in the face of uncertainty because it anchors our souls and our future in him. Begin by being honest with God about where you place your hope. Meditate on the wonderful promises in his Word and allow these truths to grow your hope in him alone.

Prayer Prompts

Lord, sometimes I place my hope in . . .
Your Word declares that those who hope in you alone will experience . . .

hopelessness

What can I do when things seem hopeless?

———————— ❧ ————————

Hannah was in deep anguish, crying bitterly as she prayed to the Lord.
+ 1 SAMUEL 1:10

*The jailer put them into the inner dungeon and
clamped their feet in the stocks. Around midnight,
Paul and Silas were praying and singing hymns to God.*
+ ACTS 16:24-25

Wait patiently for the Lord. Be brave and courageous.
+ PSALM 27:14

*"I know the plans I have for you," says the Lord.
"They are plans for good and not for disaster, to give you a future and a hope."*
+ JEREMIAH 29:11

And so, Lord, where do I put my hope? My only hope is in you.
+ PSALM 39:7

HOPE IS a powerful thing. Losing our hope puts us in danger of depression and despair. Is a difficult situation, struggling relationship, or daunting task leaving you feeling hopeless? Hope returns when you remember that God is still in charge and he has the power to change any situation. The Bible assures you that God will either deliver you from your troubles or bring you through them—for his glory and your joy. How might this hope change the way you face your trial today? Turn your attention to God, pray to him, praise him, and wait patiently for him to act on your behalf.

Prayer Prompts

Lord, I need hope in the area of . . .
When I feel hopeless, your Word encourages me to . . .

✿ hospitality

How can I practice hospitality when I don't have much to share with others?

———— ✿ ————

Martha welcomed him into her home. Her sister, Mary, sat at the Lord's feet, listening to what he taught. But Martha was distracted by the big dinner she was preparing. She came to Jesus and said, "Lord, doesn't it seem unfair to you that my sister just sits here while I do all the work? Tell her to come and help me." But the Lord said to her, "My dear Martha, you are worried and upset over all these details! There is only one thing worth being concerned about. Mary has discovered it, and it will not be taken away from her."

+ LUKE 10:38-42

Don't forget to show hospitality to strangers, for some who have done this have entertained angels without realizing it!

+ HEBREWS 13:2

SOME OF US avoid hospitality because our home or cooking feels inadequate. Others may find it too difficult to share time, space, and resources. But beautiful decorations and gourmet meals have very little to do with hospitality. Hospitality is about cultivating a safe space for others to experience the welcoming presence of God. And God promises many blessings to those who show hospitality. Don't be distracted with making the perfect meal or having a spotless house. Just share what you have generously, set aside your insecurities, and enjoy the people you are with. It is your presence, not your presentation, that makes others feel welcome.

Prayer Prompts

Lord, the insecurity that keeps me from being hospitable is . . .
Your Word describes true hospitality as . . .

humility

What is the difference between humility and low self-esteem?

――――――――― ❧ ―――――――――

Those who are left will be the lowly and humble,
for it is they who trust in the name of the LORD.
+ ZEPHANIAH 3:12

I recognize my rebellion; it haunts me day and night. Against you, and
you alone, have I sinned; I have done what is evil in your sight. You will
be proved right in what you say, and your judgment against me is just.
+ PSALM 51:3-4

The humble will see their God at work and be glad.
Let all who seek God's help be encouraged.
+ PSALM 69:32

Humble yourselves under the mighty power of God,
and at the right time he will lift you up in honor.
+ 1 PETER 5:6

"CHRISTIAN HUMILITY is not thinking less of yourself; it is thinking of yourself less," wrote C. S. Lewis. We often mistake low
self-esteem for humility, but humility according to God is much
different. True humility begins with knowing who God is and who
we are in comparison. It is the antithesis of pride. It is not about
seeing ourselves as less, but rather seeing God as so much more. He
is in ultimate control of everything, and his plans for our lives are
far better than our own. He promises to bless, honor, refresh, lead,
and rescue those whose hearts are humble. Ask the Lord to help you
think about yourself less so that you may think about him more.

Prayer Prompts

Lord, I have mistaken low self-esteem as humility in thinking that . . .
Your Word describes the humble as . . .

hurry

Why is it important to resist hurry in my life?

———————— ❧ ————————

How do you know what your life will be like tomorrow?
Your life is like the morning fog—it's here a little while, then it's gone.
+ JAMES 4:14

Be still, and know that I am God!
+ PSALM 46:10

Jesus said, "Come to me, all of you who are weary and carry heavy burdens,
and I will give you rest. Take my yoke upon you. Let me teach you, because
I am humble and gentle at heart, and you will find rest for your souls."
+ MATTHEW 11:28-29

Teach us to realize the brevity of life, so that we may grow in wisdom.
+ PSALM 90:12

AS WOMEN, many of us feel like we can never slow down. If we pause and take a break, who will handle the hundreds of details we carry in our minds all the time? Whether it's responsibilities with work, family, home, or church, we rush because we feel responsible to make sure everything gets done. The truth is, when we hurry, we are actually trying to do too much. God did not intend for us to race through the only life we have been given. In fact, he promises that our busy rushing is useless because we never know what tomorrow will bring. Intentionally fight against hurry by taking the time to read the Bible verses on this page once again. Take a deep breath and allow yourself to trust in God's promises that slowing down is actually good for you. It reminds us that our lives are more than to-do lists, that God is in control, and that our ultimate purpose is to glorify him.

Prayer Prompts

Lord, one way I can slow down today is by . . .
When I slow down, remind me that your Word says this is good because . . .

hurts 🌿

How can I heal from the hurts in my relationships?

———————— ❧ ————————

Don't say, "I will get even for this wrong."
Wait for the Lord to handle the matter.
+ PROVERBS 20:22

If you forgive those who sin against you, your heavenly Father will forgive
you. But if you refuse to forgive others, your Father will not forgive your sins.
+ MATTHEW 6:14-15

Make allowance for each other's faults, and forgive anyone who offends you.
Remember, the Lord forgave you, so you must forgive others.
+ COLOSSIANS 3:13

Love each other as brothers and sisters. Be tenderhearted, and keep a
humble attitude. Don't repay evil for evil. Don't retaliate with insults
when people insult you. Instead, pay them back with a blessing.
That is what God has called you to do, and he will grant you his blessing.
+ 1 PETER 3:8-9

He heals the brokenhearted and bandages their wounds.
+ PSALM 147:3

WHEN OTHERS hurt us, it can be very tempting to retaliate—especially with our words. However, God assures us that he is in control and will handle the matter. And he will always handle it better than we could. Our part, with God's help, is to work toward forgiveness. This could very well be the hardest thing God calls us to do. But he tells us to forgive because he knows that is the best antidote for healing. Trust that God is in control of your relationships and will give you the strength to begin the process of healing through forgiveness.

Prayer Prompts
Lord, my heart still hurts over my relationship with . . .
Your Word encourages me to handle this pain by . . .

 # identity

How can I become a woman who identifies herself with Christ above all else?

———————— ❧ ————————

Once you had no identity as a people; now you are God's people. Once you received no mercy; now you have received God's mercy.
+ 1 PETER 2:10

Because we are his children, God has sent the Spirit of his Son into our hearts, prompting us to call out, "Abba, Father." Now you are no longer a slave but God's own child. And since you are his child, God has made you his heir.
+ GALATIANS 4:6-7

See how very much our Father loves us, for he calls us his children, and that is what we are!
+ 1 JOHN 3:1

WE OFTEN base our identity on what we do—our career, talents, accomplishments, and what others say about us. But Dallas Willard states, "It's not what you do; it's who you become. That's what you will take into eternity. . . . It's the most important thing about you. It is your life." Becoming a woman who identifies herself with Christ is the most important thing we can do for our lives on earth and into eternity. How we identify ourselves will impact every action, thought, and relationship. When you recognize that you're basing your identity on worldly things, look to God's Word to show you who you really are. He calls you his child and heir, and he says you are known and loved by him. This is the most important thing about you; this is who you are.

Prayer Prompts

Lord, I often base my identity on . . .
Your Word says that who I really am is based on . . .

idolatry

How do I know if I have created idols in my life?

————————— ❦ —————————

Wherever your treasure is, there the desires of your heart will also be.
+ MATTHEW 6:21

Then Samuel said to all the people of Israel, "If you want to return to the LORD with all your hearts, get rid of your foreign gods and your images of Ashtoreth. Turn your hearts to the LORD and obey him alone; then he will rescue you."
+ 1 SAMUEL 7:3

May you experience the love of Christ, though it is too great to understand fully. Then you will be made complete with all the fullness of life and power that comes from God.
+ EPHESIANS 3:19

So, my dear friends, flee from the worship of idols.
+ 1 CORINTHIANS 10:14

WE OFTEN try to live a "full" life by filling the holes in our hearts with things other than God. When we use something else to meet a deep need inside us, it becomes an idol. God is the only one who can meet our needs. The first step in getting rid of idols is to come out of hiding. Many believers try to conceal the things that have become most precious to them, but it is only when we acknowledge idols that we can begin to be free of them. This may be something we need to do over and over because idols have a way of popping back up. Have an honest conversation with God about the treasures of your heart so that he can replace your idols with himself.

Prayer Prompts

Lord, to fill the deep need inside me, I often turn to . . .
But your Word says to get rid of idols by . . .

 imagination

How can I use my imagination to grow closer to God?

— ❧ —

God created human beings in his own image.
+ GENESIS 1:27

*Fix your thoughts on what is true, and honorable, and right,
and pure, and lovely, and admirable. Think about things that
are excellent and worthy of praise.*
+ PHILIPPIANS 4:8

*Those who are dominated by the sinful nature think about
sinful things, but those who are controlled by the Holy Spirit
think about things that please the Spirit.*
+ ROMANS 8:5

OUR GOD is a creative God, and he made us in his image. God was able to imagine the heavens, earth, animals, and humans, and we are patterned after him, so he has certainly instilled some imaginative abilities within us. Using our imaginations can be a powerful tool to help us engage with God and Scripture in a new way. We can engage our imaginations as we read God's Word by placing ourselves in a Bible story. Richard Foster writes in his book *Prayer*, "We begin to enter the story and make it our own. We move from detached observation to active participation." So pick a story from the Bible and imagine yourself in the scene. What do you see? What do you feel? How do you experience God? Remember that your imagination is a gift from God. Ask the Holy Spirit to use this gift to deepen your relationship with Jesus as you experience him through his Word.

Prayer Prompts

Lord, I would like to use my imagination to engage in the Bible story about . . .
As I placed myself in this story, your Word taught me that . . .

179

impossibilities 🍃

How can I believe that God can do what sometimes seems impossible?

— ❧ —

This is what the LORD of Heaven's Armies says: All this may seem impossible to you now, a small remnant of God's people. But is it impossible for me?
+ ZECHARIAH 8:6

"What do you mean, 'If I can'?" Jesus asked.
"Anything is possible if a person believes."
+ MARK 9:23

"You don't have enough faith," Jesus told them. "I tell you the truth, if you had faith even as small as a mustard seed, you could say to this mountain, 'Move from here to there,' and it would move. Nothing would be impossible."
+ MATTHEW 17:20

THE BIBLE is filled with seemingly impossible stories: A flood covers the earth. A sea is divided so people can walk through on dry land. A man survives three days in the belly of a fish. A virgin gives birth to a baby boy. To the person who does not believe in God or his Word, these stories defy logic. But those who believe in the Creator of all things also believe that he can alter what he has created. In order for you to recognize and experience the impossible, you need faith. Faith helps you to understand that what you see is not all there is. Learn to recognize and appreciate the "impossible" things God does for you and around you each day: unexpected forgiveness, healing for the heart, the intricate systems of the human body, or the birth of a baby. The more you see the "impossible" acts of God with eyes of faith, the stronger your faith in God will become.

Prayer Prompts

Lord, I need to see you work in this impossible situation: . . .
Your Word reminds me that nothing is impossible for you when it says . . .

 # inadequacy

I feel so inadequate.
How can I be sure God can use me?

❧

The Sovereign LORD is my strength!
He makes me as surefooted as a deer, able to tread upon the heights.
+ HABAKKUK 3:19

I can do everything through Christ, who gives me strength.
+ PHILIPPIANS 4:13

We now have this light shining in our hearts, but
we ourselves are like fragile clay jars containing this great treasure.
This makes it clear that our great power is from God, not from ourselves.
+ 2 CORINTHIANS 4:7

FEELINGS OF INADEQUACY not only cause us to doubt our abilities, they cause us to doubt our worth. God promises that he loves us, not because of our abilities, strengths, or talents, but because he is our Father. He sees us as holy, as if we'd never sinned. How can we not have overwhelming victory today when this is how the God of the universe sees us? He is our strength and is able to do more through us than we could ever imagine. On days when you just don't feel like you are enough, rest in God's promises that he loves you more than you know. You are a woman of great worth, and a woman of great worth can do mighty things for God because his Spirit and power live in her.

Prayer Prompts

Lord, I feel underqualified and incapable of . . .
Your Word assures me that I can have victory because . . .

inexperience 🗨

How can God use my limited experience?

───────── ❧ ─────────

Moses pleaded with the Lord, *"O Lord, I'm not very good with words.
I never have been, and I'm not now, even though you have spoken to me.
I get tongue-tied, and my words get tangled." Then the* Lord *asked Moses,
"Who makes a person's mouth? Who decides whether people speak or do not
speak, hear or do not hear, see or do not see? Is it not I, the* Lord? *Now go!
I will be with you as you speak, and I will instruct you in what to say."*
+ EXODUS 4:10-12

*[God] chose his servant David, calling him from the sheep pens.
He took David from tending the ewes and lambs and made him the
shepherd of Jacob's descendants—God's own people, Israel. He cared
for them with a true heart and led them with skillful hands.*
+ PSALM 78:70-72

*[Jesus said,] "You didn't choose me. I chose you.
I appointed you to go and produce lasting fruit,
so that the Father will give you whatever you ask for, using my name."*
+ JOHN 15:16

G OD USES EVERYTHING—even our inexperience—to further
his purposes. David's years of shepherding groomed him to
become a future monarch. The lessons he learned on the hills with
the sheep taught him to rule not as a tyrant but as a shepherd. When
you feel discouraged because you're being asked to do something
you feel unequipped for, remember that God has good plans for you.
His plan is unfolding right now. So do the best you can wherever you
are. Instead of questioning God's decision to use you, step out in faith
and trust that he is able to carry out his plans through you.

Prayer Prompts

Lord, I feel unequipped to . . .
When I doubt myself, your Word reminds me that . . .

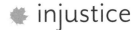 # injustice

What will God do about injustice?

———— ❧ ————

You will bring justice to the orphans and the oppressed,
so mere people can no longer terrify them.
+ PSALM 10:18

The Lord replies, "I have seen violence done to the helpless, and
I have heard the groans of the poor. Now I will rise up to rescue them,
as they have longed for me to do."
+ PSALM 12:5

The Lord loves justice, and he will never abandon the godly.
He will keep them safe forever, but the children of the wicked will die.
+ PSALM 37:28

If you do what is wrong, you will be paid back
for the wrong you have done. For God has no favorites.
+ COLOSSIANS 3:25

WE OFTEN TALK about God being loving, merciful, and forgiving. And although God is all these things, that is only part of who he is. God is also just and holy; he will not allow the wicked to go unchecked. God's Word tells us that he is an advocate for the poor, oppressed, and helpless, and that there will be consequences for all who persist in doing what is unjust and evil, whether they happen on earth or in eternity. If you are watching an unjust situation unfold in the news or are experiencing it personally, take heart in God's promises. He assures us that he cares about the oppressed and promises that someday he will bring them justice.

Prayer Prompts

Lord, I need to know you will bring justice to . . .
I can be sure that you are a holy and just God because your Word says . . .

inspiration 🍂

How can I inspire others to know God?

———————— ✃ ————————

*You are the light of the world—like a city on a hilltop that cannot
be hidden. No one lights a lamp and then puts it under a basket.
Instead, a lamp is placed on a stand, where it gives light to everyone
in the house. In the same way, let your good deeds shine out for all to
see, so that everyone will praise your heavenly Father.*
+ MATTHEW 5:14-16

*There was a believer in Joppa named Tabitha (which in Greek is Dorcas).
She was always doing kind things for others and helping the poor.*
+ ACTS 9:36

If someone asks about your hope as a believer, always be ready to explain it.
+ 1 PETER 3:15

GOD ASKS his followers to be lights in this dark world. This means
following God's Word, helping the poor, and, above all, going
out of our way to love people well. When we live lives overflowing
with love and hope, others can't help but notice. There's nothing more
powerful than an act of love toward someone who doesn't expect it or
deserve it. When someone asks about our behavior, we must always
be ready to explain our faith with gentleness and respect. We cannot
just live a good life and expect others to know why. We must connect
our good deeds to the name of Jesus. Wake up each morning asking
God to show you an opportunity to bless someone that day in a way
that may inspire him or her to ask about your faith. And when you
feel afraid to act or speak, ask God for help, remembering his promise
to be with you wherever you go.

Prayer Prompts

Lord, one person I want to inspire to know you is . . .
Your Word encourages me to inspire others by . . .

 # integrity

What does it mean to be a woman of integrity?

—————— ❧ ——————

To the faithful you show yourself faithful;
to those with integrity you show integrity.
+ PSALM 18:25

If you are faithful in little things, you will be faithful in large ones. But if you
are dishonest in little things, you won't be honest with greater responsibilities.
+ LUKE 16:10

I know, my God, that you examine our hearts and
rejoice when you find integrity there.
+ 1 CHRONICLES 29:17

Declare me innocent, O LORD, for I have acted with integrity;
I have trusted in the LORD without wavering. Put me on trial, LORD,
and cross-examine me. Test my motives and my heart. For I am always
aware of your unfailing love, and I have lived according to your truth.
+ PSALM 26:1-3

INTEGRITY is the unity between our character and God's. This union results in greater purity of our hearts, minds, and actions, which reflect the heart, mind, and actions of God. But integrity isn't something we can achieve instantly; developing it is a process that happens choice by choice. When you face a small decision and feel tempted to cut a corner, tell a white lie, or act apart from God's character, remember that this one act impacts your integrity. The pressure and troubles of everyday life test your integrity. When this happens, ask God to give you the wisdom and strength to follow him step by step.

Prayer Prompts

Lord, I feel tempted to compromise my integrity regarding . . .
Your Word promises that those who strive to live with integrity will . . .

intercession

Does it really make a difference when others pray for me or I pray for others?

———— ❧ ————

Abraham said, "Lord, please don't be angry with me if I speak one more time. Suppose only ten are found there?" And the Lord replied, "Then I will not destroy it for the sake of the ten."
+ GENESIS 18:32

While Peter was in prison, the church prayed very earnestly for him.
+ ACTS 12:5

The earnest prayer of a righteous person has great power and produces wonderful results.
+ JAMES 5:16

We have not stopped praying for you since we first heard about you. We ask God to give you complete knowledge of his will and to give you spiritual wisdom and understanding.
+ COLOSSIANS 1:9

INTERCESSORY PRAYER is going before the Lord on another's behalf. We are called to pray earnestly for others, trusting God to produce wonderful results from our faithful prayers. It is easy to become discouraged if we think our prayers are ineffective or unimportant. But in ways beyond our understanding, intercessory prayer is a channel for the love and power of God to work in another's life. We may not understand the power our prayers have on another until we get to heaven. Ask God to help you become a woman of prayer, one who faithfully intercedes for those around her.

Prayer Prompts
Lord, today I would like to pray for . . .
Your Word instructs me to pray for them in this way: . . .

🍁 internal conflict

I want to please God, but I know that often I don't. How can I resolve this internal conflict?

— ❧ —

There is no condemnation for those who belong to Christ Jesus. And because you belong to him, the power of the life-giving Spirit has freed you from the power of sin that leads to death.
+ ROMANS 8:1-2

Who will free me from this life that is dominated by sin and death? Thank God! The answer is in Jesus Christ our Lord. So you see how it is: In my mind I really want to obey God's law, but because of my sinful nature I am a slave to sin.
+ ROMANS 7:24-25

The LORD is like a father to his children, tender and compassionate to those who fear him. For he knows how weak we are; he remembers we are only dust.
+ PSALM 103:13-14

MOST OF US struggle with inner conflict. We have given our lives to follow Christ, but our old human nature still exists. We don't want to do wrong, but we often do. We know the attitudes and behavior Christ desires, but we find it hard to live that way all the time. When we fail to please God, we have two choices: Either we condemn ourselves, allowing our shame to separate us from God, or we let our shortcomings remind us of our need for Jesus. God deeply desires you to choose him. The power of the Cross is greater than the power of sin. Allow this inner conflict to lead you toward receiving God's forgiveness, acceptance, and grace.

Prayer Prompts

Lord, I feel like I continually disappoint you when I . . .
I still struggle with sin, but your Word assures me of grace because . . .

intimacy

What does intimacy with God look like?

—— ❧ ——

The LORD is close to all who call on him, yes, to all who call on him in truth.
+ PSALM 145:18

Come close to God, and God will come close to you.
+ JAMES 4:8

O LORD, you have examined my heart and know everything about me. You know when I sit down or stand up. You know my thoughts even when I'm far away. You see me when I travel and when I rest at home. You know everything I do.
+ PSALM 139:1-3

SOME OF US have experienced the joy of being in an intimate relationship with another person. But no matter how deep we go with a friend, family member, or husband, that intimacy is nothing compared to intimacy with God. God knows *every* thought we have, *every* action we take, and *every* motive behind our actions. And the best part about God is that even though he knows us this intimately, he still loves us. We don't need to change any part of ourselves for God to love us more. All he wants is for us to come to him with our sin, accept his forgiveness, and experience abundant life with him. Practically, this means accepting that he intimately knows us and loves us, learning about him though his Word, and inviting him into every part of our lives through prayer. Take comfort that true intimacy awaits those who strive to live close to him.

Prayer Prompts

Lord, I desire to deepen my relationship with you by . . .
Your Word tells me I can experience intimacy with you when I . . .

🍂 invitation

What does it mean to invite Jesus into my day?

— ❦ —

My heart has heard you say, "Come and talk with me."
And my heart responds, "Lord, I am coming."
+ PSALM 27:8

You will show me the way of life, granting me the joy of
your presence and the pleasures of living with you forever.
+ PSALM 16:11

I hold you by your right hand—I, the Lord your God.
And I say to you, "Don't be afraid. I am here to help you."
+ ISAIAH 41:13

God . . . has invited you into partnership
with his Son, Jesus Christ our Lord.
+ 1 CORINTHIANS 1:9

God's word is full of descriptions of his presence with us: He holds our right hand, he invites us to talk with him, he shows us the way, and he partners with us. When we invite God into our days, it isn't to convince him to be present; he has already promised to be with us in every moment. We invite God into our days to grow our awareness of his presence. If you are facing a challenging conversation, meeting, or crisis today, take a deep breath and prayerfully invite God to be with you in it. This reminder of his presence will give you peace and help you enter the situation with God at the forefront of your mind. As you encounter challenges throughout your day, use this simple breath prayer as a way to remember and acknowledge him.

Prayer Prompts
Lord, I invite you to be present with me today when I . . .
Your Word assure me of your presence when it says . . .

involvement 🍃

How can I know where God wants me to serve or be involved?

———— ❧ ————

Learn to do good. Seek justice. Help the oppressed.
Defend the cause of orphans. Fight for the rights of widows.
+ ISAIAH 1:17

God has given each of you a gift from his great variety of spiritual gifts.
Use them well to serve one another.
+ 1 PETER 4:10

All the believers devoted themselves to the apostles' teaching, and to fellowship,
and to sharing in meals (including the Lord's Supper), and to prayer.
+ ACTS 2:42

This is my commandment: Love each other
in the same way I have loved you.
+ JOHN 15:12

THERE ARE MANY general tasks God asks all believers to involve themselves in: caring for the needy and oppressed, defending and upholding justice, exercising our spiritual gifts for the service of the church, joining in worship and fellowship with other believers, and loving others well. We don't need to wait for an opportunity to do these things; they are all ways that we can get involved in serving God right now! However, sometimes God places specific tasks on our hearts to meet special needs. It takes courage to get involved, and it often feels uncomfortable in the beginning. Start with prayer, ask for advice and wisdom from godly friends, and trust in God to guide you right where he wants you to be.

Prayer Prompts

Lord, one area where I can serve my church or community is . . .
Your Word encourages me to get involved by . . .

 # jealousy

What is the danger of jealousy?

❧

Get rid of all evil behavior. Be done with all deceit,
hypocrisy, jealousy, and all unkind speech.
+ 1 PETER 2:1

A peaceful heart leads to a healthy body; jealousy is like cancer in the bones.
+ PROVERBS 14:30

Wherever there is jealousy and selfish ambition,
there you will find disorder and evil of every kind.
+ JAMES 3:16

Don't worry about the wicked or envy those who do wrong.
For like grass, they soon fade away. Like spring flowers, they soon wither.
+ PSALM 37:1-2

ALL OF US are familiar with jealousy. We might wish for another woman's house, marriage, style, income, or dress size. If we aren't careful, our jealous thoughts will become more frequent and come more naturally. When this happens, we need to remember that jealous thoughts embitter us and eventually lead to harmful actions. God's Word warns that jealousy, if left unchecked, has the power to steal our joy, cause us to miss God's blessings, divide families, and destroy relationships. When you begin to wish you were someone else or feel angry that someone else has what you don't, praise God for what you have. Changing your attitude from jealousy to gratitude has the power to change your life.

Prayer Prompts

Lord, if I am honest, I feel a little jealous of . . .
Your Word warns me that jealousy is dangerous because . . .

joy

How can I choose to be joyful when I don't feel like it?

———— ❧ ————

Because of our faith, Christ has brought us into this place of undeserved privilege where we now stand, and we confidently and joyfully look forward to sharing God's glory.
+ ROMANS 5:2

Let all who take refuge in you rejoice; let them sing joyful praises forever. Spread your protection over them, that all who love your name may be filled with joy.
+ PSALM 5:11

This is the day the LORD has made. We will rejoice and be glad in it.
+ PSALM 118:24

Let all that I am praise the LORD; may I never forget the good things he does for me.
+ PSALM 103:2

GOD DOES NOT PROMISE constant happiness; in fact, the Bible assures us that in this world, problems will come our way because we live in a fallen world. But God does promise lasting joy for all who faithfully follow him. Joy happens in two ways. Temporary joy is a response to happy events, while lasting joy is what we experience despite our circumstances. Lasting joy comes only when we follow God, choose to respond to his gifts with thanksgiving, and strive to live with an eternal perspective. Ask the Lord to help you be aware of his goodness in your life and to develop an appreciative and thankful heart so that you may experience lasting joy, regardless of your circumstances.

Prayer Prompts

Lord, it's hard for me to feel joyful because . . .
In spite of my circumstances, I am choosing joy because your Word says . . .

❧ judgment

What should I do when I find myself judging others?

Do not judge others, and you will not be judged. For you will be treated as you treat others. The standard you use in judging is the standard by which you will be judged.

+ MATTHEW 7:1-2

Make allowance for each other's faults, and forgive anyone who offends you. Remember, the Lord forgave you, so you must forgive others.

+ COLOSSIANS 3:13

Don't use foul or abusive language. Let everything you say be good and helpful, so that your words will be an encouragement to those who hear them.

+ EPHESIANS 4:29

A JUDGMENTAL PERSON offers hurtful criticism that is not helpful. Constructive criticism, by contrast, is offered for the purpose of building a relationship and helping someone become who God has created them to be. As Christian women, we have a responsibility to be accountable to our community of believers, and sometimes that means giving or receiving feedback about how we can better follow God. But it is much easier to receive when it is offered gently and in love rather than in a harsh or humiliating way. Before you offer suggestions to others about how you think they should live, check your heart by asking God, "Are my words helpful? Kind? Encouraging? Needed?" If you can't answer yes, refrain from commenting. Ask God to teach you the difference between judging and encouraging another person in the faith.

Prayer Prompts

Lord, whenever I'm tempted to make a judgment call, help me to . . .
Your Word instructs me to keep my heart clear of judgment by . . .

justice

How does God call me to be a woman of justice?

———— ❦ ————

Turn from evil and do good, and you will live in the land forever.
For the Lord loves justice, and he will never abandon the godly.
+ PSALM 37:27-28

The LORD has told you what is good, and this is what he requires of you:
to do what is right, to love mercy, and to walk humbly with your God.
+ MICAH 6:8

Learn to do good. Seek justice. Help the oppressed.
Defend the cause of orphans. Fight for the rights of widows.
+ ISAIAH 1:17

My mercy and justice are coming soon. My salvation is on the way.
My strong arm will bring justice to the nations.
+ ISAIAH 51:5

JUSTICE is about fairness in protecting rights and punishing wrongs. We often worry about how God is going to protect us, but God's Word makes it clear that he has given us the responsibility of protecting others. What injustices in the world break your heart? What can you do to help the poor, vulnerable, and oppressed? Being a follower of God requires more than knowing what is good; it demands *doing* what is good. Someday God will set the whole world right. But for now, he wants you to partner with him to bring justice to the world. Be attentive to the injustices that break your heart; pray that God would lead you to act and would shape you into a woman who values justice.

Prayer Prompts

Lord, the injustice that breaks my heart is . . .
Your Word calls me to respond by . . .

# kindness

Am I always supposed to be kind—even to difficult people?

❦

*A servant of the Lord must not quarrel but must be kind to everyone,
be able to teach, and be patient with difficult people.*
+ 2 TIMOTHY 2:24

*Never let loyalty and kindness leave you! . . . Then you will find favor with
both God and people, and you will earn a good reputation.*
+ PROVERBS 3:3-4

*The LORD is merciful and compassionate, slow to get angry
and filled with unfailing love. . . . The LORD is righteous
in everything he does; he is filled with kindness.*
+ PSALM 145:8, 17

How kind the LORD is! How good he is! So merciful, this God of ours!
+ PSALM 116:5

IT CAN FEEL impossible to show kindness to those we feel don't
deserve it. But God's Word encourages us to be merciful, compassionate, and loving toward *all* people. Kindness is behaving toward
others mercifully, the way God behaves toward us. It is not limited to
a single act; it is a lifestyle. If you are struggling to show kindness to
someone today, reflect on how God has been kind to you. Remember
that when you practice kindness, God promises that your soul will
be nourished and refreshed, you will gain a good reputation, and, in
the process, you will come to know him better.

Prayer Prompts

Lord, sometimes it is hard for me to be kind to . . .
Your Word encourages me to live a life full of kindness by . . .

knowing God 🍃

How does knowing more about God deepen my relationship with him?

———————— ❧ ————————

May you have the power to understand, as all God's people should, how wide, how long, how high, and how deep his love is. May you experience the love of Christ, though it is too great to understand fully. Then you will be made complete with all the fullness of life and power that comes from God.
+ EPHESIANS 3:18-19

This is the way to have eternal life—to know you, the only true God, and Jesus Christ, the one you sent to earth.
+ JOHN 17:3

You must grow in the grace and knowledge of our Lord and Savior Jesus Christ.
+ 2 PETER 3:18

WHEN WE make the effort to learn about others, we begin to understand them better. It is the same with God. We cannot expect to go deeper with God without learning more about who he is. Thankfully, God has given us his Word to help us know him. From cover to cover, the Bible describes God's character and attributes, the things he cares about, and how he interacts with his creation. And one thing is clear—God cares deeply about relationship. He is not an elusive being; he is a God who desires to be known. As you read God's Word, ask yourself, *What does this teach me about who God is?* As you get to know God better, you will find yourself noticing him more and more, praising him for who he is, and trusting him at all times.

Prayer Prompts

Lord, something I am learning about you is . . .
These verses from your Word encourage me to continue to know you more: . . .

 laziness

Is laziness a sin? What is the difference between rest and laziness?

— ❧ —

Lazy people want much but get little, but those who work hard will prosper.
+ PROVERBS 13:4

Never be lazy, but work hard and serve the Lord enthusiastically.
+ ROMANS 12:11

*[A virtuous and capable wife] is energetic and strong,
a hard worker. . . . She carefully watches everything in
her household and suffers nothing from laziness.*
+ PROVERBS 31:17, 27

LAZINESS is traditionally considered one of the "seven deadly sins," yet it is often overlooked. We tend to think of sin as doing something we should not do, but sin is also failing to do what we should. Signs of laziness could be neglecting our responsibilities, putting off obligations, failing to notice temptation, or being complacent in our faith. Everyone needs times of rest, but rest is different from laziness. Rest is purposeful. It refreshes us so that we can better love and serve God and others. Laziness is self-centered and is a sign of avoidance, detachment, and emptiness. Are you the kind of person who asks, "What needs to be done today?" or the kind who asks, "How can I avoid today's tasks?" When you feel tempted by laziness, ask God to help you find purpose in work and refocus on what is most important today.

Prayer Prompts

Lord, I struggle with laziness in the area of . . .
Your Word encourages me to find purpose in work and service by . . .

leadership 🍃

How can I develop my leadership
potential for God's Kingdom?

—— ❧ ——

*In his grace, God has given us different gifts for doing certain things well.
So if God has given you the ability to prophesy, speak out with as much
faith as God has given you. If your gift is serving others, serve them well. . . .
If God has given you leadership ability, take the responsibility seriously.*

+ ROMANS 12:6-8

*The rulers in this world lord it over their people, and officials flaunt
their authority over those under them. But among you it will be
different. Whoever wants to be a leader among you must be your
servant, and whoever wants to be first among you must be the slave
of everyone else. For even the Son of Man came not to be served but
to serve others and to give his life as a ransom for many.*

+ MARK 10:42-45

THE WORLD says that in order to be leaders, we must be powerful
and successful and assert our authority over others. But Jesus calls
his followers to a different kind of leadership; we are called to lead
others with humility and a servant's heart. This can happen only when
our motive is to advance God's Kingdom instead of our own. Each
time we set aside our own desires or needs for the good of others and
for God's glory, we grow more into a leader who brings joy to God's
heart. Whether God has called you to be a leader within your church,
home, or group of friends, ask him to help you lead with a servant attitude. Whose needs can you put above your own today? Keep close to
God as you love others well, and he will show you how to lead his way.

Prayer Prompts

Lord, the world thinks of leadership this way: . . .
Help me to become the kind of leader described in your Word—a leader who . . .

# legacy

How can I make lasting memories of God's work in my life?

———— ❧ ————

Moses said, "This is what the LORD has commanded: Fill a two-quart container with manna to preserve it for your descendants. Then later generations will be able to see the food I gave you in the wilderness when I set you free from Egypt."

+ EXODUS 16:32

We will use these stones to build a memorial. In the future your children will ask you, "What do these stones mean?" Then you can tell them, "They remind us that the Jordan River stopped flowing when the Ark of the Lord's Covenant went across."

+ JOSHUA 4:6-7

IT IS EASY to forget the work and blessings of God in our lives, especially when hard times come along. But God knows that humans are forgetful and has graciously given us the Bible as the record of his work in history. Reading it reminds us of who God is and what he has done. As the Israelites set up stones to remind them of God's miraculous parting of the Jordan River, we can find creative ways to remind ourselves of God's work. We can celebrate special anniversaries, write in spiritual journals, sing worship songs, or tell stories to remind ourselves of God's blessing in our lives. What can you do today to show God's faithfulness to future generations? The legacy you leave behind could significantly impact the spiritual lives of many generations to follow.

Prayer Prompts

Lord, I want future generations to know about the time when you . . .
As I read your Word, I am reminded that in the past you . . .

letting go 🍃

How can I do better at letting go of certain things and trusting God with them?

Those who love their life in this world will lose it.
Those who care nothing for their life in this world will keep it for eternity.
+ JOHN 12:25

If you cling to your life, you will lose it,
and if you let your life go, you will save it.
+ LUKE 17:33

My old self has been crucified with Christ. It is no longer I who live,
but Christ lives in me. So I live in this earthly body by trusting in
the Son of God, who loved me and gave himself for me.
+ GALATIANS 2:20

THE THINGS we hold most dear are the hardest to trust God with. God warns us that when we cling to our lives, we will lose them. But if we let our lives go, they will be saved. What does this actually mean? We must let go of one thing before we can grasp something else. Not only does letting go of our lives help build our trust in God, but eventually it also results in true freedom. We are free when we no longer need anyone or anything besides God for our fulfillment, satisfaction, and identity. Is there something in your life you need to release your grip from? The hard choice to "let go" is one you will need to make over and over, but it becomes easier as you find God to be faithful each time. Ask God to help you recognize the things you are clinging to too tightly and rebuild your trust in him alone.

Prayer Prompts

Lord, I'm struggling to let go of . . .
Your Word promises that those who release control to you will experience . . .

🍂 limitations

What does God think when he looks at me with all my faults and limitations?

— ✵ —

Gideon son of Joash was threshing wheat at the bottom of a winepress to hide the grain from the Midianites. The angel of the LORD appeared to him and said, "Mighty hero, the LORD is with you!"
+ JUDGES 6:11-12

I [Paul] thank Christ Jesus our Lord, who has given me strength to do his work. He considered me trustworthy and appointed me to serve him, even though I used to blaspheme the name of Christ.
+ 1 TIMOTHY 1:12-13

All glory to God, who is able, through his mighty power at work within us, to accomplish infinitely more than we might ask or think.
+ EPHESIANS 3:20

THROUGHOUT GOD'S WORD, we see him choosing less-than-perfect people to use for his work. Gideon, who hid from his enemies in a winepress and claimed he was "the least" of his family, was called a mighty hero by the angel of the Lord. Paul, who was famous for persecuting Christians, was called by God to spread the gospel after his conversion. God's message to Gideon and Paul—and to us—is clear: Our limitations do not define us. God calls out the best in us. He sees more in us than we see in ourselves. We may look at our limitations, but God looks at our potential. Read God's Word to learn how to see yourself through his eyes. He promises he is able to do more through you than you could ever imagine.

🍂 Prayer Prompts

Lord, I feel held back from doing your work because of . . .
Your Word assures me I am useful in spite of my limitations because . . .

listing to others

How do I become a good listener?

———————— ❧ ————————

The heart of the godly thinks carefully before speaking.
+ PROVERBS 15:28

Understand this, my dear brothers and sisters:
You must all be quick to listen, slow to speak, and slow to get angry.
+ JAMES 1:19

Come and listen to my counsel.
I'll share my heart with you and make you wise.
+ PROVERBS 1:23

If you listen to correction, you grow in understanding.
+ PROVERBS 15:32

GOD CALLS US to be "quick to listen, slow to speak, and slow to get angry." Sadly, too often we are slow to listen, quick to speak, and quick to get angry. Listening is an art, one that is close to God's heart. Since God always listens to us, we minister to others by listening to them. Listening is a form of love. We show others they are valuable when we listen with respect, care, and patience and refrain from interrupting with our own thoughts and advice. Can you set aside your schedule and distractions to be fully present to hear another? If this is hard for you, ask God to show you how you could lovingly listen better—both to him and to others. Be encouraged that God desires to shape your heart into one that loves others well through the ministry of listening.

Prayer Prompts

Lord, I feel called to love these people through listening well: . . .
Your Word instructs me to listen well by . . .

 # loneliness

If God is always with me, why do I feel so alone?

❦

O LORD, how long will you forget me? Forever? How long will you look the other way? How long must I struggle with anguish in my soul, with sorrow in my heart every day?
+ PSALM 13:1-2

Lord, through all the generations you have been our home!
+ PSALM 90:1

[Jesus said,] "Teach these new disciples to obey all the commands I have given you. And be sure of this: I am with you always, even to the end of the age."
+ MATTHEW 28:20

You know when I sit down or stand up. You know my thoughts even when I'm far away. . . . I can never escape from your Spirit! I can never get away from your presence!
+ PSALM 139:2, 7

THE GREATER our troubles, the farther away God sometimes seems. In our darkest hours, we may feel that God has left us. In times like these, when it feels as if God is absent, we can't trust our feelings. We must trust God's promise that he will never leave us alone. We rely on what the Bible tells us is true, not on what our feelings are telling us. Even though we may feel as if God is far away, actually he is always near. No matter how troubled you are, trust that God is with you. When you are hurting the most, he most wants to walk beside you.

Prayer Prompts

Lord, I feel a deep sense of loneliness when . . .
Your Word promises me that . . .

loss

How can I deal with loss in my life?

— ❧ —

"Where have you put him?" [Jesus] asked them. They told him,
"Lord, come and see." Then Jesus wept. The people who were
standing nearby said, "See how much he loved him!"
+ JOHN 11:34-36

Job stood up and tore his robe in grief [and said,]
"The LORD gave me what I had, and the LORD has taken it away."
+ JOB 1:20-21

The thought of my suffering and homelessness is bitter beyond words. I will
never forget this awful time, as I grieve over my loss. Yet I still dare to hope
when I remember this: The faithful love of the LORD never ends! His mercies
never cease. Great is his faithfulness; his mercies begin afresh each morning.
+ LAMENTATIONS 3:19-23

LOSS ALWAYS brings pain. Expressing that pain is not wrong or sinful; rather, it is a healthy expression of how God created us. Jesus' tears over the death of Lazarus forever validate our tears of grief. Whether we have lost a loved one, a job, a friendship, or a dream, we must allow ourselves the necessary time to grieve The process should not be denied or hurried. You may find that birthdays, holidays, certain aromas, or special places bring the grief back up. But each time you allow yourself to grieve, it will help you move toward acceptance. Those who don't know God grieve alone and without hope. However, those who know God face loss with hope and the assurance of his love. No matter what loss you're facing, take comfort in knowing that one day you will be with God in heaven, where all grief will be gone forever.

Prayer Prompts

Lord, I don't know how to deal with the loss of . . .
Your Word validates my grief because it says . . .

 # love of God

How can I be sure God loves me?

❧

How precious is your unfailing love, O God!
All humanity finds shelter in the shadow of your wings.
+ PSALM 36:7

Each day the LORD pours his unfailing love upon me.
+ PSALM 42:8

Yahweh! The LORD! The God of compassion and mercy! I am slow to anger
and filled with unfailing love and faithfulness. I lavish unfailing love
to a thousand generations. I forgive iniquity, rebellion, and sin.
+ EXODUS 34:6-7

Praise the LORD! Give thanks to the LORD, for he is good!
His faithful love endures forever.
+ PSALM 106:1

SOMETIMES IT'S HARD to believe that God *really* loves us. Perhaps we know about his love but haven't personally experienced it. But God intended his love to be the foundation for how we live, make decisions, and relate to others. God's Word is all about his love for us. He doesn't love us because he has to. He loves us because he created us, knows us, and calls us his children. The only way to really allow God's love for us to sink in is to meditate on his love in his Word and open our eyes to the multitude of ways he shows us his love every day. Sometimes he shows us love through a sunset with our favorite colors. Other times it's through the kindness of a friend or a child. Sometimes it's through a whisper to our hearts. Ask God to help you fully accept and experience his one-of-a-kind love for you.

Prayer Prompts

Lord, I feel your love most when . . .
Your Word reminds me you love me this much: . . .

loving others 🍃

What are some practical ways God calls me to love others?

The whole law can be summed up in this one command: "Love your neighbor as yourself."
+ GALATIANS 5:14

Love is patient and kind. Love is not jealous or boastful or proud or rude. It does not demand its own way. It is not irritable, and it keeps no record of being wronged. It does not rejoice about injustice but rejoices whenever the truth wins out. Love never gives up, never loses faith, is always hopeful, and endures through every circumstance.
+ 1 CORINTHIANS 13:4-7

Encourage each other and build each other up, just as you are already doing.
+ 1 THESSALONIANS 5:11

EVERY PERSON HAS a deep need to be known and loved. God's Word has special instructions to help us know how to love others well: (1) Respect. Respecting others means giving them honor and dignity. It can be shown through listening to others' stories, being patient and kind, and affirming their worth. (2) Encourage. Finding the good in others and pointing it out is a powerful way to build up their confidence and help them feel valued. Encouraging means taking the attention off ourselves to focus instead on others. (3) Sacrifice. We are called to love others as we would want to be loved. We show them we care by giving our time, attention, energy, and resources. Ask the Lord to help you love others practically because of the love he has shown you.

Prayer Prompts
Lord, someone I would like to love better is . . .
Your Word encourages me to show practical love by . . .

lust

Is lust really that bad if I'm not acting on it?

❧

God's will is for you to be holy, so stay away from all sexual sin. Then each of you will control his own body and live in holiness and honor—not in lustful passion.
+ 1 THESSALONIANS 4:3-5

It is what comes from inside that defiles you. For from within, out of a person's heart, come evil thoughts, sexual immorality, . . . lustful desires.
+ MARK 7:20-22

Guard your heart above all else, for it determines the course of your life.
+ PROVERBS 4:23

THE OLD TESTAMENT law commanded God's people not to commit adultery. But Jesus took it one step further by saying that if we even look at someone lustfully, we have already committed adultery in our hearts. Temptation begins with the eyes and travels quickly to the heart. If we let our eyes linger where they shouldn't be looking, our minds will find ways to justify our gaze, and our hearts will start tugging us in that direction. Lust is not a sin that only men struggle with. Both the physical and emotional aspects of lust can tempt women as well. Don't underestimate the power of sin. God's Word sternly warns us to flee from all sexual sin, including lustful passion. We avoid temptation by taking our eyes off that which is tempting as a way to guard our hearts. The Bible says that the heart is "deceitful" (Jeremiah 17:9). Therefore, as sinful people, we can't trust our emotions to tell us what is right and good. Trust God's Word, for it comes from God's heart, which is good and perfect.

Prayer Prompts

Lord, the temptation I need to flee from is . . .
Your Word warns me that lustful thoughts are dangerous because . . .

marriage 🌿

How can I have a strong and happy marriage?

*Since they are no longer two but one, let no one split apart
what God has joined together.*
+ MATTHEW 19:6

Submit to one another out of reverence for Christ.
+ EPHESIANS 5:21

She brings [her husband] good, not harm, all the days of her life.
+ PROVERBS 31:12

*Love is patient and kind. Love is not jealous or boastful or
proud or rude. It does not demand its own way. It is not
irritable, and it keeps no record of being wronged.*
+ 1 CORINTHIANS 13:4-5

MARRIAGE was God's idea from the beginning. He knew it wasn't good for men and women to be alone, so he designed marriage to bring us joy, intimacy, and companionship. For that reason God has given us specific instructions for relationships. A wife who pleases the Lord is filled with love, honors her husband by staying faithful, responds with grace, and does her best to exemplify Jesus to her spouse. If you are married, try to understand your husband's differences and celebrate them. No marriage is perfect because when two imperfect people come together, times of conflict and disappointment are bound to happen. Marriage will experience hardships, some passing and some lasting. Whether your marriage feels fulfilling or lonely, come to God for wisdom and encouragement. Allow his Word to convict and encourage you to be a wife who loves and honors her husband.

Prayer Prompts

Lord, this is how I feel about marriage: . . .
Your Word gives me these instructions for relating to my husband: . . .

mediocrity

I often feel average and ordinary.
What can I do to live an extraordinary life?

———————— ❧ ————————

I knew you before I formed you in your mother's womb.
Before you were born I set you apart and appointed you.
+ JEREMIAH 1:5

He chose to give birth to us by giving us his true word.
And we, out of all creation, became his prized possession.
+ JAMES 1:18

You are members of God's family.
+ EPHESIANS 2:19

I cry out to God Most High, to God who will fulfill his purpose for me.
+ PSALM 57:2

YOU ARE NOT MEDIOCRE. God formed you, knows you, chose you, and calls you a member of his family when you put your trust in his Son. No matter how ordinary and insignificant your life may seem, God has promised that you are special and have purpose. Don't be tempted to believe your life doesn't matter. Walk with confidence and start living like you are a child of the Most High God because that is who you are. Your Father doesn't just have something great in store for your future; he has something great in store for you *today*. If you feel trapped in mediocrity, reflect on God's Word. Allow the truth to sink in that the almighty God will fulfill his purpose for you.

Prayer Prompts

Lord, sometimes my life seems dull and insignificant because . . .
When I feel mediocre, your Word reminds me that . . .

meditation

Does meditation have a place in my relationship with God?

———————— ❧ ————————

They delight in the law of the LORD, meditating on it day and night.
+ PSALM 1:2

I lie awake thinking of you, meditating on you through the night.
+ PSALM 63:6

*I recall all you have done, O LORD; I remember your
wonderful deeds of long ago. They are constantly in
my thoughts. I cannot stop thinking about your mighty works.*
+ PSALM 77:11-12

*You will keep in perfect peace all who trust in you,
all whose thoughts are fixed on you!*
+ ISAIAH 26:3

THE WORD *MEDITATION* has become associated with Eastern spirituality and mysticism, but biblical meditation simply means thinking deeply on God's Word and what it reveals about him. The concept of meditation is mentioned throughout the Bible. Joshua and David talk about meditating on God's law day and night. David prayed that his meditations would be pleasing to God. Meditation goes beyond the study of God to communion with him that ultimately leads to godly actions. How would your life be different if you filled your thoughts daily with God and his Word? Think deeply about God's Word, his actions, and his presence in your life. Weave these thoughts into the fabric of your life. Meditating on God and his Word is an essential part of keeping your spiritual walk strong and focused.

Prayer Prompts

Lord, I want to take time to meditate on this verse: . . .
As I think deeply about your Word, I am reminded of . . .

❧ memorization

With so much access to the Internet, is it still necessary to memorize Scripture?

————————— ❧ —————————

My child, never forget the things I have taught you.
Store my commands in your heart. If you do this,
you will live many years, and your life will be satisfying.
✝ PROVERBS 3:1-2

Listen to the words of the wise; apply your heart to my instruction. For it is
good to keep these sayings in your heart and always ready on your lips.
✝ PROVERBS 22:17-18

I have hidden your word in my heart, that I might not sin against you.
✝ PSALM 119:11

Commit yourselves wholeheartedly to these words of mine. Tie them to
your hands and wear them on your forehead as reminders.
✝ DEUTERONOMY 11:18

MEMORIZATION has become a lost art. Even though many of us can access Bible programs on our phones, it is more important to have Scripture in our hearts than in our pockets. Something important happens in the heart when we meditate on and memorize God's Word: Our minds and hearts become a closer reflection of God's image and character. Take time to store God's Word in your heart. Memorization isn't a race, so give yourself grace if committing Scripture to memory is difficult. Trust in the many benefits God promises to those who memorize his Word. The passages you commit to memory will always be with you, and they may come to mind when you need them most.

Prayer Prompts

Lord, when it comes to memorizing Scripture, I feel that . . .
Your Word reminds me that memorization is important because . . .

mentoring

How could God use me to encourage godliness in younger generations?

———— ❧ ————

You have heard me teach things that have been confirmed by many reliable witnesses. Now teach these truths to other trustworthy people who will be able to pass them on to others.
+ 2 TIMOTHY 2:2

Jesus said, . . . "Let me teach you, because I am humble and gentle at heart, and you will find rest for your souls."
+ MATTHEW 11:28-29

Whoever wants to be a leader among you must be your servant, and whoever wants to be first among you must be the slave of everyone else.
+ MARK 10:43-44

M ENTORING is more than formal training; it is sharing life. A mentor shares wisdom, life experience, and support to help the mentee learn and grow. Even if we feel like we have nothing to offer, God can use our unique life experiences and lessons. Perhaps he wants us to pass on what we have learned to the next generation of women. Is there someone younger or with less life experience that you can commit to building a relationship with? Remember that you are called to lead as a servant, and you are not solely responsible for someone else's spiritual growth. Simply love another by listening, showing compassion, and being intentional. Keep in mind that God sent the Holy Spirit as your spiritual mentor. Spend time with God and he will help you to love and build relationships with others.

Prayer Prompts

Lord, something I could offer to younger women is . . .
Your Word gives me this practical wisdom about mentoring: . . .

How does God's mercy affect my daily life?

*The LORD is compassionate and merciful, slow to get angry
and filled with unfailing love. . . . He does not punish us for
all our sins; he does not deal harshly with us, as we deserve.*
✦ PSALM 103:8, 10

*The LORD has told you what is good, and this is what he requires of you:
to do what is right, to love mercy, and to walk humbly with your God.*
✦ MICAH 6:8

*All praise to God, the Father of our Lord Jesus Christ.
It is by his great mercy that we have been born again.*
✦ 1 PETER 1:3

MERCY is undeserved favor. And God's mercy is beyond anything
we've ever experienced. He not only exempts us from the punishment for our sins, he also gives us the undeserved gift of salvation.
Our rebellion against God deserves his punishment, but instead he
offers us forgiveness and eternal life. Even more, God's mercies never
end. He never stops giving us his undivided attention and his faithful
presence, as well as spiritual gifts, provision for our needs, and hope for
our future—all undeserved and yet lavishly poured out in our lives. It is
by his mercies that our very lives are sustained. Every breath is a merciful gift from an all-loving God. God's mercy changes our perspective
when we understand what it feels like to be loved even when we have
not loved in return. Allow this truth to inspire you toward living with
gratitude and loving others the same way that God loves you.

Prayer Prompts

Lord, because you have shown me mercy, I can show mercy to . . .
When it's hard to show mercy, your Word reminds me . . .

miracles

Does God still perform miracles today?
How can I see more miracles in my life?

———————— ❧ ————————

*"This is the finger of God!" the magicians exclaimed to
Pharaoh. But Pharaoh's heart remained hard. He wouldn't
listen to them, just as the LORD had predicted.*
+ EXODUS 8:19

*Come and see what our God has done,
what awesome miracles he performs for people!*
+ PSALM 66:5

*You made all the delicate, inner parts of my body
and knit me together in my mother's womb.*
+ PSALM 139:13

*The heavens proclaim the glory of God. The skies display his craftsmanship.
Day after day they continue to speak; night after night they make him known.*
+ PSALM 19:1-2

THE MIRACLES of God recorded in the Bible can seem like
ancient myths if we fail to recognize God's intervention in our
lives today. Just as Pharaoh was blind to the miracles God performed
right before his eyes, we too can blind ourselves to God's miracles
all around us. Maybe we think a miracle is always a dramatic event
such as raising a dead person to life. But miracles happen every day:
the birth of a baby, an awesome sunset, the restoration of a hopeless
relationship, the rebirth of the earth in spring. These are just a few. If
you think you've never seen a miracle, look closer. Ask God to help
you see the miracles that are happening all around you.

Prayer Prompts
Lord, one miracle I see today is . . .
Your Word reminds me that there are miracles all around me when it says . . .

# mistakes

Can God still use me even though I make so many mistakes?

———— ❧ ————

[Jesus said,] "Simon, Simon, Satan has asked to sift each of you like wheat. But I have pleaded in prayer for you, Simon, that your faith should not fail. So when you have repented and turned to me again, strengthen your brothers."
+ LUKE 22:31-32

Jesus said, "Peter, let me tell you something. Before the rooster crows tomorrow morning, you will deny three times that you even know me."
+ LUKE 22:34

We know that God causes everything to work together for the good of those who love God and are called according to his purpose for them.
+ ROMANS 8:28

KNOWING that Simon Peter was heading for disaster, Jesus prayed for him, making two requests of his heavenly Father: first, that Peter's mistakes would not cause him to lose his faith, and second, that Peter would eventually use the lessons he had learned from his error to strengthen others spiritually. Eventually, both of these prayers were answered, and Peter went on to become the leader of the first church in Jerusalem and an encourager of those who were suffering for their faith. Mistakes are part of being human. However, we must decide to learn and grow from our mistakes instead of repeating them. God's heart for us is that we will remain teachable and teach others. Remember that God can use your worst failures to strengthen your faith and enable you to better comfort and help those around you.

Prayer Prompts

Lord, I still feel bad about the mistake I made when . . .
Your Word reminds me that this is how you see my mistakes: . . .

money

Why can't money buy happiness? Sometimes I feel like I would be happier if I didn't need to worry about money.

———— ❧ ————

Those who love money will never have enough.
How meaningless to think that wealth brings true happiness!
+ ECCLESIASTES 5:10

Teach those who are rich in this world not to be proud and not to trust
in their money, which is so unreliable. Their trust should be in God,
who richly gives us all we need for our enjoyment.
+ 1 TIMOTHY 6:17

Don't love money; be satisfied with what you have. For God has said,
"I will never fail you. I will never abandon you."
+ HEBREWS 13:5

IT IS TEMPTING to believe that money has the power to fix all our problems. Money can cultivate a dangerous craving—the more we have, the more we want. So how can we live with the tension of needing money to live, yet not depending on it for our happiness? First, we need to remember that money itself is not evil; however, the love of money is! Our souls were made for relationship with God, and because of that, he is the only one who can truly satisfy us. If we had all the money in the world yet lacked a relationship with God, something would still be missing. When you notice yourself fixating on finances, desiring more things, or trusting in the next paycheck or big break, bring your thoughts back to God. Strive to know him more and he will become the greatest love of your heart.

Prayer Prompts

Lord, this is one way I think money would make me happy: . . .
Your Word assures me money can't buy true happiness because . . .

❧ motivation

How can I stay motivated when I am discouraged?

— ❧ —

So, my dear brothers and sisters, be strong and immovable.
Always work enthusiastically for the Lord, for you know
that nothing you do for the Lord is ever useless.
+ 1 CORINTHIANS 15:58

My life is worth nothing to me unless I use it
for finishing the work assigned me by the Lord Jesus.
+ ACTS 20:24

"I know the plans I have for you," says the LORD. "They are plans for good and
not for disaster, to give you a future and a hope. In those days when you pray,
I will listen. If you look for me wholeheartedly, you will find me."
+ JEREMIAH 29:11-13

LACK OF MOTIVATION often comes from lack of purpose. We lose inspiration and enthusiasm when we feel our actions and efforts are meaningless. However, we must remember that nothing we do for God is ever useless. Sometimes we just need to take time to refocus on him to give us a clearer vision for the future and our part in his eternal plan. If you feel discouraged right now, don't allow your circumstances to lead you toward hopelessness. Focus instead on God's promise to guide you into the wonderful future he has planned for you as his daughter. Ask him to give you a renewed sense of motivation, energy, and confidence as you trust him to help you. Anticipation for your future can compel you to move forward today.

Prayer Prompts

Lord, I feel unmotivated in this area of life: . . .
When I lack motivation, your Word encourages me that . . .

motives

As long as I do the right thing, what difference do my motives make?

―――――――― ❧ ――――――――

Even when you ask, you don't get it because
your motives are all wrong—you want only what will give you pleasure.
+ JAMES 4:3

I, the LORD, search all hearts and examine secret motives.
I give all people their due rewards, according to what their actions deserve.
+ JEREMIAH 17:10

Search me, O God, and know my heart; test me and know my thoughts.
+ PSALM 139:23

OUR MOTIVES are everything to God because they reveal what is most important to us and what is driving our choices. The condition of our heart is essential to the condition of our relationship with him. Do you ever pray out of obligation? Do you ever follow God's ways because you think it will keep him from getting angry with you? Have you ever tried to manipulate him to give you something you want? We've all had times when our motives were not exactly pure. But when we come to God out of a desire for authentic relationship, that pleases him. Where are your motives misguided? Confess these to God, tell him the kind of relationship you want to have with him, and take time to listen to his voice. God invites you to ask him to search you, examine your heart, and test your motives. It is only through honest confession and conversation that God is able to change your motives into ones that please him.

Prayer Prompts

Lord, some misguided motives that I need to confess are . . .
Your Word guides me to align my motives with your heart when it says . . .

 # mystery

Why is it important that there are mysteries about God we'll never fully understand?

❧

Just as you cannot understand the path of the wind or the mystery of a tiny baby growing in its mother's womb, so you cannot understand the activity of God, who does all things.
+ ECCLESIASTES 11:5

"My thoughts are nothing like your thoughts," says the LORD. "And my ways are far beyond anything you could imagine. For just as the heavens are higher than the earth, so my ways are higher than your ways and my thoughts higher than your thoughts."
+ ISAIAH 55:8-9

Truly, O God of Israel, our Savior, you work in mysterious ways.
+ ISAIAH 45:15

WHEN WE CANNOT make sense of something, it often makes us uncomfortable and distrusting. Therefore, when God acts in mysterious ways, naturally it challenges our faith. However, would we really want to have a God we knew everything about? If humans could completely understand God's nature and knowledge, we would cease to be in awe of him. God's mysteries are opportunities for faith. God has given you all you need to know in order to believe in him. If you pursue learning what he has already revealed about himself, you will discover him in new and exciting ways. God's ways are higher than ours and greater than we could ever understand, which makes following him a lifelong adventure of discovery.

Prayer Prompts

Lord, when I can't understand something about you, it makes me feel . . .
Even when you work in mysterious ways, your Word assures me I can know . . .

nature 🍃

What does nature's beauty tell me about God?

— ❦ —

The heavens proclaim the glory of God. The skies display his craftsmanship.
Day after day they continue to speak; night after night they make him known.
+ PSALM 19:1-2

Ever since the world was created, people have seen the earth
and sky. Through everything God made, they can clearly see
his invisible qualities—his eternal power and divine nature.
+ ROMANS 1:20

Everything was created through him and for him.
He existed before anything else, and he holds all creation together.
+ COLOSSIANS 1:16-17

O LORD, what a variety of things you have made!
In wisdom you have made them all. The earth is full of your creatures.
+ PSALM 104:24

ALTHOUGH SCRIPTURE—God's story in written form—is the best way to understand who God is, he has provided another way for people to begin to know him: through his creation. God intended his creation to bring him glory and to point people to himself. The breadth of creation makes us feel small, reminding us of God's majesty and eternal power. And yet the small, intricate details assure us of his tender and personal care. Scripture makes clear that he alone is the reason that the universe holds together. When you feel disconnected from God, take a walk outside, look at the vastness of the sky or the small intricacies of a flower, and reflect on how much nature reveals about your Creator.

Prayer Prompts

Lord, when I go out in nature, I think . . .
One of my favorite Scriptures about your role as Creator is . . .

 # neediness

How is being needy actually a good thing for my relationship with God?

— ❧ —

God blesses those who are poor and realize their need for him,
for the Kingdom of Heaven is theirs.
+ MATTHEW 5:3

Fear the LORD, you his godly people,
for those who fear him will have all they need.
+ PSALM 34:9

He has not ignored or belittled the suffering of the needy.
He has not turned his back on them, but has listened to their cries for help.
+ PSALM 22:24

Your Father knows exactly what you need even before you ask him!
+ MATTHEW 6:8

OUR CULTURE often looks down on the needy and praises those who are independent and self-sufficient. However, God teaches that neediness, whether emotional, financial, or physical, can actually be a blessing because it puts us in a position of humble dependence on him. This kind of dependence strengthens our faith as we wait for God to supply our needs—and he can be trusted to do this. God doesn't promise to give us everything we want; he promises to give us everything we need. Because of this truth, we can face tomorrow without worry. Your needs allow God to show you his power and provision and to teach you that he is sufficient. Take one day at a time, surrendering your needs to him. One day you will look back and see that God kept his promise to give you everything you need.

Prayer Prompts

Lord, something that I need from you is . . .
In my neediness, I can be encouraged because your Word says . . .

needs

How can I keep a clear distinction between my needs and my wants?

———————— ❧ ————————

The LORD is my shepherd; I have all that I need.
+ PSALM 23:1

If we have enough food and clothing, let us be content.
+ 1 TIMOTHY 6:8

Give me neither poverty nor riches!
Give me just enough to satisfy my needs.
+ PROVERBS 30:8

IN ORDER TO SURVIVE and thrive on this earth, all people have basic needs: food, water, shelter, and love. If you have these basic things, consider yourself blessed because there are many throughout the world who lack them due to the nature of our fallen world. So if there are people who don't have such things as food and shelter, what does it mean when God says he will give us everything we need? Perhaps God's definition of needs and wants is different from ours. In God's mind, persevering in our faith and having a close relationship with him are what we need most. Confusing wants with needs takes our focus off of what is really important. When we want something beyond our basic needs, we will be dissatisfied, discontent, greedy, and impatient when we don't get it. If you find yourself struggling with whether something is a need or a want, ask God to reveal to you what holds eternal importance.

Prayer Prompts

Lord, I confess that my "wants" include . . .
Your Word reminds me that you have met my needs through . . .

negativity

How can I protect myself from a negative attitude?

&

*Let the Spirit renew your thoughts and attitudes. Put on your new nature,
created to be like God—truly righteous and holy.*
+ EPHESIANS 4:23-24

*I have learned how to be content with whatever I have. I know how to live on
almost nothing or with everything. I have learned the secret of living in every
situation, whether it is with a full stomach or empty, with plenty or little.
For I can do everything through Christ, who gives me strength.*
+ PHILIPPIANS 4:11-13

*Be thankful in all circumstances,
for this is God's will for you who belong to Christ Jesus.*
+ 1 THESSALONIANS 5:18

GIVING IN TO DISCOURAGEMENT during hard times is a slippery slope. Once we allow negative thoughts to take over, they have enormous power to make us sink into despair. However, when challenges come our way, we can consider this: What if hard times and life struggles are raw materials that God uses to show us his mighty work in our lives? While it is hard to be thankful *for* the tough times, what if God promised to help us be thankful *in* them? Our outlook on life is a powerful factor in how we view our problems. If we see them only as obstacles, our attitude will likely be bitter, cynical, and hopeless. If we see our problems as opportunities to deepen our trust and relationship with God, we will rise above them and even thank God for them. And when future problems come our way, we will have the strength and faith to face them with God's perspective.

Prayer Prompts

Lord, I notice myself having a negative attitude about . . .
When I notice negativity, your Word encourages me to . . .

neglect

How can I keep from neglecting God?

This is what the LORD says to the family of Israel: "Come back to me and live!"
+ AMOS 5:4

If we confess our sins to him, he is faithful and just to forgive us our sins and to cleanse us from all wickedness.
+ 1 JOHN 1:9

Come close to God, and God will come close to you. Wash your hands, you sinners; purify your hearts, for your loyalty is divided between God and the world.
+ JAMES 4:8

WE ALL HAVE moments when we suddenly realize the distance between us and God has become vast. Before we can close the gap, we must determine what caused the distance in the first place. We can ask ourselves why we have neglected our relationship with God and then confess it. True confession brings God's forgiveness and restores our relationship with him. Then we can reprioritize our lives in order to guard against neglecting our relationship with God in the future. What can we let go of in order to put him first? Finally, we can recognize the excuses that cause our neglect of God to become a habit. Sometimes we claim it isn't the right time to become serious about our relationship with God. Any excuse that separates us from God is the work of the enemy trying to grow that distance between us. Move a step closer to God today by making time with him your top priority. Recognize the excuses that hinder your relationship. These steps will help you experience his presence, peace, and blessing in your life.

Prayer Prompts

Lord, I tend to neglect my relationship with you when . . .
In order to close the distance between us, your Word instructs me to . . .

 # neighbors

I know God calls me to love my neighbor, but what does this look like in a practical sense?

— ❧ —

"Which of these three would you say was a neighbor to the man who was attacked by bandits?" Jesus asked. The man replied, "The one who showed him mercy." Then Jesus said, "Yes, now go and do the same."
+ LUKE 10:36-37

Obey the royal law as found in the Scriptures: "Love your neighbor as yourself."
+ JAMES 2:8

If someone has enough money to live well and sees a brother or sister in need but shows no compassion—how can God's love be in that person?
+ 1 JOHN 3:17

JESUS' TEACHINGS mean that our "neighbor" is anyone around us who needs his love and care. However, sometimes when we think of everyone as our neighbor, we miss opportunities to love anyone. While it is important to love all people we come in contact with, sometimes we forget to love our actual neighbors. God has placed you in your city, your neighborhood, and your home for a reason—that those right around you might experience the love of Jesus through you. Do you know the needs of your neighbors? How might you practically meet one need in your neighborhood in order to show someone the love of Christ? Even as you read this, is God bringing a particular neighbor to mind? Sometimes it can feel scary to step out of your comfort zone to love those on your street. However, God promises to be with you and will bless your efforts to know and love your neighbors well.

Prayer Prompts

Lord, one practical way I can meet a need of my neighbor is by . . .
Your Word gives me encouragement to . . .

obedience

How can I be encouraged to obey when following God feels hard?

———— ❧ ————

*Jesus said to his disciples, "If any of you wants to be my follower,
you must give up your own way, take up your cross, and follow me."*
+ MATTHEW 16:24

*Remember how the LORD your God led you through the wilderness for
these forty years, humbling you and testing you to prove your character.*
+ DEUTERONOMY 8:2

*God blesses those who patiently endure testing and temptation. Afterward they
will receive the crown of life that God has promised to those who love him.*
+ JAMES 1:12

FOLLOWING GOD will inevitably lead us to a crossroad in our
lives: Do we take the difficult road of obedience to God, or do
we take the easy and comfortable route to satisfy our own desires?
We know what we "should" do, but obeying God does not always
come naturally or feel joyful in the moment. God doesn't promise
us that following him will be easy. In fact, the more important a
task is, the more we may be tempted toward disobedience. But God
does promise that his commandments are not burdensome obligations but pathways to joyful, meaningful, and satisfying lives. Since
God is the creator of all things, he knows how life is supposed to
work. Obedience demonstrates both your trust that God's way is
best for you and your desire to live as a woman in close relationship
with him.

Prayer Prompts

Lord, one area where I struggle to obey you is . . .
When obedience feels hard, your Word encourages me to . . .

 # obligation

Is it wrong to serve out of obligation?

———— ❧ ————

We know we love God's children if we love God and obey his commandments.
+ 1 JOHN 5:2

Work willingly at whatever you do, as though you were working for the Lord rather than for people. Remember that the Lord will give you an inheritance as your reward, and that the Master you are serving is Christ.
+ COLOSSIANS 3:23-24

This is real love—not that we loved God, but that he loved us and sent his Son as a sacrifice to take away our sins. Dear friends, since God loved us that much, we surely ought to love each other.
+ 1 JOHN 4:10-11

SERVING OTHERS can become obligatory and wearing when we take on activities and responsibilities for the wrong reasons. But when we serve with the intention to love others the way God loves us, our hearts will be in the right place. And God promises that when we serve others, we are actually serving him and will be greatly rewarded. Of course, there will always be times when we don't feel like serving— maybe we are tired, the weather is bad, or a better opportunity has come along. However, we have to do the right thing and trust that our hearts will follow. After all, if we only served others when we felt like it, then we would probably never serve! As you consider upcoming involvements, ask God to help you do things with the right motives and to reveal any area where they are less than pure. Trust that he will help you serve from your heart as you lead with your body.

Prayer Prompts

Lord, I feel obligated to serve when . . .
Your Word encourages me to serve by reminding me that . . .

opportunity

When an opportunity arises, how do I know if God wants me to walk through that open door?

Never stop praying.
+ 1 THESSALONIANS 5:17

Your word is a lamp to guide my feet and a light for my path.
+ PSALM 119:105

Without wise leadership, a nation falls; there is safety in having many advisers.
+ PROVERBS 11:14

We must quickly carry out the tasks assigned us by the one who sent us. The night is coming, and then no one can work.
+ JOHN 9:4

OPPORTUNITIES seized or missed often become defining moments in our lives. God gives us many chances to participate in his purpose; therefore we must be prepared to recognize when God opens a door for us, and then walk through it with boldness. But how do we know if an open door is from God? First, we know that any opportunity that contradicts God's Word or violates its principles is not from the Lord. The Bible may not directly address a particular opportunity, but it gives clear guidelines about what God desires for our lives and what he warns us to avoid. Second, we must pray that God will lead us. And third, we can seek wise advice from godly people in our lives. Keep your eyes open for what God will bring your way. And when you believe that God is presenting you with an opportunity, respond quickly and work hard to carry out the task he has put before you.

Prayer Prompts

Lord, I wonder if you have opened this door: . . .
Before I decide to walk through it, your Word tells me to . . .

 outsider

What can I do when my faith make me feel like an outsider?

❦

You Gentiles are no longer strangers and foreigners. You are citizens along with all of God's holy people. You are members of God's family.
+ EPHESIANS 2:19

What blessings await you when people hate you and exclude you and mock you and curse you as evil because you follow the Son of Man.
+ LUKE 6:22

When we get together, I want to encourage you in your faith, but I also want to be encouraged by yours.
+ ROMANS 1:12

We are citizens of heaven, where the Lord Jesus Christ lives.
+ PHILIPPIANS 3:20

WE CAN BE ENCOURAGED that the power of God is for us, regardless of how many are against us. God used a young David to overcome the giant Goliath. He used Gideon's three hundred soldiers to defeat the vast armies of Midian. And he used twelve disciples to establish the worldwide church. Even if our faith excludes us or hinders certain friendships, God is still able to do great things through us. Strive to follow him each day. Don't compromise your beliefs in order to have friends; instead, ask God to bring you into relationship with women who will strengthen your faith as well as women who are in need of faith. And when discouragement begins to creep in, remember that feeling like an outsider in this world is natural, for your true home is in heaven, and you will fully belong there.

Prayer Prompts

Lord, I feel like an outsider when . . .
When I feel like I don't belong, your Word encourages me that . . .

overcoming 🍃

How can God help me overcome the impossible obstacles in my life?

———— ❧ ————

I hold you by your right hand—I, the LORD your God. And I say to you,
"Don't be afraid. I am here to help you."
+ ISAIAH 41:13

I can do everything through Christ, who gives me strength.
+ PHILIPPIANS 4:13

Jesus looked at them intently and said, "Humanly speaking,
it is impossible. But with God everything is possible."
+ MATTHEW 19:26

LIFE WILL PRESENT immense obstacles and invincible opponents, and God does not promise to help us escape them. But we can take heart! The ability to overcome is the birthright of believers. God has given us his Holy Spirit to help us rise above the obstacles and temptations in our lives. However, this doesn't mean that we won't struggle. Being filled with the Holy Spirit did not prevent Jesus from being tempted, but it did help him overcome temptation. As long as you live on this earth, you will never be free from trouble, but you have the power to overcome it through the Holy Spirit's help. If you are currently facing an obstacle in your life, see it as an opportunity for God to show his incredible power. The very hardships and weaknesses that frighten you may be the tools God wants to use to teach you that nothing is impossible for him to overcome.

Prayer Prompts

Lord, I'm not sure I can rise above this problem: . . .
Your Word tells me I am able to overcome obstacles because . . .

 # overwhelmed

How can I cope when I feel overwhelmed with the tasks of my day?

— ❧ —

God is our refuge and strength, always ready to help in times of trouble.
+ PSALM 46:1

We also pray that you will be strengthened with all his glorious power so you will have all the endurance and patience you need. May you be filled with joy, always thanking the Father.
+ COLOSSIANS 1:11-12

Give your burdens to the LORD, and he will take care of you. He will not permit the godly to slip and fall.
+ PSALM 55:22

I cry out to the LORD; I plead for the LORD's mercy. I pour out my complaints before him and tell him all my troubles. When I am overwhelmed, you alone know the way I should turn.
+ PSALM 142:1-3

OUR LIVES are often packed full of responsibilities. It can feel like there aren't enough hours in a day to accomplish all we need to get done. When we feel overwhelmed, the most important thing we can do is to take a break with the Lord. We can read a passage of Scripture, take a walk around the block to pray, or take some deep breaths, remembering that God is with us. This may feel like a waste of precious time, but reconnecting with God is actually the most productive thing you can do. Only when you spend time in his presence can you find strength, perseverance, and perspective to tackle the tasks of the day.

Prayer Prompts
Lord, I feel overwhelmed by . . .
When I feel overwhelmed, your Word tells me . . .

pain

What hope do I have for living through painful circumstances?

———————— ✿ ————————

We believers also groan, even though we have the Holy Spirit within us as a foretaste of future glory, for we long for our bodies to be released from sin and suffering. We, too, wait with eager hope for the day when God will give us our full rights as his adopted children, including the new bodies he has promised us.
✝ ROMANS 8:23

After you have suffered a little while, he will restore, support, and strengthen you, and he will place you on a firm foundation.
✝ 1 PETER 5:10

What we suffer now is nothing compared to the glory he will reveal to us later.
✝ ROMANS 8:18

ALMOST EVERYONE has felt the physical tension or the chest-tightening ache that comes from a broken heart. Whether our pain comes from betrayal, neglect, abandonment, or failing health, our greatest (and only) hope is healing from God. Sometimes agony feels so intense that we can't see anything except our pain. But even when we can't see God, he is right beside us. He never takes a day off or forgets to care for us. He has promised to help us in every difficulty. If you doubt God's ability to heal your pain, that is okay. Start by telling him how you feel. When you allow him into your pain through your honest, vulnerable prayers, you can experience healing through his loving presence.

Prayer Prompts

Lord, it is hard for me to find hope in this painful circumstance: . . .
When I can't see past my pain, your Word encourages me to remember . . .

 # panic

How can I keep from panicking when life seems to be falling apart?

❦

*Be strong and courageous! Do not be afraid and do not panic
before them. For the LORD your God will personally go
ahead of you. He will neither fail you nor abandon you.*
+ DEUTERONOMY 31:6

When I am afraid, I will put my trust in you.
+ PSALM 56:3

With his love, he will calm all your fears.
+ ZEPHANIAH 3:17

*You will keep in perfect peace all who trust in you,
all whose thoughts are fixed on you!*
+ ISAIAH 26:3

PANIC IS physically and emotionally paralyzing—it is where
worry and fear meet in an instant crisis. If we aren't prepared
for it, we will feel incapable of dealing with it properly. Good preparation expels fear, gives us peace about the future, and provides
daily confidence to deal with an instant crisis. The best way to avoid
panic is to gain wisdom through a daily relationship with God.
Every moment we spend with God strengthens and prepares us for
any circumstance. The more we are connected with God, the more
equipped we will be to deal with panic rationally. Remember, God
is in control of your life. Stay close to God by keeping your focus
on him, and he will help protect you against panic with his perfect peace.

Prayer Prompts
Lord, I tend to panic when . . .
Your Word encourages me to protect myself from panic by . . .

passion

Why can't I always be on fire for God?

※

*We must listen very carefully to the truth we have heard,
or we may drift away from it.*
+ HEBREWS 2:1

*I had to feed you with milk, not with solid food, because
you weren't ready for anything stronger. And you still aren't ready.*
+ 1 CORINTHIANS 3:2

*You must love the LORD your God with
all your heart, all your soul, and all your mind.*
+ MATTHEW 22:37

MOST PEOPLE have experienced the hunger to know God more and the excitement of growing closer to him. But just like in any relationship, feelings of passion ebb and flow. Sometimes sin hinders our experience of God, but it doesn't mean that God is no longer present. And when the passion dies, it doesn't necessarily mean that we are doing something wrong. Maybe God withdraws his closeness because he wants to grow our faith. God wants us to pursue him because we love and trust him, not because he gives us feelings of excitement. Your relationship with God takes effort and energy. Stay committed in your efforts to know him better: Consistently study God's Word, be thankful, serve others, and look for him in every circumstance. Ask God to help you fight off feelings of apathy and reignite your passion for him.

Prayer Prompts

Lord, I was most passionate about following you when . . .
When apathy hinders our relationship, your Word encourages me to . . .

past

Can I live a healthy, godly life despite my past?

❧

> [The LORD said,] "Though your sins are like scarlet,
> I will make them as white as snow."
> + ISAIAH 1:18

> I focus on this one thing: Forgetting the past and looking forward to what
> lies ahead, I press on to reach the end of the race and receive the heavenly
> prize for which God, through Christ Jesus, is calling us.
> + PHILIPPIANS 3:13-14

> Fear not; you will no longer live in shame. Don't be afraid; there is no more
> disgrace for you. You will no longer remember the shame of your youth.
> + ISAIAH 54:4

OUR MEMORIES of the past are like photo albums that contain snapshots of our lives. Some snapshots are of happy moments and celebrations; others record our failures, tragedies, and shameful actions. Most of us would like to tear out the snapshots that expose the parts we'd prefer to forget. The apostle Paul, considered one of the great leaders in the New Testament, had a past he wished he could forget: persecuting and killing Christians. But Paul understood that his past had been redeemed through God's healing and forgiveness. How we view our pasts will affect how we live in the present and the future. Some of us have a positive past with a strong spiritual heritage. We shouldn't take that for granted but should use it to help others. Some of us have a past filled with regrets. No matter what you've done, God is ready (and able!) to forgive you and give you a fresh start.

Prayer Prompts

Lord, when I think about my past, I feel . . .
Your Word assures me I can courageously face the future because . . .

patience 🍃

How can I learn patience?

———————— ❧ ————————

Patient endurance is what you need now, so that you will continue to
do God's will. Then you will receive all that he has promised.
+ HEBREWS 10:36

The Holy Spirit produces this kind of fruit in our lives:
love, joy, peace, patience . . .
+ GALATIANS 5:22

Be still in the presence of the LORD, and wait patiently for him to act.
+ PSALM 37:7

If you suffer for doing good and endure it patiently, God is pleased with you.
+ 1 PETER 2:20

PATIENCE is not a personality trait; it is a by-product of God's
work in our hearts. Patience is an active choice to wait gracefully
for something to unfold. Learning to be patient comes from taking
small, faithful steps each day. God promises that when we face situations with perseverance and endurance, he will help us, encourage
us, and give us patience. What situation in life is currently testing
your patience? How might God's Word encourage you to respond to
this frustrating circumstance with grace and self-control? Whether
you spent two hours stuck in rush-hour traffic today or held a crying
baby at 2:00 a.m., God is using these moments to grow you into a
patient woman. Ask him to help you continue on with patient endurance, and watch for the fruit it will produce in your life.

Prayer Prompts
Lord, it's so hard for me to be patient with . . .
Your Word encourages me to grow in patience by . . .

 # peace

How can I have peace in a world that is anything but peaceful?

— ❧ —

You will keep in perfect peace all who trust in you,
all whose thoughts are fixed on you!
+ ISAIAH 26:3

[Jesus said,] "I am leaving you with a gift—peace of mind and heart. And the
peace I give is a gift the world cannot give. So don't be troubled or afraid."
+ JOHN 14:27

[Jesus said,] "Don't let your hearts be troubled. Trust in God, and
trust also in me. There is more than enough room in my Father's
home. If this were not so, would I have told you that I am going to
prepare a place for you? When everything is ready, I will come and
get you, so that you will always be with me where I am."
+ JOHN 14:1-3

MOST OF US long for peace in our unpredictable lives. Yet no matter how frayed our nerves are or how unsettled our hearts feel, God is able to calm us. God's Word advises us to actively pursue his peace. He promises peace to those who strive to know his Word, follow his commands, trust him at all times, live in harmony with others, and keep their thoughts focused on him. Which of these areas do you need to work on with God's help? You can't prevent bad things from invading your life, but you can have peace—a quiet, unshakable confidence. When the world feels scary, remember that God is keeping a safe place for you in heaven. Let that assurance keep you from panicking in today's storms. God is with you, and the outcome is certain.

Prayer Prompts

Lord, I long to feel peace about . . .
Your Word settles my heart when I read . . .

perfectionism

How can I embrace my imperfections?

———— ❧ ————

He has reconciled you to himself through the death of Christ in his physical body. As a result, he has brought you into his own presence, and you are holy and blameless as you stand before him without a single fault.
+ COLOSSIANS 1:22

By that one offering he forever made perfect those who are being made holy.
+ HEBREWS 10:14

*How foolish can you be? After starting your new lives in the Spirit, why are you now trying to become perfect by your own human effort? . . .
The real children of Abraham, then, are those who put their faith in God.*
+ GALATIANS 3:3, 7

STRIVING FOR PERFECTION can be exhausting. We know perfection is an impossible standard, yet we often believe that if we work hard enough, we can reach it. The truth is, no matter how much we try, we will never live without mistakes in this world. But maybe God is calling us to a different kind of perfection. We cannot be made perfect by our own efforts, but we can be made holy and blameless before God because of his efforts. Because he offered his Son as a sacrifice for our sins, we are made holy, without fault, by his grace! Isn't that kind of perfectionism much better than the world's? Relinquish perfectionism and accept who you really are—an imperfect woman who has been declared faultless because of what God has done.

Prayer Prompts

*Lord, I try hard to be perfect in the areas of . . .
Instead of striving toward perfection, your Word encourages me to . . .*

# persecution

I fear being persecuted because of my faith. How can I face the future with courage?

———— ❧ ————

Dear friends, don't be surprised at the fiery trials you are going through, as if something strange were happening to you. Instead, be very glad— for these trials make you partners with Christ in his suffering.
+ 1 PETER 4:12-13

That's why I take pleasure in my weaknesses, and in the insults, hardships, persecutions, and troubles that I suffer for Christ. For when I am weak, then I am strong.
+ 2 CORINTHIANS 12:10

Can anything ever separate us from Christ's love? Does it mean he no longer loves us if we have trouble or calamity, or are persecuted, or hungry, or destitute, or in danger, or threatened with death? . . . No, despite all these things, overwhelming victory is ours through Christ, who loved us.
+ ROMANS 8:35, 37

THE EARLY CHURCH was constantly threatened with persecution. And yet, Peter and Paul encouraged these believers to pray not for the threats to end but for courage to face them. Sometimes God removes the things that frighten us. But more often, the Holy Spirit gives us boldness to turn those threats into opportunities to grow spiritually and declare our faith. Ask God to help you see beyond the immediate crisis and place both your current problem and your eternal future in his hands. When fear grips your heart, hold on to the truth that nothing will ever be able to separate you from the love of Christ.

Prayer Prompts

Lord, when I think about the possibility of facing persecution, I feel . . .
Your Word inspires me to be bold because it promises . . .

perseverance 🍃

How can I persevere through difficult seasons in a way that pleases God?

— ❧ —

We think you ought to know, dear brothers and sisters, about the trouble we went through in the province of Asia. We were crushed and overwhelmed beyond our ability to endure, and we thought we would never live through it. In fact, we expected to die. But as a result, we stopped relying on ourselves and learned to rely only on God, who raises the dead.
+ 2 CORINTHIANS 1:8-9

May the Lord lead your hearts into a full understanding and expression of the love of God and the patient endurance that comes from Christ.
+ 2 THESSALONIANS 3:5

We also pray that you will be strengthened with all his glorious power so you will have all the endurance and patience you need. May you be filled with joy.
+ COLOSSIANS 1:11

PERSEVERANCE means enduring with courage, even when the end is not in sight. We persevere in the midst of our trials by continuing to be faithful and do what is right, whether or not we can see good results right now. Problems have a way of testing our faith— they either strengthen us or break us down. It all depends on our attitude. When we persevere with God's help, we come out on the other side with a stronger faith, experiencing the benefits of obedience and growing in confidence that will help us deal with future problems. Be encouraged that God is able not only to help you endure but to help you persevere joyfully!

Prayer Prompts

Lord, I need perspective as I persevere through the difficult situation of . . .
Your Word reminds me to persevere with an attitude of . . .

place

Why do certain places help me feel closer to God?

I saw a new heaven and a new earth, for the old heaven and the old earth had disappeared. And the sea was also gone. And I saw the holy city, the new Jerusalem, coming down from God out of heaven like a bride beautifully dressed for her husband. I heard a loud shout from the throne, saying, "Look, God's home is now among his people! He will live with them, and they will be his people. God himself will be with them. He will wipe every tear from their eyes, and there will be no more death or sorrow or crying or pain. All these things are gone forever."
+ REVELATION 21:1-4

There is more than enough room in my Father's home. If this were not so, would I have told you that I am going to prepare a place for you?
+ JOHN 14:1-2

CERTAIN PLACES are special because they offer glimpses of our eternal home. The glory of the old Jerusalem gave believers a glimpse of the new Jerusalem in heaven. The beauty of this earth, genuine love between friends or family members, and places of rest and renewal are all tastes of the beauty, love, and joy we will experience in heaven. Whether your special place is a local park bench or your living-room chair, God has provided it for you as a gift. Thank God for giving you glimpses of heaven during your time on earth, and allow your special place to encourage you to look forward to your future with him.

Prayer Prompts

Lord, this place is special to me because . . .
Special places give me a glimpse of how your Word describes heaven: . . .

planning

Why should I plan for the future if God is ultimately in control of it?

Look here, you who say, "Today or tomorrow we are going to a certain town and will stay there a year. We will do business there and make a profit." How do you know what your life will be like tomorrow? Your life is like the morning fog—it's here a little while, then it's gone. What you ought to say is, "If the Lord wants us to, we will live and do this or that." Otherwise you are boasting about your own pretentious plans, and all such boasting is evil.
+ JAMES 4:13-16

A prudent person foresees the danger ahead and takes precautions. The simpleton goes blindly on and suffers the consequences.
+ PROVERBS 22:3

Don't begin until you count the cost. For who would begin construction of a building without first calculating the cost to see if there is enough money to finish it?
+ LUKE 14:28

You can make many plans, but the LORD's purpose will prevail.
+ PROVERBS 19:21

PLANNING is a wise and necessary part of life. Preparing for the future does not come naturally to some of us, while for others, planning serves as a coping mechanism to help us feel like we are in control. Thankfully, God is the ultimate planner. He promises a great plan for all of humanity as well as for us personally. Make your plans, but allow God to change them as he sees fit.

Prayer Prompts

Lord, something that would be wise for me to plan for is . . .
As I make plans, your Word reminds me to keep in mind that . . .

 # pleasure

Does it please God when we enjoy the things he's given us?

—— ❦ ——

*I decided there is nothing better than to enjoy food and drink
and to find satisfaction in work. Then I realized that these
pleasures are from the hand of God.*
+ ECCLESIASTES 2:24

*Since everything God created is good, we should not reject
any of it but receive it with thanks. For we know it is made
acceptable by the word of God and prayer.*
+ 1 TIMOTHY 4:4-5

*Nehemiah continued, "Go and celebrate with a feast of rich foods and sweet
drinks, and share gifts of food with people who have nothing prepared.
This is a sacred day before our Lord."*
+ NEHEMIAH 8:10

*You have given me greater joy than those who have
abundant harvests of grain and new wine.*
+ PSALM 4:7

GOODNESS is part of God's character, and therefore he is pleased when we celebrate special occasions or enjoy food, friends, and beauty. Just as a mother experiences joy while watching her child delight in a gift, so God delights when his people enjoy the good things he has given them. What gifts has God given you today? How can you remember to thank him for them? Accept and appreciate God's gifts and live life as God intended you to enjoy it—to the fullest!

Prayer Prompts

Lord, I love enjoying your gift of . . .
I know my delighting in your gifts brings you joy because your Word says . . .

possessions 🍃

How do I keep from being overly attached to my possessions?

— ⚭ —

If you try to hang on to your life, you will lose it.
But if you give up your life for my sake, you will save it.
+ MATTHEW 16:25

The earth is the LORD's, and everything in it.
The world and all its people belong to him.
+ PSALM 24:1

Seek the Kingdom of God above all else, and he will give you
everything you need. So don't be afraid, little flock. For it gives
your Father great happiness to give you the Kingdom.
+ LUKE 12:31-32

MANY OF US don't worship our actual possessions but rather what they give us. The things we own can make us feel secure, significant, or admired. However, money and wealth can be dangerously deceptive. When we become overly focused on our material possessions, they end up owning us instead of the other way around. However, our relationship with Jesus ought to change our relationship with our possessions, because everything we have is from God. If you feel like your heart has become overly focused on what belongs to you, one of the best things you can do is invest your money in the things of God. Your heart will follow your money, and you will start caring about the ministries or people you are contributing to. Ask God to help you view your possessions as he does, know what is really worth being concerned over, and invest your heart in what matters most.

Prayer Prompts

Lord, sometimes my possessions make me feel . . .
Your Word reminds me to view what I own with this perspective: . . .

 # power of God

How can I experience God's power working through me?

— ❧ —

[The Lord] said, "My grace is all you need. My power works best in weakness." So now I am glad to boast about my weaknesses, so that the power of Christ can work through me.
+ 2 CORINTHIANS 12:9

This is the secret: Christ lives in you. This gives you assurance of sharing his glory. . . . That's why I work and struggle so hard, depending on Christ's mighty power that works within me.
+ COLOSSIANS 1:27, 29

Be strong in the Lord and in his mighty power. Put on all of God's armor so that you will be able to stand firm against all strategies of the devil.
+ EPHESIANS 6:10-11

With God's help we will do mighty things.
+ PSALM 60:12

GOD'S POWER is not dependent on human strength. In fact, his power is most evident when we are weak, because it is only by God's strength that we are able to accomplish what we cannot do on our own. If we merely imitate him or try through our own efforts to do right and please God, we will fail. But we have God's power, through his Holy Spirit, working in us and on our behalf. When opposition or problems arise, try not to look at the size of the problem but at the size of your God. When you feel unable to keep going, God says, "It's okay. I've got this." Pray, wait, and watch what he is able to do through your weakness.

Prayer Prompts

Lord, I need to see your power in the area of . . .
Your Word assures me that you are able to . . .

praise

How can praise become a natural response to the presence of God in my life?

———— ❧ ————

As [Jesus] rode along, the crowds spread out their garments on the road ahead of him. . . . All of his followers began to shout and sing as they walked along, praising God for all the wonderful miracles they had seen.
+ LUKE 19:36-37

Great is the LORD! He is most worthy of praise! He is to be feared above all gods. The gods of other nations are mere idols, but the LORD made the heavens!
+ 1 CHRONICLES 16:25-26

When I look at the night sky and see the work of your fingers—the moon and the stars you set in place—what are mere mortals that you should think about them, human beings that you should care for them?
+ PSALM 8:3-4

GOD IS THE CREATOR of the universe. He fashioned the heavens, placing the planets and stars in motion; carved out the canyons, valleys, and mountains; and breathed life into every human being. How amazing is it that this same God desires a personal relationship with us and even provides a way for us to live forever with him in heaven? As the creator and sustainer of life, he is worthy of our highest praise. Before you come into prayer or worship, take a few moments to think about God's awesome power and greatness. As you meditate on his unlimited and unconditional love for you personally, despite your limitations, you will begin to find yourself responding to him with more adoration, joy, and praise.

Prayer Prompts

Lord, I confess that I often forget to praise you for . . .
Your Word reminds me you are worthy of praise because . . .

 prayer

How do I talk to God?

—— ❧ ——

Keep on asking, and you will receive what you ask for. Keep on seeking, and you will find. . . . If you sinful people know how to give good gifts to your children, how much more will your heavenly Father give good gifts to those who ask him.
+ MATTHEW 7:7, 11

Don't worry about anything; instead, pray about everything. Tell God what you need, and thank him for all he has done. Then you will experience God's peace, which exceeds anything we can understand. His peace will guard your hearts and minds as you live in Christ Jesus.
+ PHILIPPIANS 4:6-7

Pray in the Spirit at all times and on every occasion.
+ EPHESIANS 6:18

PRAYER IS NOT just about telling God what our needs are. It is engaging with the ever-present Christ in all our moments. Talking with him includes praising and thanking him, confessing our sins, making requests, expressing pain and frustration, or simply sharing what is happening in our lives. Good conversation also includes listening, so we need to allow time for God to speak back to us. God often does as much in our hearts through our act of praying as he does in actually answering our prayers. Prayer softens our hearts, gives us wisdom and direction, turns our worry into peace, and helps us tune in to the very heart of God. God always welcomes you with open arms into his presence. Every time you talk to God, remember that you are forming and deepening the most important relationship you will ever have.

Prayer Prompts

Lord, the issue on my heart today is . . .
Your Word encourages me to pray that . . .

presence of God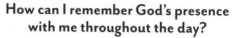

How can I remember God's presence with me throughout the day?

If you look for me wholeheartedly, you will find me.
+ JEREMIAH 29:13

The LORD your God is living among you.
+ ZEPHANIAH 3:17

I know the LORD is always with me.
I will not be shaken, for he is right beside me.
+ PSALM 16:8

Jacob awoke from his sleep and said,
"Surely the LORD is in this place, and I wasn't even aware of it!"
+ GENESIS 28:16

THE BIBLE tells many stories of people who were in the very presence of God but completely unaware of it. Jesus' own disciples didn't realize they were walking with him on the road to Emmaus (Luke 24:36-37). What causes us to miss the presence and activity of God in our days? Often it's simply our own busyness and distractions. We need to train ourselves to be constantly aware of the truth that God is always with us. No matter what we feel, the truth is that God is with us every moment. Remind yourself of this truth by putting Bible verses around your home, carrying something with you as a tangible reminder, or even setting an alarm on your phone that simply says, "God is with you." Don't miss what he is doing right in front of you!

Prayer Prompts

Lord, one way I can remind myself of your presence is by . . .
Even when I feel like you are far away, your Word reminds me that . . .

 # pressure

How can I best deal with the pressures of life?

❦

*Martha was distracted by the big dinner she was preparing. She came to Jesus
and said, "Lord, doesn't it seem unfair to you that my sister just sits here while
I do all the work? Tell her to come and help me." But the Lord said to her,
"My dear Martha, you are worried and upset over all these details!"*
+ LUKE 10:40-41

As pressure and stress bear down on me, I find joy in your commands.
+ PSALM 119:143

*"This is not good!" Moses' father-in-law exclaimed.
"You're going to wear yourself out—and the people, too.
This job is too heavy a burden for you to handle all by yourself."*
+ EXODUS 18:17-18

THE PRESSURES of daily life can squeeze our perspectives inward,
causing us to lose our ability to look beyond ourselves. Pressure
makes us focus on the trivial and miss the significant. What can
we do when we're feeling pressure? First, we can begin our days by
asking what is most important to God. God's agenda for our days is
often drastically different from our own. Second, we can open God's
Word, where we will find the secrets to peace. God's Word shifts our
perspective away from external pressures and onto him. Finally, we
can allow others to help us with the load. God never intended us
to handle the pressures of life alone, and accepting assistance from
others will give them an opportunity to serve. When pressure weighs
you down, shift your perspective on what's most important, gain
wisdom from God's Word, and don't be afraid to ask for help.

Prayer Prompts

Lord, I feel burdened by these pressures of life: . . .
Your Word gives me this practical advice for dealing with pressure: . . .

pretending 🍃

I'm tired of pretending I have it all together. How can I bring authenticity to my relationships?

———— ❧ ————

We have depended on God's grace, not on our own human wisdom.
+ 2 CORINTHIANS 1:12

Joyful are people of integrity, who follow the instructions of the LORD.
+ PSALM 119:1

Give all your worries and cares to God, for he cares about you.
+ 1 PETER 5:7

ALL OF US have that closet or bedroom where we shove our mess when others come over. It is human nature to try to cover up the mess in our lives. As women, we often believe that if we portray a picture-perfect image, others will see us as successful and self-sufficient. Yet if we are truly honest, we have to admit that none of us *really* have it all together. Some of us struggle with anxiety or depression. Others have fragile marriages or are drowning in debt. It is humbling to realize we are just pretending to be okay. It is even more humbling to admit that we need help, yet this is the first step in bringing authenticity to our lives with God and others. Being vulnerable is to allow another person into the messiness of our lives. Wouldn't it feel refreshing if we all admitted we are struggling? If you find it difficult to be honest with others about your hardships, start by being honest with God. You don't need to have it all together before you pray because God already knows you. Allow God to sit with you in your mess in order to experience his help and his grace.

Prayer Prompts
Lord, if I am really honest, I need help with . . .
Your Word encourages me toward a life of authenticity when it says . . .

pride

What is pride, and why is it so dangerous?

— ❦ —

Just as the heavens are higher than the earth, so my ways are higher than your ways and my thoughts higher than your thoughts.
+ ISAIAH 55:9

Pride goes before destruction, and haughtiness before a fall.
+ PROVERBS 16:18

Fools think their own way is right, but the wise listen to others.
+ PROVERBS 12:15

Those who exalt themselves will be humbled, and those who humble themselves will be exalted.
+ LUKE 18:14

THE MOST DANGEROUS sins are often those we cannot see. Pride, at its core, is the desire to live apart from God. It is convincing ourselves that, on any particular issue, we know better than he does. However, God's Word assures us that he is perfect in goodness and all-loving toward his creation. His plans for us are good, and therefore he can be trusted with our future. Do you tend to be stubborn? Do you struggle to trust that God's Word is true? Do you lack respect for his authority? How do you respond when God changes your plans? Do you respond in anger, saying, "Fine, have it your way," or in humility, saying, "Lord, your will be done"? If you see signs of pride in your life, ask God to move your heart toward humility. Read God's Word to grow in your knowledge of who he is and who you are in comparison. Learn to be teachable so that you don't miss out on growing with God.

Prayer Prompts

Lord, sometimes I see these signs of pride in my heart: . . .
Your Word warns me that pride is dangerous because . . .

priorities 🌿

How can I set the right priorities?

───────── ❧ ─────────

Seek [the LORD's] will in all you do, and he will show you which path to take.
+ PROVERBS 3:6

*The most important commandment is this: . . . "You must love the LORD
your God with all your heart, all your soul, all your mind, and all your
strength." The second is equally important: "Love your neighbor as yourself."
No other commandment is greater than these.*
+ MARK 12:29-31

*Seek the Kingdom of God above all else, and live righteously,
and he will give you everything you need.*
+ MATTHEW 6:33

WHEN WE FEEL STRESSED, exhausted from rushing from one thing to the next, it may be time to sit with God in the quiet to reset our priorities. It can feel difficult to take time to listen to God's voice in times of stress, but that is when we need it most. The more time we spend with the Lord, the more certainly we will recognize his voice. Knowing how to listen to him will give us confidence to do what is most important, helping us decide what to say yes to and what to let go. Put God first and watch how much simpler life becomes. When you seek him and trust that he is in control, you become free from feeling like you need to do it all. Take time to rest in his company and get his insights on your obligations, and he will show you how to live with freedom and simplicity.

Prayer Prompts

Lord, perhaps it would be wise for me to let go of . . .
As I read your Word, I realize that my top priority should be . . .

 # problems

What can I do when problems overwhelm me?

❧

Dear brothers and sisters, when troubles of any kind come your way, consider it an opportunity for great joy. For you know that when your faith is tested, your endurance has a chance to grow.
+ JAMES 1:2-3

The LORD helps the fallen and lifts those bent beneath their loads.
+ PSALM 145:14

Why am I discouraged? Why is my heart so sad? I will put my hope in God! I will praise him again—my Savior and my God! Now I am deeply discouraged, but I will remember you.
+ PSALM 42:5-6

Joyful are those who have the God of Israel as their helper, whose hope is in the LORD their God.
+ PSALM 146:5

UNEXPECTED PROBLEMS have the power to make us feel trapped in discouragement, hopelessness, and self-pity. However, overwhelming problems are opportunities to experience God's help. When we feel overwhelmed, we can remember God's faithfulness in the past. That encourages us to trust him today and gives us hope for tomorrow. Remembering what God has done has the power to drive away the darkest times of despair and protect us against self-pity. God is reaching out his hand to help you. Don't wait until you can't go another step to grab his hand. Pray earnestly, asking God to shoulder your load, ease your burden, and ease your stress.

Prayer Prompts
Lord, this problem feels too heavy to bear: . . .
When my problems overwhelm me, your Word encourages me that . . .

productivity

How can I let go of my desire to always "do" and instead just "be"?

━━━━━━━━━ ❧ ━━━━━━━━━

He told them, "This is what the LORD commanded: Tomorrow will be a day of complete rest, a holy Sabbath day set apart for the LORD."
+ EXODUS 16:23

The LORD is my shepherd; I have all that I need. He lets me rest in green meadows; he leads me beside peaceful streams. He renews my strength.
+ PSALM 23:1-3

Be still, and know that I am God!
+ PSALM 46:10

IT CAN FEEL challenging and unnatural to force ourselves to stop accomplishing tasks and instead just be present in the moment. Perhaps this is because productivity makes us feel empowered and important; it gives us a sense of purpose. However, throughout the Bible, God encourages—and even commands—his people to have times of stillness and silence with him. Slowing down to spend intentional time with God helps us refocus, gain strength, and remember that God is the one in control. If setting aside your productivity feels hard, try incorporating rest throughout your day in small ways. Walk more slowly, take your time in a conversation you would typically rush through, do one task at a time rather than trying to juggle multiple things, or let go of items on your to-do list. When life gets too busy, ask God what you need to let go of in your schedule so that you can find time to stop and be still.

Prayer Prompts

Lord, my productivity makes me feel . . .
Instead of filling my day with activity, I'm encouraged by your Word to . . .

 promises of God

How does knowing God help me believe his promises?

❧

*I praise your name for your unfailing love and faithfulness;
for your promises are backed by all the honor of your name.*
+ PSALM 138:2

God can be trusted to keep his promise.
+ HEBREWS 10:23

*Jesus Christ, the Son of God, does not waver between "Yes" and "No." . . .
As God's ultimate "Yes," he always does what he says. For all of God's promises
have been fulfilled in Christ with a resounding "Yes!" And through Christ,
our "Amen" (which means "Yes") ascends to God for his glory.*
+ 2 CORINTHIANS 1:19-20

PROMISES hold great power. When they are kept, they put our hearts at ease and give us assurance for the future. When they are broken, they shatter our trust and leave us feeling disheartened and hopeless. God knows the immense power a promise holds and has filled his Word with promises for his people. Learn God's promises and allow them to sink deep into your heart. God can be trusted to keep his promises for two reasons. First, he is truthful and dependable. Second, he is able to carry out what he has promised. Both character and power are crucial, and God possesses them in perfect degree. Even when circumstances lead you to doubt, you can be sure that God's promises will come true. The more you know God, the more his promises will provide you with strength, perseverance, and encouragement.

Prayer Prompts
*Lord, one of your promises I need to hold on to today is . . .
Your Word assures me you keep your promises to . . .*

protection 🍃

Why does God protect some people but not others? How can I trust he will protect me?

— ❧ —

The LORD is my light and my salvation—so why should I be afraid?
The LORD is my fortress, protecting me from danger, so why should I tremble?
+ PSALM 27:1

Through your faith, God is protecting you by his power until you receive
this salvation, which is ready to be revealed on the last day for all to see.
+ 1 PETER 1:5

The LORD says, "I will rescue those who love me.
I will protect those who trust in my name."
+ PSALM 91:14

HOW CAN WE UNDERSTAND God's promises of protection in a world filled with sadness and tragedy? This is a difficult question that we may never be able to fully answer. God's view of protection is much larger and more significant than ours. While God cares for us and our physical safety, he is more concerned about our spiritual protection. When we view our earthly life and eternal future with this perspective, God's protection takes on a much deeper meaning. Bad things will continue to happen in our lifetime, but nothing so bad that it will separate us from him. Sad things will happen too, but nothing so sad that God cannot redeem it. God's protection is a shield for those who have chosen to trust him as their Savior. No matter what happens, God assures us he will watch over our souls and guard them for all eternity. This is our ultimate security and hope.

Prayer Prompts

Lord, I ask you to protect me from . . .
When I feel afraid, your Word gives me hope because it says . . .

 # purity

Sexual purity seems old-fashioned.
Is purity really so important to God?

*Don't you realize that your body is the temple of the Holy Spirit, who lives
in you and was given to you by God? You do not belong to yourself, for God
bought you with a high price. So you must honor God with your body.*
+ 1 CORINTHIANS 6:19-20

*Run from sexual sin! No other sin so clearly affects the body as this one does.
For sexual immorality is a sin against your own body.*
+ 1 CORINTHIANS 6:18

*Let there be no sexual immorality, impurity, or greed among you. . . .
Instead, be filled with the Holy Spirit.*
+ EPHESIANS 5:3, 18

IN A DRAMATIC CONTRAST to culture, Jesus calls his people to a
standard of sexual purity that is very different from the world's.
He calls us to purity in thought as well as in action. This means not
only keeping all sexual acts within marriage but also refraining from
impure thoughts. These specific boundaries for sex are not meant
to frustrate us but rather to protect us. Since our bodies and hearts
are connected, when we think impurely or engage in sexual activity
outside of marriage, we are also causing damage to our hearts. God
knows how good sexuality is when kept within the boundaries he
created for us. Sex outside these boundaries often results in regret,
shame, heartbreak, and damaged intimacy. To walk in freedom
with a free conscience, ask God to help you live a pure life and be
an example to a culture that holds a distorted view of sexuality.

Prayer Prompts
Lord, sometimes culture tempts me to believe that . . .
Your Word tells me that purity is important because . . .

257

purpose

How can I lead a purposeful life?

---- ❧ ----

I cry out to God Most High, to God who will fulfill his purpose for me.
+ PSALM 57:2

*Always work enthusiastically for the Lord, for you
know that nothing you do for the Lord is ever useless.*
+ 1 CORINTHIANS 15:58

A spiritual gift is given to each of us so we can help each other.
+ 1 CORINTHIANS 12:7

*The LORD has told you what is good, and this is what he requires of you:
to do what is right, to love mercy, and to walk humbly with your God.*
+ MICAH 6:8

GOD HAS both a general purpose and a specific purpose for us.
Our general purpose is to love others as Jesus has loved us.
More specifically, God has also given each of us spiritual gifts and
wants us to use them to make a unique contribution in our own
sphere of influence. God has placed us in our countries, neighborhoods, and homes for a specific purpose. And he has given us special
gifts to love those around us. Sometimes we feel like we need to do
big things for God to fulfill our purpose. But most often, we can follow God by obeying him in ways that feel small: telling others about
what God has done in our lives, working enthusiastically, doing what
is right, loving mercy, obeying his Word, and caring for the needy.
When you're not sure what God's purpose is for you, ask him to help
you find meaning in purpose as you obey him in small ways.

Prayer Prompts

Lord, I struggle with feeling purposeful when . . .
Your Word assures me I have purpose today because . . .

pursuit

How does God pursue me?

—— ✿ ——

See how very much our Father loves us,
for he calls us his children, and that is what we are!
+ 1 JOHN 3:1

This is how God loved the world: He gave his one and only Son, so
that everyone who believes in him will not perish but have eternal life.
+ JOHN 3:16

Since our friendship with God was restored by the death of his Son while we
were still his enemies, we will certainly be saved through the life of his Son.
+ ROMANS 5:10

I have loved you, my people, with an everlasting love.
With unfailing love I have drawn you to myself.
+ JEREMIAH 31:3

JUST AS A MOTHER longs to have a relationship with her child, so
God longs to have a relationship with us. And similar to a parent,
he wants to spend time with us, talk with us, show us his love, and
offer us the best life possible. He pursues us not to get something but
to give us something wonderful: help, hope, joy, peace, and eternal
life. God calls everyone to turn away from sin and turn to a loving
relationship with him. While he gives each person the freedom to
choose how to respond to his love, his desire is that no one reject
him. And because God is so loving, he convicts us of wrongful ways
and guides us back to the right path. You are worthy of being pur-
sued, not because of what you do but because of who you are as a
daughter of God.

Prayer Prompts
Lord, knowing that you pursue me makes me feel . . .
Your Word assures me that you pursue me because . . .

questions 🍃

Is it wrong to question God's plans
and actions in my life?

— ∞ —

*Moses said to the LORD, "You have been telling me, 'Take these people up
to the Promised Land.' But you haven't told me whom you will send with
me. You have told me, 'I know you by name, and I look favorably on you.'
If it is true that you look favorably on me, let me know your ways so I may
understand you more fully and continue to enjoy your favor. And remember
that this nation is your very own people." The LORD replied, "I will personally
go with you, Moses, and I will give you rest—everything will be fine for you."*
+ EXODUS 33:12-14

*If you need wisdom, ask our generous God, and he will give it to you.
He will not rebuke you for asking.*
+ JAMES 1:5

BEFORE THE EXODUS, God revealed a plan to Moses without
explaining how it would unfold. Moses knew what God had
promised, but he became concerned when he didn't know the details
of how those promises would be fulfilled. Despite Moses' impatience,
God was patient, reminding Moses that he was with him and that
what he had promised would happen. God doesn't always yield all of
the details of how a plan will play out, but he gives us an even better
answer: "Don't worry about the details. I am with you and will help
you." If you are questioning God's actions, perhaps it is time for an
honest conversation with him. Bringing tough questions to God in
prayer actually draws us closer to him. God invites your honesty and
heartfelt questions; he will not rebuke you for asking.

Prayer Prompts
Lord, sometimes I wonder why . . .
Even when I question, your Word reminds me . . .

❧ quietness

Why are times of quietness important?

— ❧ —

Jesus said, "Let's go off by ourselves to a quiet place and rest awhile." He said this because there were so many people coming and going that Jesus and his apostles didn't even have time to eat. So they left by boat for a quiet place.
+ MARK 6:31-32

"Go out and stand before me on the mountain," the LORD told [Elijah]. . . . The LORD passed by, and a mighty windstorm hit the mountain. It was such a terrible blast that the rocks were torn loose, but the LORD was not in the wind. After the wind there was an earthquake, but the LORD was not in the earthquake. And after the earthquake there was a fire, but the LORD was not in the fire. And after the fire there was the sound of a gentle whisper.
+ 1 KINGS 19:11-12

Let all that I am wait quietly before God, for my hope is in him.
+ PSALM 62:5

QUIETNESS can feel unfamiliar and even uncomfortable. However, when we quiet the inner and outer voices around us, we are able to hear God's voice more clearly. People think that God speaks in a booming voice from heaven, but most often he speaks to people in the silence. It can be difficult to hear God when our days are filled with noise, interruptions, and distractions. Find a quiet moment with God today. It can be in your bedroom, while you're driving, or even when you're in the shower. Talk to him about what is on your heart, and then listen. As you spend time in silence with God, he slowly teaches you to recognize his voice.

Prayer Prompts

Lord, I need a quiet moment with you to . . .
Your Word says quiet moments are important because . . .

quitting 🍂

How do I know when to keep going and when it's time to quit?

— ❧ —

David continued, "Be strong and courageous, and do the work. Don't be afraid or discouraged, for the LORD God, my God, is with you. He will not fail you or forsake you."
+ 1 CHRONICLES 28:20

We are pressed on every side by troubles, but we are not crushed. We are perplexed, but not driven to despair. . . . We know that God, who raised the Lord Jesus, will also raise us with Jesus and present us to himself together with you. . . . That is why we never give up.
+ 2 CORINTHIANS 4:8, 14, 16

Let's not get tired of doing what is good. At just the right time we will reap a harvest of blessing if we don't give up.
+ GALATIANS 6:9

NO ONE WANTS to be a quitter. However, there are times when it's appropriate to let go and times when we should keep going—and it is wise to know the difference. It is time to quit when we are doing something wrong or are hurting ourselves or others. Even if our behavior is not inherently wrong, if an activity takes too much time and attention away from God and others, then we need to let it go. However, if God has called us to a task, we shouldn't give up when it gets difficult. Just because God asks us to do something doesn't mean it will be easy. If your task is focused on and for God and you know that he is taking you in a certain direction, don't give up when it gets tough. Keep moving forward with faith.

Prayer Prompts

Lord, I am struggling with whether it is time to give up or keep going with . . . But your Word gives me this wisdom: . . .

 # reassurance

I have prayed and accepted Christ as my Savior, but how can I be sure I'm saved?

———————— ❦ ————————

If you openly declare that Jesus is Lord and believe in your heart that God raised him from the dead, you will be saved. For it is by believing in your heart that you are made right with God, and it is by openly declaring your faith that you are saved.
+ ROMANS 10:9-10

Then he said to Thomas, "Put your finger here, and look at my hands. Put your hand into the wound in my side. Don't be faithless any longer. Believe!" "My Lord and my God!" Thomas exclaimed. Then Jesus told him, "You believe because you have seen me. Blessed are those who believe without seeing me."
+ JOHN 20:27-29

"What do you mean, 'If I can'?" Jesus asked. "Anything is possible if a person believes." The father instantly cried out, "I do believe, but help me overcome my unbelief!"
+ MARK 9:23-24

WHEN DOUBT about our salvation creeps into our minds, we can be left desperate for reassurance. During these times, God's promises can soothe our fears and offer us the encouragement we need. If you have accepted God's forgiveness of your sin and believe in your heart that Jesus is Lord and Savior, you are saved. Our salvation doesn't depend on how confident we are, how much we trust God, or our degree of faith—it depends on Jesus. However, Jesus promises blessings to those with great faith. If you are in a season of doubt, ask the Lord to help your unbelief.

Prayer Prompts

Lord, I'm tempted to doubt my salvation when . . .
When I doubt, your Word reassures me that . . .

reconciliation 🍃

Why it important to God that I'm at peace with others?

— ❧ —

*If you are presenting a sacrifice at the altar in the Temple and
you suddenly remember that someone has something against you,
leave your sacrifice there at the altar. Go and be reconciled to that person.
Then come and offer your sacrifice to God.*
+ MATTHEW 5:23-24

*God was in Christ, reconciling the world to himself, no longer counting people's
sins against them. And he gave us this wonderful message of reconciliation.*
+ 2 CORINTHIANS 5:19

God blesses those who work for peace, for they will be called the children of God.
+ MATTHEW 5:9

RECONCILIATION is at the heart of what it means to follow
Jesus. Jesus suffered the agony of the Cross to redeem sinful
human beings and reconcile them to a holy God. Our reconciliation
with God is a picture of how we are to be reconciled with others.
Harmony in human relationships is so important that Jesus even
commands us to leave worship to reconcile with the people in our
lives with whom we have conflict. It's clear that unresolved conflict
actually hinders our relationship with God. Is there anyone in your
life with whom Jesus wants you to pursue reconciliation? If so,
remember that even if he or she does not accept your attempts to
reconcile, it will please God that you tried. It's never easy to be the
person who takes the high road, but God promises that if you do,
you will experience his love, peace, and goodness in your life.

Prayer Prompts

Lord, I know I must reconcile with . . .
Your Word reminds me that reconciliation is important because . . .

 # redemption

How can God possibly redeem the bad choices I've made?

—— ❧ ——

I have swept away your sins like a cloud. I have scattered your offenses like the morning mist. Oh, return to me, for I have paid the price to set you free.
+ ISAIAH 44:22

Though your sins are like scarlet, I will make them as white as snow. Though they are red like crimson, I will make them as white as wool.
+ ISAIAH 1:18

You have turned my mourning into joyful dancing. You have taken away my clothes of mourning and clothed me with joy.
+ PSALM 30:11

We know that God causes everything to work together for the good of those who love God and are called according to his purpose for them.
+ ROMANS 8:28

REDEMPTION resonates deeply with the human heart; we love seeing good come out of bad situations. Perhaps it is because we long for the broken pieces in our own lives to somehow be made whole. This is exactly what God promises to those who trust in Jesus as their Savior. They are 100 percent forgiven, made clean and holy, restored to right relationship with him, and guaranteed eternal life. No matter how messy, broken, or dirty your life is, God is able to use it for his good. If this truth is difficult for you to accept, reflect on the promises in God's Word. Trust that as time passes, you will experience him bringing beauty out of your life that you never thought possible.

Prayer Prompts

Lord, I wonder how you will redeem these wrong choices I've made: . . .
Your Word promises me that you are able to . . .

rejection

Will God ever reject me?

———— ✦ ————

Jesus stood up again and said to the woman, "Where are your accusers? Didn't even one of them condemn you?" "No, Lord," she said. And Jesus said, "Neither do I. Go and sin no more."
+ JOHN 8:10-11

This High Priest of ours understands our weaknesses, for he faced all of the same testings we do, yet he did not sin. So let us come boldly to the throne of our gracious God. There we will receive his mercy, and we will find grace to help us when we need it most.
+ HEBREWS 4:15-16

The LORD will not reject his people; he will not abandon his special possession.
+ PSALM 94:14

ONE OF THE GREATEST struggles for many women is the fear of rejection. Perhaps this is because rejection confirms the biggest lie that Satan whispers in our ear—that we aren't good enough. However, we never need to worry about this with God. We can approach God knowing he gladly welcomes us and will always accept us. God's voice will never say, "Sorry, you just don't measure up" or "If only you had tried a little harder." He always listens, always hears, always responds, and always loves. Even at your weakest moment, he does not reject you but rather embraces and strengthens you to be all he intends you to be. If you worry about God rejecting you, remind yourself of this truth from Scripture: You are his special possession, and he promises never to abandon you.

Prayer Prompts

Lord, sometimes I fear you will reject me if I . . .
Your Word opposes this lie by assuring me that . . .

 # relationship

What does a relationship with God actually look like?

❧

Surely your goodness and unfailing love will pursue me all the days of my life.
+ PSALM 23:6

Long ago the LORD said to Israel: "I have loved you, my people, with an everlasting love. With unfailing love I have drawn you to myself."
+ JEREMIAH 31:3

When the cool evening breezes were blowing, the man and his wife heard the LORD God walking about in the garden. So they hid from the LORD God among the trees. Then the LORD God called to the man, "Where are you?"
+ GENESIS 3:8-9

ADAM AND EVE disobeyed God and rebelled against God. And yet the first thing God did after they sinned was pursue them to restore their relationship. Although Adam and Eve would have to experience the consequences of their actions, God had no intention of severing his connection with them. It's hard to imagine this kind of unconditional love, which pursues us no matter what we have done. When we do wrong, or when we reject God, he does not give up on us but rather pursues us for the purpose of forgiving us and restoring us to a right relationship with him. This is the very essence of why you were created—to be in relationship with God and to experience his goodness, presence, and unfailing love. God's faithful pursuit is a beautiful call to friendship with him.

Prayer Prompts

Lord, I describe my relationship with you as . . .
Your Word uses these words to show what relationship with you is like: . . .

relevance 🍃

Are God's promises still relevant to my life today?

———— ❧ ————

The LORD your God will personally go ahead of you.
He will neither fail you nor abandon you.
+ DEUTERONOMY 31:6

If we confess our sins to him, he is faithful and
just to forgive us our sins and to cleanse us from all wickedness.
+ 1 JOHN 1:9

We have peace with God because of what
Jesus Christ our Lord has done for us.
+ ROMANS 5:1

GOD'S PROMISES are not only for his people in general; they are for us *personally*. Maybe you are in a season of great joy and blessing. Or perhaps you are in a place of great anxiety, fear, grief, and stress. No matter what season you are in, God has assurances he wants to communicate to you through the promises in his Word. How would your life be different if you really believed all God's promises? You would probably be a more confident, peaceful, courageous, and secure woman. The more you meditate and reflect on God's promises, the more you will see real change in your life. And because God's Word is eternal for all times and ages, his promises are perfectly relevant to you today. Take heart that the one who loves you has promised wonderful things for your future.

Prayer Prompts
Lord, when I apply your promises to my personal life, I feel . . .
The one promise from your Word I want to hold on to today is . . .

# religion

Why does religion sometimes feel burdensome?

❧

I hate all your show and pretense—the hypocrisy of your religious festivals and solemn assemblies. . . . Instead, I want to see a mighty flood of justice, an endless river of righteous living.
✛ AMOS 5:21, 24

The Lord says, "These people say they are mine. They honor me with their lips, but their hearts are far from me. And their worship of me is nothing but man-made rules learned by rote."
✛ ISAIAH 29:13

If you claim to be religious but don't control your tongue, you are fooling yourself, and your religion is worthless. Pure and genuine religion in the sight of God the Father means caring for orphans and widows in their distress and refusing to let the world corrupt you.
✛ JAMES 1:26-27

Now we live in fellowship with the true God because we live in fellowship with his Son, Jesus Christ. He is the only true God, and he is eternal life.
✛ 1 JOHN 5:20

SOMETIMES FAITH gets reduced to a list of rules and religious obligations. Perhaps we do this to feel in control of our lives or because keeping the rules makes us feel "good enough." When the focus of our faith is on rituals instead of relationship, religion feels empty. God longs for us to pursue a deep relationship with him. As our hearts connect with the one true God, our lives then overflow with love and acts of devotion to him. Talk to God and receive his grace as he invites you to exchange empty rules for a true relationship with him.

Prayer Prompts

Lord, my religion feels burdensome when . . .
Your Word encourages me to let go of empty rules by . . . remembering

remembering

What can help me remember God's work in my past?

---- ❦ ----

Watch out! Be careful never to forget what you yourself have seen.
Do not let these memories escape from your mind as long as you live!
And be sure to pass them on to your children and grandchildren.
+ DEUTERONOMY 4:9

Remember the things I have done in the past. For I alone am God!
I am God, and there is none like me.
+ ISAIAH 46:9

Let all that I am praise the LORD;
may I never forget the good things he does for me.
+ PSALM 103:2

He causes us to remember his wonderful works.
How gracious and merciful is our LORD!
+ PSALM 111:4

As HUMANS, we tend to forget God's blessings and goodness, especially during difficult seasons. That is why God instructs us to remember the good things he has done: so that we will never forget his faithfulness. If you need reminders of God's work in the past, ask yourself, *How has God answered previous prayers? What was one unexpected gift he has given me? When was a time when he allowed me to experience his presence?* Answering these questions will help you gain perspective and encouragement, no matter what difficulty you are going through. Set aside time to remember God's work in the past in order to find hope for the future.

Prayer Prompts

Lord, a time when I especially felt your presence and answer to prayer was . . .
Your Word encourages me when I remember how you . . .

 # renewal

My life is a mess, and I wish I could start over again. How can I experience renewal?

———————————— ❧ ————————————

Create in me a clean heart, O God. Renew a loyal spirit within me.
+ PSALM 51:10

I will give you a new heart, and I will put a new spirit in you. I will take out your stony, stubborn heart and give you a tender, responsive heart.
+ EZEKIEL 36:26

Throw off your old sinful nature and your former way of life, which is corrupted by lust and deception. Instead, let the Spirit renew your thoughts and attitudes. Put on your new nature, created to be like God—truly righteous and holy.
+ EPHESIANS 4:22-24

Anyone who belongs to Christ has become a new person. The old life is gone; a new life has begun!
+ 2 CORINTHIANS 5:17

ISN'T IT TRUE that we are often harder on ourselves than on anyone else? God doesn't beat us up for our mistakes and shortcomings, so why should we? God is a huge fan of second chances, third chances, fourth chances, and more. Every day begins with fresh mercy and grace. No matter what circumstances have caused you to feel like a mess, God promises that he is faithful to forgive and help you start over. Those who don't want his forgiveness are beyond its reach. But a heart that truly wants to change is a heart that is ready for the kind of renewal only God's Spirit can bring. Accept his help and watch how his power shines best through your weakness.

Prayer Prompts

Lord, starting over feels impossible because . . .
Your Word promises this for those who desire to be renewed: . . .

repentance 🍃

What is repentance and why is it so important?

———————————— ❧ ————————————

When I refused to confess my sin, my body wasted away, and
I groaned all day long. Day and night your hand of discipline was
heavy on me. My strength evaporated like water in the summer heat.
Finally, I confessed all my sins to you and stopped trying to hide
my guilt. I said to myself, "I will confess my rebellion to the LORD."
And you forgave me! All my guilt is gone.
+ PSALM 32:3-5

There is joy in the presence of God's angels when even one sinner repents.
+ LUKE 15:10

REPENTANCE is the decision to make a U-turn away from
the wrong and toward the good. Sometimes we take a wrong
turn in life and end up on a dangerous path. But admitting our sin
before God can change the direction of our lives. Repentance has
the power to remove our guilt, restore our joy, and heal our broken
souls. When we have truly repentant hearts, we feel remorse for our
sin and want to commit to a new way of life—that of serving God.
When God forgives our sins, our life journey moves to a new direction without looking back. Do you long to turn away from something in order to turn back to God? His Word promises that he will
show mercy and great patience to those who come back to him. It
only takes one step.

Prayer Prompts

Lord, I know I need to repent from . . .
Your Word says if I turn away from sin and toward you, I will experience . . .

# reputation

Is it biblical to care what others think about me?

+ ≪ +

We are traveling together to guard against any criticism. . . .
We are careful to be honorable before the Lord, but
we also want everyone else to see that we are honorable.
+ 2 CORINTHIANS 8:20-21

Store my commands in your heart. . . . Never let loyalty and kindness
leave you! Tie them around your neck as a reminder. Write them deep
within your heart. Then you will find favor with both God and people,
and you will earn a good reputation.
+ PROVERBS 3:1, 3-4

You are the light of the world—like a city on a hilltop that cannot be hidden.
+ MATTHEW 5:14

SOME PEOPLE care too much about what others think of them. Others couldn't care less about the opinion of those around them. How does God want us to view our reputation? His Word says having a good reputation is honorable. It is important to work hard, be kind and loyal, and live morally excellent lives—not to please others, but to please God. Our relationship with God determines our reputation; our focus on loving God and loving others will become what we are known for. If you care too much about the opinions of others, remind yourself that what matters most is not what others think of you but what God thinks of you. And if you care too little about your reputation, remember that God calls you to be a light to those around you.

Prayer Prompts

Lord, I want to be known for . . .
Your Word says the way to gain a good reputation is by . . .

rescue

What can I do when I long to be rescued from something in my life?

———————— ❧ ————————

We put our hope in the LORD. He is our help and our shield.
+ PSALM 33:20

*The LORD replies, "I have seen violence done to the helpless,
and I have heard the groans of the poor. Now I will rise up
to rescue them, as they have longed for me to do."*
+ PSALM 12:5

*Don't be afraid. Just stand still and watch the LORD rescue you. . . .
The LORD himself will fight for you.*
+ EXODUS 14:13-14

*Jesus gave his life for our sins, just as God our Father planned,
in order to rescue us from this evil world in which we live.*
+ GALATIANS 1:4

IS THERE SOMETHING you need to be rescued from? Maybe you long to be free from an impossible situation, a certain person, or even your own sin. Instead of trying to escape your circumstances, come to God. Ask him to rescue you and protect you. God promises to help us, save us, defend us, and protect us in everything we face. God also promises he will ultimately rescue those who believe in him from this evil world. The next time you wonder whether God can rescue you, remember that through his Son, he already has.

Prayer Prompts

Lord, I long for you to rescue me from . . .
Your Word gives me hope and comfort because it says . . .

 # resentment

How can I keep my heart from resentment and bitterness?

— ❧ —

When you are praying, first forgive anyone you are holding a grudge against, so that your Father in heaven will forgive your sins, too.
+ MARK 11:25

Don't grumble about each other, brothers and sisters, or you will be judged. For look—the Judge is standing at the door!
+ JAMES 5:9

Look after each other so that none of you fails to receive the grace of God. Watch out that no poisonous root of bitterness grows up to trouble you, corrupting many.
+ HEBREWS 12:15

WHEN ANOTHER PERSON has wronged us, sometimes we protect ourselves by reacting to the situation with anger rather than with sadness. However, when we allow anger to linger within our hearts, it results in resentment. God doesn't promise we won't be betrayed, misunderstood, or unappreciated in this world. Each one of us will have our feelings hurt. But the key to keeping our hearts from resentment and bitterness is the power of forgiveness. It is not easy to forgive someone who has caused us pain. But if we choose to resent instead of forgive, the Bible warns us that our souls will be in danger. Is there resentment in your heart today? Whom might God be calling you to forgive in order to experience freedom? Ask God to help you let go of your grudges and choose the path of forgiveness. If forgiveness feels impossible, reflect on all the times your Father has forgiven you.

Prayer Prompts

Lord, I still feel angry about . . .
To keep my anger from turning to resentment, Your Word reminds me . . .

respect 🍃

How can I become a woman others respect?

— ❦ —

Whoever wants to be a leader among you must be your servant.
+ MATTHEW 20:26

[Jesus] must become greater and greater, and I must become less and less.
+ JOHN 3:30

There will be glory and honor and peace from God for all who do good.
+ ROMANS 2:10

Charm is deceptive, and beauty does not last;
but a woman who fears the LORD will be greatly praised.
+ PROVERBS 31:30

AS WOMEN, we sometimes believe that we'll receive respect when we look good from the outside—like when our homes are tidy, our children are obedient, or we are successful in our careers. These external things might cause others to envy us, but they won't bring real respect. Respect comes from serving rather than being served, taking responsibility for our actions instead of trying to save face in front of others, speaking up against injustice instead of blending in with the group, building others up instead of trying to make ourselves look good. The world teaches us to look beautiful at all costs, to speak with irreverence, and to live by what's best for us. These self-centered practices may bring us attention but not anything deeper. True respect is reserved for people who consistently practice kindness, live with integrity, and are motivated by a deep love for others. The more you reflect the character of God, the more you will become the kind of woman who earns genuine respect.

Prayer Prompts

Lord, sometimes I try to gain the respect of others by . . .
Your Word reminds me that real respect comes from . . .

🌿 responsibility

How much responsibility do I bear for my actions? Sometimes I feel like I can't help doing certain things.

———————— ❧ ————————

Do not let sin control the way you live; do not give in to sinful desires. . . .
Sin is no longer your master, for you no longer live under the
requirements of the law. Instead, you live under the freedom of God's grace.
+ ROMANS 6:12, 14

Don't you realize that you become the slave of whatever you choose
to obey? You can be a slave to sin, which leads to death, or
you can choose to obey God, which leads to righteous living.
+ ROMANS 6:16

[The LORD God asked,] "Have you eaten from the tree whose
fruit I commanded you not to eat?" The man replied, "It was
the woman you gave me who gave me the fruit, and I ate it."
+ GENESIS 3:11-12

ONE OF SATAN'S GREAT LIES is that we are victims who have no power to resist our impulses. In reality, everything we do is the result of choices we make, and we are responsible for those choices. While it's hard to resist certain temptations and always make good decisions, blaming others for our bad choices hinders us from lives of freedom and happiness. The good news is that God is more powerful than anything that tries to control us. Whenever you feel powerless to resist your impulses or trapped in your sin, stop and pray for God's help. The more you move toward God in moments of temptation, the more you move away from your temptation. God can break the chains that hold you and help you develop the strength to say no.

Prayer Prompts

Lord, sometimes I use this excuse for my sinful actions: . . .
Your Word encourages me to take responsibility for my actions by . . .

rest

Why is rest so important for me?

※

*In six days the Lord made heaven and earth, but
on the seventh day he stopped working and was refreshed.*
+ EXODUS 31:17

*The Lord is my shepherd; I have all that I need. He lets me rest in green
meadows; he leads me beside peaceful streams. He renews my strength.*
+ PSALM 23:1-3

*It is useless for you to work so hard from early morning until late at night,
anxiously working for food to eat; for God gives rest to his loved ones.*
+ PSALM 127:2

*Jesus said, "Come to me, all of you who are weary and
carry heavy burdens, and I will give you rest."*
+ MATTHEW 11:28

MANY OF US see rest as a luxury we can't afford. However, God's Word is clear that we can't afford *not* to rest. One of the most important things we can do for our bodies, minds, and souls is to rest with God. When we sit with him quietly, he ministers to us by refreshing our souls. Make time to receive from him. What gives you rest? Reading a book? Going for a run? Cooking? Invite God into that restful activity by praying, "Lord, you are with me in this moment. I am so thankful you care about giving me the rest you know I need." Work hard and make the most of every opportunity, but don't forget to prioritize rest. If it's important to God's heart, it ought to be important to ours, too.

Prayer Prompts

Lord, the idea of setting aside time to rest makes me feel . . .
Your Word reminds me that rest is important because . . .

🍂 restoration

How does God restore me to himself after I have sinned?

———————— ❧ ————————

"My wayward children," says the LORD, "come back to me,
and I will heal your wayward hearts."
    + JEREMIAH 3:22

You will have compassion on us. You will trample our sins
under your feet and throw them into the depths of the ocean!
    + MICAH 7:19

Though your sins are like scarlet, I will make them as white as snow.
Though they are red like crimson, I will make them as white as wool.
    + ISAIAH 1:18

I will forgive their wickedness, and I will never again remember their sins.
    + HEBREWS 8:12

WHEN WE HURT SOMEONE, it often takes time to restore the relationship. Sometimes others hold grudges, frequently bring up past offenses, or refuse to forgive us. This is not how God responds when we confess our sins and ask for his forgiveness. His Word gives many different images for what happens when he forgives: He tramples our sin under his feet, he throws it into the ocean depths, he removes the stain of our sin, and he never remembers it again. His forgiveness means he has restored our relationship as though we had never sinned. What a gracious and merciful God! Do you long to experience a restored relationship with God? All you need to do is ask. He is always eager to bring you back to him.

Prayer Prompts

Lord, I confess that I have sinned by . . .
Your Word assures me that you want to restore me by . . .

risks

How do I decide when to take a risk and when to play it safe?

———————— ❦ ————————

Be careful then, dear brothers and sisters. Make sure that your own hearts are not evil and unbelieving, turning you away from the living God.
+ HEBREWS 3:12

Listen, O Israel! The LORD is our God, the LORD alone. And you must love the LORD your God with all your heart, all your soul, and all your strength.
+ DEUTERONOMY 6:4-5

Commit everything you do to the LORD. Trust him, and he will help you.
+ PSALM 37:5

GOD'S WORD gives clear warnings to guide us away from risky behaviors that could be hurtful and destructive. But God also encourages us to take certain risks that will result in healthy and godly lives. For these things, God's Word tells us to go ahead and take a chance. God might say, "Go ahead. Start a conversation with that person, take that mission trip, accept that job, help that friend, take on that challenge." But before you do, ask yourself, *Does what I think God is saying align with his Word?* and *Is my motive behind this risk to serve God or serve myself?* Taking the risks that help you grow in your faith and avoiding risks that will harm your relationship with God will turn your life into a healthy and exciting adventure.

Prayer Prompts

Lord, I need wisdom about whether I should take this risk: . . .
Your Word tells me that before I act, I must make sure my heart is . . .

🍂 romance

How can I keep romance alive in my marriage?

———————— ❧ ————————

*Come, my love, let us go out to the fields and spend the night among
the wildflowers. Let us get up early and go to the vineyards to see if
the grapevines have budded, if the blossoms have opened, and if the
pomegranates have bloomed. There I will give you my love.*
+ SONG OF SONGS 7:11-12

*Love never gives up, never loses faith,
is always hopeful, and endures through every circumstance.*
+ 1 CORINTHIANS 13:7

Live a life filled with love, following the example of Christ.
+ EPHESIANS 5:2

Love each other with genuine affection, and take delight in honoring each other.
+ ROMANS 12:10

THOSE OF US who are married probably believed that romance
would always be a part of our marriages. But over the years that
feeling of romance sometimes fades. Yet the truth is, love is not a feeling—it is a choice. On our wedding day, we didn't promise to always
feel in love. We promised to *choose* to love each other with our words,
actions, and faithfulness. How can you choose to love your husband
today? Can you surprise him with something unexpected and spon-
taneous? Stick a love note on the bathroom mirror? Call him just to
tell him you love him? What would it be like to show love to your
spouse in a tangible way, without expecting something in return? Just
as God pursues you with his unconditional love, romance is the art of
pursuing your mate with that same unconditional love.

Prayer Prompts

Lord, help me show romantic love to my husband today by . . .
Your Word specifically encourages me to love my spouse by . . .

Sabbath 🍃

Why is it so important to God that I take a day off work?

---- ❧ ----

On the seventh day God had finished his work of creation, so he rested from all his work. And God blessed the seventh day and declared it holy, because it was the day when he rested from all his work of creation.
+ GENESIS 2:2-3

Remember to observe the Sabbath day by keeping it holy. You have six days each week for your ordinary work, but the seventh day is a Sabbath day of rest dedicated to the LORD your God.
+ EXODUS 20:8-10

The Sabbath was made to meet the needs of people, and not people to meet the requirements of the Sabbath.
+ MARK 2:27

WE LIVE IN AN AGE of anxiety, stress, and perpetual motion. How ironic that we actually take pride in explaining how busy we are. God did not intend for his people to live in this state of frenzied activity. Throughout the entire Bible, it is clear from God's words and example that he wants us to set aside time for rest and refreshment to restore both body and soul. God, in ceasing from his work, called his rest "holy." God knows that no matter how much we may like our work, it takes a toll on our minds, bodies, and souls. Sabbath gives us permission to let go of our to-do lists for twenty-four hours and trust God with the things left undone. Don't miss out on restorative moments with God that can only be experienced through regular rhythms of worship and rest.

Prayer Prompts

Lord, it's hard for me to take a day of rest because . . .
Your Word calls me to take a Sabbath rest because . . .

 # sacredness

When is something sacred?
What does it mean to be sacred?

————— ❧ —————

Finally, they made the sacred medallion—the badge of holiness—of pure gold.
They engraved it like a seal with these words: HOLY TO THE LORD.
+ EXODUS 39:30

Do not make idols or set up carved images, or sacred pillars.
+ LEVITICUS 26:1

Don't you realize that your body is the temple of the Holy Spirit . . . ?
+ 1 CORINTHIANS 6:19

May the God of peace make you holy in every way, and may your whole spirit
and soul and body be kept blameless until our Lord Jesus Christ comes again.
+ 1 THESSALONIANS 5:23

SACRED **MEANS SET APART** to be used by God for a holy purpose. When objects are deemed sacred, it usually means they are
regarded with respect and honor and used in worship. The sacred
medallion we read about in Exodus 39:30 served as a visual reminder
to the Israelites that the high priest was set apart as God's appointed
servant for bringing them into God's holy presence. What places or
objects are kept sacred in your life as a reminder of who God is? Your
church? Your home? Your Bible and journal? Remember, *you* are also
set apart for God. Your body is the dwelling place of the Holy Spirit.
Dedicate yourself, your home, and the things in it to be used to glorify
God. When you commit everything you are and have to God's purposes, all of life becomes a sacred act of worship to him.

Prayer Prompts

Lord, a sacred space or item in my home is . . .
Your Word reminds me that the purpose of this sacred thing is to . . .

sacrifice 🍃

How can I become more willing to sacrifice for others?

———— ✦ ————

Lay your hand on the animal's head, and the Lord will accept its death in your place to purify you, making you right with him.
+ LEVITICUS 1:4

The law of Moses was unable to save us because of the weakness of our sinful nature. So God did what the law could not do. He sent his own Son in a body like the bodies we sinners have. And in that body God declared an end to sin's control over us by giving his Son as a sacrifice for our sins.
+ ROMANS 8:3

This is real love—not that we loved God, but that he loved us and sent his Son as a sacrifice to take away our sins.
+ 1 JOHN 4:10

IT CAN FEEL EXHAUSTING to continually sacrifice our time, desires, comfort, or finances for others. If we look only at the sacrifice involved, it will be impossible to have a good attitude. Sacrifice does not just involve giving things up; rather, it is a kind of substitution. We give up one thing to obtain something of greater value. Every time we sacrifice for another, our hearts are shaped more and more like God's heart. He uses your sacrifices to shape you into a woman who is more loving, selfless, and generous. God sacrificed what was most precious to him, his Son, so that you would be saved from your sins and be made right with him. Anytime you make a sacrifice by giving something up for someone else, you are reminded, in some small way, of God's greatest sacrifice of all.

Prayer Prompts

Lord, it is hard for me to sacrifice these specific things for others: . . .
Your Word reminds me of your sacrifice for me when you . . .

 # safety

I often feel afraid that something will happen to my loved ones. Is it wrong to worry about their safety?

The LORD is good, a strong refuge when trouble comes.
He is close to those who trust in him.
✦ NAHUM 1:7

He will feed his flock like a shepherd. He will carry
the lambs in his arms, holding them close to his heart.
He will gently lead the mother sheep with their young.
✦ ISAIAH 40:11

If God cares so wonderfully for wildflowers that are here today
and thrown into the fire tomorrow, he will certainly care for you.
Why do you have so little faith?
✦ MATTHEW 6:30

Such love has no fear, because perfect love expels all fear.
✦ 1 JOHN 4:18

WHEN WE LOVE PEOPLE deeply, our fears for them can run just as deep. But fear is never from God; it is a tactic Satan uses to hurt us. Fear tries to break our relationships, our hearts, our hope, and our connection to God. But the only thing greater than the power of fear is the power of love. And the Bible describes God's love for his people as perfect and able to expel all fear. So when fear for another's safety grips your heart, use it as a reminder to pray. The power of prayer leads us to experience the power of God's love. When we meditate on how much God loves us and our loved ones, our worries over their safety lose their power.

Prayer Prompts

Lord, I often worry about the safety of . . .
When I feel afraid, I meditate on these truths from your Word: . . .

salvation 🔖

If I am saved, does that mean I am free to do what I want?

─────── ✑ ───────

We know that our old sinful selves were crucified with Christ so that sin might lose its power in our lives. We are no longer slaves to sin. For when we died with Christ we were set free from the power of sin.
+ ROMANS 6:6-7

Anyone who belongs to Christ has become a new person. The old life is gone; a new life has begun!
+ 2 CORINTHIANS 5:17

Dear friends, let us continue to love one another, for love comes from God. Anyone who loves is a child of God and knows God. But anyone who does not love does not know God, for God is love.
+ 1 JOHN 4:7-8

THE ANCIENT church father Augustine famously said, "Love God and do whatever you please." We are free to do what we want, but those who truly love God and have accepted his beautiful gift of salvation will not want to do anything that would hurt him. When we accept Jesus Christ as Lord, we have a guaranteed inheritance of eternal life in a perfect world, with everything we could want or need. And when we truly grasp this truth, it will change the way we live. We will no longer feel the need to live for this world and the empty promises it holds for us. Instead, our hearts will live for eternity and for the one we will spend it with. Ask God to give you a heart that truly seeks and loves him, and watch how he aligns your desires with his.

Prayer Prompts

Lord, when I really stop to think about the gift of salvation, I feel . . .
Your Word reminds me of these promises to those who are saved: . . .

 # satisfaction

Why can't I ever feel satisfied with my life?

———— ❧ ————

You don't have what you want because you don't ask God for it.
And even when you ask, you don't get it because your motives are
all wrong—you want only what will give you pleasure.
+ JAMES 4:2-3

Let them praise the LORD for his great love and for the wonderful things he has
done for them. For he satisfies the thirsty and fills the hungry with good things.
+ PSALM 107:8-9

O God, you are my God. . . . My soul thirsts for you. . . .
You satisfy me more than the richest feast.
+ PSALM 63:1, 5

GOD HAS PLACED a longing for heaven inside of every human heart. C. S. Lewis states, "If we find ourselves with a desire that nothing in this world can satisfy, the most probable explanation is that we were made for another world." Nothing on this earth will bring true fulfillment or lasting happiness. The Bible promises over and over that only God is able to fully satisfy—to meet that deep emptiness inside us that longs to be filled. Only a relationship with him can lead to a life that is truly rich and satisfying. If you feel unsatisfied with life, perhaps it is because you doubt that God is enough. The next time you find yourself longing for more, come to God with your disappointments. Remember his promises to satisfy those who believe in him and continually strive to know him.

Prayer Prompts

Lord, I have not found satisfaction in . . .
Your Word promises that I can have a satisfied soul when . . .

secrets 🍃

Is it always a bad thing to keep secrets?

― ❧ ―

*When you pray, go away by yourself, shut the door behind you, and pray to
your Father in private. Then your Father, who sees everything, will reward you.*
+ MATTHEW 6:6

*A gossip goes around telling secrets, but those who are
trustworthy can keep a confidence.*
+ PROVERBS 11:13

*When you give to someone in need, don't let your left hand know
what your right hand is doing. Give your gifts in private, and
your Father, who sees everything, will reward you.*
+ MATTHEW 6:3-4

*Carefully determine what pleases the Lord. Take no part in the
worthless deeds of evil and darkness; instead, expose them.*
+ EPHESIANS 5:10-11

SECRETS ARE OFTEN seen as negative, and sometimes they are.
When shame, guilt, or embarrassment motivates us to keep secrets
from our loved ones, this usually ends up causing damage to our
relationships. God wants us to live as though we have nothing to hide.
However, Scripture does state that some secrets are intended to be
kept just between us and God. First, our good deeds are meant to be
kept secret so they don't draw the attention of others. And second, any
secrets we know about others are not ours to tell. The ability to keep
a secret is an important character trait we can develop. Are you trustworthy to keep a secret? Look to God's Word to help you gain wisdom
about when to reveal the truth and when to keep things hidden.

Prayer Prompts

Lord, I am unsure whether or not to keep a secret about . . .
When I consider secrets, your Word says . . .

# security

How can knowing God help me feel more secure?

*Therefore, since we have been made right in God's sight by faith, we
have peace with God because of what Jesus Christ our Lord has done
for us. Because of our faith, Christ has brought us into this place of
undeserved privilege where we now stand, and we confidently and
joyfully look forward to sharing God's glory.*
+ ROMANS 5:1-2

*I give them eternal life, and they will never perish.
No one can snatch them away from me, for my Father has
given them to me, and he is more powerful than anyone else.*
+ JOHN 10:28-29

THE HEART of every woman longs for security. When we face
troubles in our finances, marriages, and homes, in our work and
in the world, we sometimes wish someone would promise us that
everything will be okay. Only God can provide security like that!
The more we know him, the more secure, strong, and confident we
will become. God's Word promises that those who believe in Christ
will be kept safe for all eternity because of their faith. God has also
guaranteed a priceless inheritance stored up in heaven for those he
loves. If you believe that Jesus Christ is the Son of God who died to
forgive your sins and rose again, then you can be assured that your
eternal future is safe and certain. Even though we live in a hostile
and unpredictable world, we can feel secure in knowing how the
story will end. Allow your heart to be at rest, trusting that God is
your refuge and nothing can snatch you from his hand.

Prayer Prompts

Lord, when I focus on this world, I feel insecure about . . .
When I focus on the promises in your Word, I feel secure because . . .

self-control 🍃

I'm not a disciplined woman.
How can I possibly learn self-control?

———— ✀ ————

I don't really understand myself, for I want to do what is right, but I don't do it. . . . When I want to do what is right, I inevitably do what is wrong. . . . Who will free me from this life that is dominated by sin and death? Thank God! The answer is in Jesus Christ our Lord.
+ ROMANS 7:15, 21, 24-25

All athletes are disciplined in their training. They do it to win a prize that will fade away, but we do it for an eternal prize.
+ 1 CORINTHIANS 9:25

Supplement your faith with a generous provision of moral excellence, and moral excellence with knowledge, and knowledge with self-control, and self-control with patient endurance.
+ 2 PETER 1:5-6

FAILURE to control ourselves inevitably results in broken hearts and damaged relationships. Self-control first involves knowing God's guidelines for living as found in the Bible. We need to know what it is we must control before we can keep it under control. We can do this by (1) honestly assessing our weaknesses; (2) deciding that with God's help, they will no longer rule us; (3) removing ourselves from places of temptation; (4) humbly confessing to God when we make a mistake; and (5) giving glory to God when we are victorious! Remember, it takes time to learn self-control. Becoming a disciplined woman happens through many small decisions that move us toward living God's way.

Prayer Prompts

Lord, I need to learn self-control in the area of . . .
Your Word encourages me to be disciplined when it says . . .

 # self-doubt

Can God use me, even when I doubt myself?

—— ❧ ——

Moses pleaded with the LORD, "O Lord, I'm not very good with words.
I never have been, and I'm not now, even though you have spoken to me.
I get tongue-tied, and my words get tangled." Then the LORD asked Moses,
"Who makes a person's mouth? Who decides whether people speak or do not
speak, hear or do not hear, see or do not see? Is it not I, the LORD? Now go!
I will be with you as you speak, and I will instruct you in what to say."
But Moses again pleaded, "Lord, please! Send anyone else."
+ EXODUS 4:10-13

Is anything too hard for the LORD?
+ GENESIS 18:14

With God's help we will do mighty things.
+ PSALM 60:12

WAY BACK IN THE BOOK OF EXODUS, Moses pleaded with God to find someone else to command Pharaoh to free the Israelites. This task was way out of his comfort zone, and Moses felt scared, unprepared, and full of doubt. But God works best through humble hearts that depend on him. Moses had two choices: walk away or let God work through him. What choice will we make when God calls us to an intimidating task? Will our doubt cause us to walk away, or will we trust God to do amazing things through us? Remember that when you doubt yourself, you are actually doubting God. He has had many good things planned for your life since before you were born. And nothing can disrupt his plans—not even you. Face the task ahead with boldness because with God's help, you will do mighty things.

Prayer Prompts

Lord, I wonder if I'm the best person for this job: . . .
Your Word encourages me to face this task confidently because . . .

self-esteem 🍃

How can I become a more secure, confident person?

*We are God's masterpiece. He has created us anew in Christ Jesus,
so we can do the good things he planned for us long ago.*
    + EPHESIANS 2:10

*Even before he made the world, God loved us and chose us in Christ to be
holy and without fault in his eyes. God decided in advance to adopt us into
his own family by bringing us to himself through Jesus Christ. This is what
he wanted to do, and it gave him great pleasure. So we praise God for the
glorious grace he has poured out on us who belong to his dear Son.*
    + EPHESIANS 1:4-6

How precious are your thoughts about me, O God.
    + PSALM 139:17

OUR SENSE OF SELF is often attacked because of how the world
says women should look or act. Our self-esteem suffers when
we see ourselves differently than God sees us. Instead of focusing
on who the world says we *should be*, we need to think about who
our Creator says we *are*. This is the only way to have a healthy self-
esteem. The words God uses to describe us are "loved," "precious,"
"a masterpiece," and "his child." How might you carry yourself if you
truly believed this is how God sees you? Ask God to take away the
lies that tempt you to doubt your worth. The best way to do this is to
read God's Word over and over, letting his encouraging words give
you confidence for each day.

Prayer Prompts
*Lord, the world says that I am valuable if I am . . .
Your Word tells me I am valuable because . . .*

 selfishness

How do I care more about what God cares for and less about myself?

Wherever your treasure is, there the desires of your heart will also be.
+ MATTHEW 6:21

Don't be concerned for your own good but for the good of others.
+ 1 CORINTHIANS 10:24

Let the Holy Spirit guide your lives. Then you won't be doing what your sinful nature craves. The sinful nature wants to do evil, which is just the opposite of what the Spirit wants. And the Spirit gives us desires that are the opposite of what the sinful nature desires. These two forces are constantly fighting each other, so you are not free to carry out your good intentions.
+ GALATIANS 5:16-17

WE ALL WANT to be generous, caring more about others than ourselves. But even with the best of intentions, we usually prioritize our own wants and needs when we make decisions. God's Word says two forces are constantly battling within us—the desire to serve ourselves and the desire to serve God. What can we do to win this battle? One of the best things is to invest our hearts in whatever God says is important. When we start investing our time, money, prayer, and resources in his priorities, we will begin caring about those things. This will not always feel easy. In fact, the more selfish we are, the harder it will be to put others first. Ask the Holy Spirit to help you take one small step each day toward investing in God's Kingdom. Watch how your heart will slowly begin to long for that which will last for eternity.

Prayer Prompts

Lord, I notice my selfishness when . . .
Your Word tells me that I can have victory over my selfishness by . . .

self-worth 🐟

How can I develop a healthier sense of self-worth?

———————— ❧ ————————

Be honest in your evaluation of yourselves,
measuring yourselves by the faith God has given us.
✝ ROMANS 12:3

What is the price of five sparrows—two copper coins? Yet God does not forget
a single one of them. And the very hairs on your head are all numbered. So
don't be afraid; you are more valuable to God than a whole flock of sparrows.
✝ LUKE 12:6-7

He saved us, not because of the righteous things
we had done, but because of his mercy.
✝ TITUS 3:5

SATAN WILL TRY to convince us that our worth is based on how we measure up to others in appearance, possessions, accomplishments, or social status. This will usually leave us feeling either inadequate and envious or full of pride. A better method of determining our worth is comparing ourselves with God's standards. Measured against his holiness, everyone falls short and is humbled; but in God's eyes, every person is valued and loved. Maintaining a balance between humility over our sin and exultation over God's lavish grace is a healthy way to live. God doesn't base your worth on your appearance or accomplishments, so neither should you. Enjoy his grace, which has no comparison, and bask in the gracious ways that God shows his love to you.

Prayer Prompts

Lord, I feel tempted to doubt my self-worth when . . .
Your Word assures me I am worth a great deal to you because . . .

How can I use my five senses to
be more aware of God?

———— ✼ ————

When I look at the night sky [I] see the work of your fingers—
the moon and the stars you set in place.
+ PSALM 8:3

"Fill your stomach with this," he said.
And when I ate it, it tasted as sweet as honey in my mouth.
+ EZEKIEL 3:3

We hear songs of praise from the ends of the earth,
songs that give glory to the Righteous One!
+ ISAIAH 24:16

Jesus reached out and touched him. "I am willing," he said.
"Be healed!" And instantly the leprosy disappeared.
+ LUKE 5:13

WHY DID GOD give most of us the ability to see, smell, taste, hear, and touch? Our senses are gifts that help us to experience and enjoy the beauty of God's creation, to soak in good times with others, and to remember his past goodness. Whenever you feel rushed or are having a hard time being present, stop for a few moments and ask these five questions: What do I see? What do I smell? What do I taste? What do I hear? What kinds of sensations do I feel against my skin? Use your senses to become more aware of God's world around you. Thank him for the gift of your senses, and use them to make each moment unique and full of meaning.

Prayer Prompts

Lord, in this very moment, my five senses are experiencing . . .
This awareness reminds me that your Word encourages me to . . .

sensitivity 🍃

How can I become more sensitive to others' needs?

————————— ❧ —————————

If your gift is to encourage others, be encouraging. If it is giving, give generously. If God has given you leadership ability, take the responsibility seriously. And if you have a gift for showing kindness to others, do it gladly.
+ ROMANS 12:8

All of you should be of one mind. Sympathize with each other. Love each other as brothers and sisters. Be tenderhearted, and keep a humble attitude.
+ 1 PETER 3:8

Don't forget to do good and to share with those in need. These are the sacrifices that please God.
+ HEBREWS 13:16

G OD'S WORD encourages us not to forget to do good, which implies that we often do. Perhaps this is because of our tendency to overcommit. Every day it seems we rush from one thing to another. We do a lot, but do we do good? When we focus on doing, we can lose sight of the needs right in front of us. Sensitivity begins by simply looking up from what we are doing. When we are aware of those around us, we are better able to stop and listen to them, consider their feelings and struggles, ask thoughtful questions, and show them compassion and care. God has equipped you in special ways to meet the needs of others around you. Who needs your help, care, and compassion today? Each time you put aside your own agenda to be genuinely present with another person, you are developing the kind of sensitive heart that is so precious to God and treasured by others.

Prayer Prompts

Lord, someone in my life to whom I should be sensitive is . . .
Your Word says I can help him or her by . . .

🍃 serving others

Why should I serve others when no one seems to appreciate what I do?

———————— ❧ ————————

I will search for faithful people to be my companions.
Only those who are above reproach will be allowed to serve me.
+ PSALM 101:6

No one can serve two masters. For you will hate one and
love the other; you will be devoted to one and despise the other.
You cannot serve God and be enslaved to money.
+ MATTHEW 6:24

You have been called to live in freedom, my brothers and sisters.
But don't use your freedom to satisfy your sinful nature.
Instead, use your freedom to serve one another in love.
+ GALATIANS 5:13

Even the Son of Man came not to be served but to serve others
and to give his life as a ransom for many.
+ MARK 10:45

SERVING OTHERS with the right attitude doesn't always come naturally, especially when our efforts go unnoticed. But God notices each time we love and serve those around us. Serving with this in mind keeps our hearts in the right place. What can you do to keep your focus on God as you serve others? Can you pray as you serve? Imagine God beside you? Meditate on a Scripture verse? Ask the Holy Spirit to help you set aside your own need for approval, desire for recognition, and self-serving agenda so that you can focus on serving your Lord as you serve another.

Prayer Prompts

Lord, it feels difficult for me to serve when . . .
When I serve, help me remember that your Word says . . .

setbacks

How do I keep going when life constantly seems to knock me down?

———————————— ❦ ————————————

Joseph's brothers pulled him out of the cistern and sold him . . . for twenty pieces of silver. And the traders took him to Egypt.
  + GENESIS 37:28

Potiphar was furious when he heard his wife's story about how Joseph had treated her. So he took Joseph and threw him into the prison where the king's prisoners were held.
  + GENESIS 39:19-20

Pharaoh's chief cup-bearer . . . forgot all about Joseph, never giving him another thought.
  + GENESIS 40:23

You intended to harm me, but God intended it all for good.
  + GENESIS 50:20

JOSEPH EXPERIENCED a series of heartbreaking setbacks—being sold into slavery by his brothers, being framed as a rapist by Potiphar's wife, and being forgotten by the cupbearer whose dream Joseph had interpreted. While God did not send these bad experiences, he allowed them, and Joseph understood that God would use them to prepare him for an important assignment later on. When you experience a setback, think about Joseph and thank God that he promises to use everything for his good. Looking at your setbacks from that perspective keeps you alert to what you can learn from them. This will help you endure them in the moment and have hope that God will redeem them to help you become all he created you to be.

Prayer Prompts

Lord, when I think about setbacks in my life, I remember the time that . . .
Your Word encourages me to have this perspective on my problems: . . .

sex

My sexual history is full of pain.
How can I view sex the way God intended?

❧

God sent his Son into the world not to judge the world, but to save the world through him. There is no judgment against anyone who believes in him.
✦ JOHN 3:17-18

Though your sins are like scarlet, I will make them as white as snow.
✦ ISAIAH 1:18

Oh, what joy for those whose disobedience is forgiven, whose sins are put out of sight. Yes, what joy for those whose record the LORD has cleared of sin.
✦ ROMANS 4:7-8

THE WORLD SAYS sex should be casual and detached. This was never what God intended because it mistreats our bodies, damages our souls, and hinders our capacity for true intimacy. God's view of sexuality is far more fulfilling than the world's. God intended sex to bring joy and blessing to those within a marriage relationship. He intended it to be a gift allowing a husband and wife to express love to each other, delight in each other, and produce future generations. Perhaps you feel discouraged because your past has not exactly been pure. Or maybe sexuality is a painful topic because someone you trusted violated you. Whatever your sexual history, God is able to heal, restore, and redeem you. Even if you feel beyond repair, remember that this is the very reason God sent his Son, Jesus, into the world. He came not to condemn those who made mistakes but rather to bring them hope, peace, comfort, forgiveness, and salvation.

Prayer Prompts
Lord, when I think about my sexual past, I feel . . .
Your Word says that no matter what my history is, you are able to . . .

299

shame 🍃

How is shame different from guilt?
Why is it important to know the difference?

⸻ ❧ ⸻

There is no condemnation for those who belong to Christ Jesus.
+ ROMANS 8:1

You, O LORD, are a shield around me; you are my glory,
the one who holds my head high.
+ PSALM 3:3

Fear not; you will no longer live in shame.
Don't be afraid; there is no more disgrace for you.
+ ISAIAH 54:4

Those who look to him for help will be radiant with joy;
no shadow of shame will darken their faces.
+ PSALM 34:5

THE MESSAGE OF GUILT is "I've done something bad." The message of shame is "I am bad." Have you experienced the difference? Shame is not something God uses for our spiritual growth. In fact, shame is not from God at all. When the evil one tries to convince us that we are unlovable, unworthy, and beyond help, we can tell ourselves that this is not God's voice. God says we are loved, known, and redeemed. His voice can clearly be heard through the promises in his Word. What you have done or where you have been does not define you. You can be a woman who walks with confidence because God's Word promises there is no condemnation for those who belong to Christ Jesus.

Prayer Prompts

Lord, the voice of shame accuses me of . . .
Your Word reminds me that I am . . .

 # sharing

How can I develop a more generous spirit?

❧

You should remember the words of the Lord Jesus:
"It is more blessed to give than to receive."
+ ACTS 20:35

I always thank my God for you and for the gracious gifts he
has given you, now that you belong to Christ Jesus.
+ 1 CORINTHIANS 1:4

May you be filled with joy, always thanking the Father. He has enabled you
to share in the inheritance that belongs to his people, who live in the light.
+ COLOSSIANS 1:11-12

They begged us again and again for the privilege of
sharing in the gift for the believers in Jerusalem.
+ 2 CORINTHIANS 8:4

ALMOST EVERYONE has been taught since early childhood to share, yet for many people it feels incredibly difficult. Why? Because at the core of sinful human nature is the desire to get, not give; to accumulate, not relinquish; to look out for ourselves, not others. The Bible calls us to share many things—our resources, faith, love, time, talents, and money. Many things are more enjoyable when we share them with others, and doing so benefits them far more than we may realize. We are called to share because God gives so generously to us. Sharing is an expression of our love for God, demonstrated in our love for others. As we use our special gifts and resources for others, we pass on God's blessings. Those who generously share discover that the benefits of giving are far greater than the temporary satisfaction of receiving.

Prayer Prompts

Lord, something that is hard for me to share is . . .
Your Word motivates me to be generous because you have shared . . .

silence

Sometimes I feel as if God is being silent. Why doesn't he respond?

Wait patiently for the Lord. Be brave and courageous.
Yes, wait patiently for the Lord.
+ PSALM 27:14

We are confident that he hears us whenever
we ask for anything that pleases him.
+ 1 JOHN 5:14

I will answer them before they even call to me. While they are still
talking about their needs, I will go ahead and answer their prayers!
+ ISAIAH 65:24

SOMETIMES SILENCE in prayer feels deafening. Why doesn't God always speak when we pray? God could be silent for a variety of reasons. Perhaps a sinful habit in our lives is getting in the way of our hearing his voice, or maybe he is testing our faith to trust him in the silence. He may want to talk about the one topic we are avoiding in prayer, or perhaps he knows what we really need right now is someone to listen to us. Do any of these reasons for his silence resonate with you? If so, then talk to God about them. Although you may never understand why God seems silent at times, don't give up and leave him. He hasn't left you. Use the opportunity to grow your faith, your patience, and your ability to listen.

Prayer Prompts

Lord, I wonder if you are being silent because . . .
Even in the silence, your Word promises . . .

# simplicity

Do I need to simplify my life?

꩜

Jesus said, . . . "Life is more than food, and your body more than clothing."
+ LUKE 12:22-23

*One day an expert in religious law stood up to test Jesus by asking him this
question: "Teacher, what should I do to inherit eternal life?" Jesus replied,
"What does the law of Moses say? How do you read it?" The man answered,
"'You must love the LORD your God with all your heart, all your soul, all
your strength, and all your mind.' And, 'Love your neighbor as yourself.'"
"Right!" Jesus told him. "Do this and you will live!"*
+ LUKE 10:25-28

*This world is fading away, along with everything that people crave. But
anyone who does what pleases God will live forever.*
+ 1 JOHN 2:17

WE OFTEN BELIEVE our success is measured by how full our
closets are and how large our bank accounts are. However,
God calls his followers to a different way of life—one that resists the
"more is better" mentality to focus instead on our purpose for being
on this earth. Simplifying our lives means letting go of things that
complicate them in order to better focus on the kind of life Jesus says
is most fulfilling. It's not about getting rid of things but rather about
experiencing freedom from being a slave to them. Which area in
your life do you feel the Lord calling you to simplify? Your possessions? Expectations? Standards? Schedule? Commitments? Ask God
to help you learn how to let go in order to experience freedom by
focusing on what really matters.

Prayer Prompts

Lord, I long to simplify this area in my life: . . .
Help me to refocus on what your Word tells me is most important: . . .

sin 🍃

What is really so bad about sin?

――――――――― ❧ ―――――――――

*"You won't die!" the serpent replied to the woman. "God knows that
your eyes will be opened as soon as you eat it, and you will be like God,
knowing both good and evil." The woman was convinced.*
+ GENESIS 3:4-6

*Temptation comes from our own desires, which entice us and
drag us away. These desires give birth to sinful actions.
And when sin is allowed to grow, it gives birth to death.*
+ JAMES 1:14-15

*The LORD says, "I will guide you along the best pathway for your life.
I will advise you and watch over you."*
+ PSALM 32:8

SIN IS BOTH subtle and serious. It subtly begins with small lies
that Satan whispers to our hearts: "God is holding out on you."
"You know better than God." "God really isn't good." When we fail to
recognize these thoughts as lies, we allow sin to take root. And the
root of all sin is the distrust of God. When we don't trust God, we
make decisions based on what we believe is best, not on what God
knows is best for us. It has been said that the beginning of sin isn't
disobedience but rather the resentment of obedience. Sin keeps you
from trusting that surrendering your whole life to God leads to the
best life you could ever have. What lies about God is Satan trying
to convince you of right now? Where is it hard to trust that God's
way is best? Ask God to help you notice subtle lies in your thoughts,
combat them with truth from his Word, and have faith to trust him.

Prayer Prompts

Lord, Satan often tries to convince me to believe that you . . .
Your Word combats this lie when it says . . .

soul

What does it mean to have a soul?
How do I care for it?

———————————— ❧ ————————————

*Jesus replied, "You must love the LORD your God
with all your heart, all your soul, and all your mind."*
+ MATTHEW 22:37

*Ask for the old, godly way, and walk in it.
Travel its path, and you will find rest for your souls.*
+ JEREMIAH 6:16

*The LORD is my shepherd; I have all that I need. He lets me rest in green
meadows; he leads me beside peaceful streams. He renews my strength.*
+ PSALM 23:1-3

*Why am I discouraged? Why is my heart so sad? I will put my hope in God!
I will praise him again—my Savior and my God!*
+ PSALM 42:11

THE SOUL encompasses the entire person. Like everything else in
the world, it has become broken as a result of the Fall. Therefore,
to care for the soul is to reunite all the broken pieces of the self with
the Lord. We can do this in many ways, including praying, meditating
on Scripture, singing songs of praise to God, being in nature, nurturing our bodies with good food, and creating spaces of intentional rest
where we can just sit with the Lord. If you had to describe the state
of your soul using one word, what would it be? Exhausted? Empty?
Scattered? Satisfied? Pray about what places, people, or activities make
your heart, mind, and body feel fully alive. Be intentional about doing
these things as often as you can in order to care for your soul.

Prayer Prompts

Lord, I would describe my soul as . . .
Your Word encourages me to care for my soul by . . .

sovereignty

If God is sovereign, why do my prayers matter?

Finally, Abraham said, "Lord, please don't be angry with me if I speak one more time. Suppose only ten are found there?" And the Lord replied, "Then I will not destroy it for the sake of the ten."

+ GENESIS 18:32

Moses tried to pacify the Lord his God. "O Lord!" he said. . . . "Turn away from your fierce anger. Change your mind about this terrible disaster you have threatened against your people!" . . . So the Lord changed his mind.

+ EXODUS 32:11-12, 14

I love the Lord because he hears my voice and my prayer for mercy. Because he bends down to listen, I will pray as long as I have breath!

+ PSALM 116:1-2

The earnest prayer of a righteous person has great power and produces wonderful results.

+ JAMES 5:16

THERE ARE MANY examples in Scripture where a person's fervent prayer changed the course of events. God's sovereignty means that he is all-knowing, has a purpose for everything he does, and is in control. In his sovereignty, God chooses to work through prayer. He wants us to partner with him as he carries out his will here on earth. The Bible promises that God hears each prayer, that our prayers are powerful, and that every prayer matters to him. Through prayer, we are connecting in holy conversation to our Creator, the one true God. This kind of connection is life-changing. As the psalmist said, pray as long as you have breath because the Lord hears and answers prayer.

Prayer Prompts

Lord, I'm tempted to believe my prayers don't matter when . . .
Your Word says my prayers are important because . . .

 # specialness

If God loves everyone,
how could I be special to him?

————————— ❧ —————————

God decided in advance to adopt us into his own family by
bringing us to himself through Jesus Christ. This is what he
wanted to do, and it gave him great pleasure.
+ EPHESIANS 1:5

The one who formed you says, "Do not be afraid, for I have ransomed you.
I have called you by name; you are mine."
+ ISAIAH 43:1

Can a mother forget her nursing child? Can she feel no love for the child
she has borne? But even if that were possible, I would not forget you!
See, I have written your name on the palms of my hands.
+ ISAIAH 49:15-16

EVERY PERSON on earth has a deep need to feel special. If others
have failed to make us feel valuable, we can take comfort that
the one who created us sees us as special. The early church father
Augustine wrote, "God loves each of us as if there were only one of
us." Is it hard to believe that God loves you personally? God's Word
says that he adopts you, thinks precious thoughts about you, calls
you by name, never forgets you, and even has your name written
on his hands. Whenever you doubt you are special to God, remind
yourself of these truths. Look for ways in which God might be showing his unique love for you today. It might be through a friend, an
unexpected gift, or a moment where you feel his presence. Ask God
to open your eyes to his extraordinary, personal love for you.

Prayer Prompts

Lord, it's hard to believe I'm special to you because . . .
Your Word assures me you love me personally because . . .

speechlessness

What can I do when I feel like I don't have any words to pray?

━━━━━━━━━━━━━ ❧ ━━━━━━━━━━━━━

The Holy Spirit helps us in our weakness. For example, we don't know what God wants us to pray for. But the Holy Spirit prays for us with groanings that cannot be expressed in words. And the Father who knows all hearts knows what the Spirit is saying, for the Spirit pleads for us believers in harmony with God's own will.

✝ ROMANS 8:26-27

Pray like this: Our Father in heaven, may your name be kept holy. May your Kingdom come soon. May your will be done on earth, as it is in heaven. Give us today the food we need, and forgive us our sins, as we have forgiven those who sin against us. And don't let us yield to temptation, but rescue us from the evil one.

✝ MATTHEW 6:9-13

D O YOU EVER find it difficult to find the words to pray? Whenever we feel speechless before God, we can open his Word to find fresh language for prayer. When we don't even know how to begin talking to God, we can start with the Lord's Prayer. As we read it out loud, we can speak directly to God. This can be done with many passages throughout the Bible. As you pray the honest, heartfelt prayers of people from thousands of years ago, notice how the words relate to your own circumstances. Whether you are in a time of great joy or are experiencing deep despair, God's Word has something to say about every season of life. Trust God to listen to any prayer you offer with a sincere heart.

Prayer Prompts

Lord, it is hard for me to find words to pray when . . .
When my prayers feel empty, your Word assures me that . . .

 spiritual disciplines

Why is it important to practice spiritual virtues and disciplines?

———— ❧ ————

Give me understanding and I will obey your instructions;
I will put them into practice with all my heart.
+ PSALM 119:34

Train yourself to be godly. "Physical training is good, but training for godliness
is much better, promising benefits in this life and in the life to come."
+ 1 TIMOTHY 4:7-8

Let the Spirit renew your thoughts and attitudes. Put on your
new nature, created to be like God—truly righteous and holy.
+ EPHESIANS 4:23-24

Never stop praying.
+ 1 THESSALONIANS 5:17

Commit everything you do to the LORD.
Trust him, and he will help you.
+ PSALM 37:5

JUST AS OUR BODIES are made up of many muscles, so it is with our souls. We all have spiritual muscles that need strengthening, which is why practicing spiritual disciplines in our everyday life is so important. Is it hard for you to trust God? Spend time in his Word? Be thankful? Control your tongue? Pray for others? Decide what area of your faith you would like to see grow, and take small steps each day to make this a habit. Spiritual disciplines are not quick fixes to make you a "good" Christian. Rather, they are ways to *slowly* shape your heart to help you become more like Jesus.

Prayer Prompts

Lord, the spiritual muscle I want to strengthen is . . .
Your Word encourages me to begin by . . .

spiritual friendships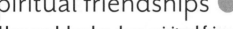

How can I develop deep spiritual friendships?

———————— ❧ ————————

When we get together, I want to encourage you in your faith,
but I also want to be encouraged by yours.
+ ROMANS 1:12

Encourage each other and build each other up, just as you are already doing.
+ 1 THESSALONIANS 5:11

Share each other's burdens, and in this way obey the law of Christ.
+ GALATIANS 6:2

If you are presenting a sacrifice at the altar in the Temple and
you suddenly remember that someone has something against you,
leave your sacrifice there at the altar. Go and be reconciled to that person.
Then come and offer your sacrifice to God.
+ MATTHEW 5:23-24

GOD'S WORD gives specific guidance for maintaining and deepening friendships. It reminds us that intentionality, authenticity, generosity, and love are essential. All women need deep friendships, but many of us struggle to develop them. Or maybe we've had close Christian friends before, but now life has taken us in different directions and we are waiting for new friends to come into our lives. Are you still searching for a place of belonging? Do you want to deepen your friendships with others? Begin by praying that God would provide trustworthy and godly women to walk alongside you. Trust that God will answer your earnest prayers and reward your efforts to invest in relationships. Then, when a person crosses your path, lean in and start getting to know her. She is most likely a gift from God.

Prayer Prompts

Lord, this is how I currently feel about my friendships: . . .
Your Word encourages me to develop and deepen friendships by . . .

# spiritual gifts

How can I discover my spiritual gifts?

— ❧ —

A spiritual gift is given to each of us so we can help each other.
To one person the Spirit gives the ability to give wise advice;
to another the same Spirit gives a message of special knowledge.
The same Spirit gives great faith to another, and to someone else the
one Spirit gives the gift of healing. . . . In fact, some parts of the body
that seem weakest and least important are actually the most necessary.
+ 1 CORINTHIANS 12:7-9, 22

God has given each of you a gift from his great variety of spiritual gifts.
Use them well to serve one another.
+ 1 PETER 4:10

WE EACH HAVE a special part in helping God advance his Kingdom on earth. The best way to participate in God's work is by using the unique spiritual gifts he has given us. Therefore, it is important to know what our gifts are. If you're not sure, start by asking God, trustworthy friends, and yourself this question: "What am I good at?" If you are good at cooking, then cook for those who need a meal. If you are good at listening, then listen well and often. If you are good at encouraging others, then look for someone to encourage every day. Make it a priority to know what your spiritual gifts are so you can fulfill the purpose for which God made you. The more you use your gifts to serve others, the more they will grow and make an even bigger impact on the lives of those around you.

Prayer Prompts

Lord, I think you have given me the spiritual gift of . . .
Your Word gives me these ideas about how to use it: . . .

spiritual warfare 🍃

Are there really spiritual enemies—
powers of darkness—trying to harm me?

———— ✂ ————

The thief's purpose is to steal and kill and destroy.
My purpose is to give them a rich and satisfying life.
+ JOHN 10:10

We are not fighting against flesh-and-blood enemies, but against evil
rulers and authorities of the unseen world, against mighty powers in
this dark world, and against evil spirits in the heavenly places.
+ EPHESIANS 6:12

Here on earth you will have many trials and sorrows.
But take heart, because I have overcome the world.
+ JOHN 16:33

SATAN, OUR SPIRITUAL ENEMY, is alive and active, working every day to steer our hearts away from God through pain, pleasure, or pride. Satan's goal is to keep us isolated from God and to drown us in misery, darkness, and despair. Whether or not we are aware of it, a spiritual battle is going on over our souls right now. Our allegiance to God puts us in the middle of the battle because we are threats to Satan's plans. Although spiritual warfare is scary, God commands us to live courageously because of Jesus' death, resurrection, and victory on the cross. We can stand firm in the Lord and in his mighty power because the Bible promises he is greater than the enemy. Whenever you feel overwhelmed or defeated by the evil one, remember that the story is not over yet. No matter what trials or sorrows Satan brings your way on earth, God has already overcome the world.

Prayer Prompts
Lord, I wonder if Satan is trying to steer my heart away from you by . . .
Your Word assures victory for those who follow you: . . .

 # starting over

Is it ever too late to start over?

— ❧ —

Anyone who belongs to Christ has become a new person.
The old life is gone; a new life has begun!
+ 2 CORINTHIANS 5:17

The one sitting on the throne said, "Look,
I am making everything new!"
+ REVELATION 21:5

Do not despise these small beginnings,
for the LORD rejoices to see the work begin.
+ ZECHARIAH 4:10

He washed away our sins, giving us a new birth
and new life through the Holy Spirit.
+ TITUS 3:5

HAVE YOU EVER DREAMED of a new beginning, where you escaped from your current life and had a chance to wipe the slate clean and start over? This is a common dream for so many of us who are haunted by regrets. But no matter what mistakes plague our past or what sins we struggle with in the present, it is never too late to start over. Escaping won't fix things; we need to be changed, to have our souls transformed. Jesus promises that those who believe he is the Son of God will become new people. Our old life disappears and a new one begins. God literally changes us from the inside out. He is doing something new within your heart today—do you see it? Rejoice in the fact that you have a God who delights in fresh starts, second chances, and new beginnings.

Prayer Prompts

Lord, sometimes I feel like it is impossible to start over because . . .
When I feel trapped in my past, your Word reminds me that . . .

steadfastness 🍃

How can I remain steadfast for God
through seasons of unanswered prayers?

※

*Keep on asking, and you will receive what you ask for. Keep on
seeking, and you will find. Keep on knocking, and the door will be
opened to you. For everyone who asks, receives. Everyone who seeks,
finds. And to everyone who knocks, the door will be opened.*
+ MATTHEW 7:7-8

Rejoice in our confident hope. Be patient in trouble, and keep on praying.
+ ROMANS 12:12

*The earnest prayer of a righteous person has great
power and produces wonderful results.*
+ JAMES 5:16

ONE OF THE BIGGEST challenges the Lord may give us is to stay
steadfast in our faith during a season of unanswered prayers.
We fail at these tests when we lose perspective about God's bigger
plans for us and lose our trust in him. Remaining steadfast means
learning to endure patiently in faith. Do you have prayers that
remain unanswered? Continue to pray courageously as you wait for
God to answer. Sometimes he graciously chooses to answer prayers
with an astounding "Yes!" Other times, he answers them in ways we
never expect. Yet we can be confident that God will *always* answer
in his timing. Whatever you have been praying for, don't give up. God
can be trusted with your prayers. He promises to faithfully answer
earnest prayers with wonderful results.

Prayer Prompts
Lord, I am still praying for . . .
Your Word assures me that I should be steadfast because . . .

 # stillness

How can I know when God wants me to take action and when I should be still?

— ❧ —

*Be still, and know that I am God! I will be honored by every nation.
I will be honored throughout the world.*
+ PSALM 46:10

*Your own ears will hear him. Right behind you a voice will say,
"This is the way you should go," whether to the right or to the left.*
+ ISAIAH 30:21

Be still in the presence of the LORD, and wait patiently for him to act.
+ PSALM 37:7

Don't be afraid. Just stand still and watch the LORD rescue you today.
+ EXODUS 14:13

INDECISION MEANS no decision. When we don't know whether to stay or go, we should pray, wait, and watch for God's guidance. Worry and anxiety often tempt us to move forward before we receive direction from God, but sometimes trusting God means taking no further action. God promises in his Word that he will guide us where we ought to go. Do you believe this? If you are facing a difficult decision and need direction from God, then set aside time to talk to him and be still, waiting for his answer. He can be trusted to lead you in his perfect timing.

Prayer Prompts

*Lord, I need direction about whether to move or stay in this area of my life: . . .
I can trust you to lead me in your timing because your Word says . . .*

strength 🍃

Where do I find the strength to deal with all my problems?

❦

I also pray that you will understand the incredible greatness of God's power for us who believe him. This is the same mighty power that raised Christ from the dead.
+ EPHESIANS 1:19-20

There is wonderful joy ahead, even though you must endure many trials for a while. These trials will show that your faith is genuine. . . . So when your faith remains strong through many trials, it will bring you much praise and glory and honor on the day when Jesus Christ is revealed to the whole world.
+ 1 PETER 1:6-7

I will never fail you. I will never abandon you.
+ HEBREWS 13:5

L IFE HAS ITS SHARE of problems and scary situations—physical danger, illness, financial hardship, job loss, conflicts, and disagreements. Where can we possibly find the strength to deal with them all? We can't fight all our problems by ourselves; we need someone to help us, someone we can count on to always be there. Whatever we are facing, we can remind ourselves that God is stronger than our biggest problems or our worst enemies. And he never leaves our side. Resist the temptation to place your confidence in your own strength. Instead, place your confidence in God's strength. Each morning, ask him to give you what you need to make it through the day. Remember that problems are opportunities to see his incredible power and strength in your life.

Prayer Prompts

Lord, I really need your strength in the area of . . .
When I feel helpless, your Word reminds me . . .

How can I best handle the daily pressures of life?

❧

As pressure and stress bear down on me, I find joy in your commands.
+ PSALM 119:143

*We are pressed on every side by troubles, but we are not
crushed. We are perplexed, but not driven to despair. We are
hunted down, but never abandoned by God.*
+ 2 CORINTHIANS 4:8-9

*Jesus said, "Come to me, all of you who are weary and carry heavy burdens,
and I will give you rest. Take my yoke upon you. Let me teach you, because
I am humble and gentle at heart, and you will find rest for your souls."*
+ MATTHEW 11:28-29

JUGGLING marriage, finances, family schedules, a career, and
church responsibilities, all while managing a home, is enough to
stress anyone out. Sometimes the crushing responsibilities of life
make us feel incapable of doing anything well. But we were not made
to handle all this pressure on our own. God doesn't place high expectations on us; we do that to ourselves. He simply asks us to come to
him when life feels like too much to handle. If you are in a season of
high stress, set your planner aside and open up your Bible. Spending
time with God puts everything else into perspective and helps you
see what is most important. Let him help you handle the stress so
that you can find peace for your soul.

Prayer Prompts
Lord, I'm really feeling stressed out about . . .
Your Word says that when I feel stressed, I need to . . .

struggle 🍂

Why is my relationship with God full of struggle whereas everyone else's seems so easy?

———————— ❧ ————————

A man came and wrestled with [Jacob] until the dawn began to break.
When the man saw that he would not win the match, he touched Jacob's
hip and wrenched it out of its socket. Then the man said, "Let me go, for the
dawn is breaking!" But Jacob said, "I will not let you go unless you bless me."
"What is your name?" the man asked. He replied, "Jacob." "Your name will
no longer be Jacob," the man told him. "From now on you will be called
Israel, because you have fought with God and with men and have won."
. . . Jacob named the place Peniel (which means "face of God"), for he said,
"I have seen God face to face, yet my life has been spared."
  ✝ GENESIS 32:24-28, 30

God's discipline is always good for us, so that we might share in his holiness.
  ✝ HEBREWS 12:10

DOES IT EVER seem like everyone else is walking peacefully with
God while you continually wrestle with him? Our spiritual
lives can feel like losing battles. Yet it is often right after the struggles
that we experience the blessings. God is using these struggles to teach
us something important. In what areas of your life are you wrestling
with God? In what areas do you rarely ask him for help? Pray about
them. God doesn't desire to defeat you with these problems; he wants
you to surrender your agendas to him. When you let him take the
lead, you will experience abundant life. Your Creator's heart for you is
to live the most joyful, fulfilling life possible.

Prayer Prompts
Lord, I'm tired of wrestling over . . .
When I stop fighting you, your Word says . . .

 # success

Is it okay to try to be successful in this life?

— ❧ —

Work willingly at whatever you do,
as though you were working for the Lord rather than for people.
+ COLOSSIANS 3:23

When someone has been given much, much will be required in return; and
when someone has been entrusted with much, even more will be required.
+ LUKE 12:48

Teach those who are rich in this world not to be proud and not to trust
in their money, which is so unreliable. Their trust should be in God,
who richly gives us all we need for our enjoyment. Tell them to use their
money to do good. They should be rich in good works and generous
to those in need, always being ready to share with others.
+ 1 TIMOTHY 6:17-18

SOMETIMES GOD ALLOWS his people to enjoy material blessings, but his standard for success differs greatly from our own. He measures success not by prestige, possessions, or power, but by our motives, devotion, and commitment to him. What motivates you as you strive for success? Do you want to build your own kingdom on earth or invest in God's Kingdom? Remember that much is expected of those to whom God has entrusted material wealth and success. So whatever you do, work hard, handle every relationship with integrity, stay committed to God's purposes for you, be generous, and work to bring him glory. That's godly success.

Prayer Prompts

Lord, I want to be successful because . . .
Your Word reminds those who are successful with material things to . . .

suffering 🍃

How can I best help someone who is experiencing suffering?

———— ❧ ————

The heartfelt counsel of a friend is as sweet as perfume and incense
+ PROVERBS 27:9

Don't look out only for your own interests, but take an interest in others, too.
+ PHILIPPIANS 2:4

Be happy with those who are happy, and weep with those who weep.
+ ROMANS 12:15

God is our merciful Father and the source of all comfort.
He comforts us in all our troubles so that we can
comfort others. When they are troubled, we will be able to
give them the same comfort God has given us.
+ 2 CORINTHIANS 1:3-4

WHETHER IT'S HAPPENED to us personally or to someone we know, we all have experienced the dark shadow of suffering. We often don't know why suffering has struck. But two things can be said about suffering: It hurts, and it helps when others bring comfort. If you know someone who is hurting, walk alongside her by offering your prayers, presence, help, and a listening ear. Don't allow the discomfort of seeing someone suffer cause you to try to explain or fix her pain. Simply choose to be with her in it and help her feel God's love and presence through you.

Prayer Prompts

Lord, one person in my life who is really suffering is . . .
Your Word suggests that I can best help her in her suffering by . . .

 surprise

How is God surprising?

※

He has brought down princes from their thrones and exalted the humble.
+ LUKE 1:52

*[Jesus] gave up his divine privileges; he took the humble position of a slave and
was born as a human being. When he appeared in human form, he humbled
himself in obedience to God and died a criminal's death on a cross.*
+ PHILIPPIANS 2:7-8

*"My thoughts are nothing like your thoughts," says the LORD.
"And my ways are far beyond anything you could imagine."*
+ ISAIAH 55:8

SOMETIMES GOD'S CREATIVITY and power are best seen when
he does the opposite of what we would expect. He chose David,
the youngest son of Jesse, to be king of Israel rather than the old-
est son, as was the custom. He used a donkey to correct the pagan
prophet Balaam. He took Saul, the most vicious opponent of the
early church, and transformed him into Paul, the most courageous
missionary of all time. He cared for and respected women in a time
when they had no rights. And God used a crucifixion, the ultimate
defeat, and made it the sign of victory over sin and death for all
eternity. Perhaps God delights in surprising his people in ways that
inspire awe, love, gratitude, and joy. Don't limit God to the horizon
of your own understanding and expectations. He can do far more
than we can ask and is far greater than we can imagine. He has
wonderful surprises in store for our future.

Prayer Prompts

Lord, one surprise in my life that has been far better than my own plan is . . .
Your Word encourages me to trust you when surprises come because . . .

surrender ●

What is the paradox of surrender?
Why must I give something up?

———————————— ❧ ————————————

If you try to hang on to your life, you will lose it.
But if you give up your life for my sake, you will save it.
+ MATTHEW 16:25

What do you benefit if you gain the whole world but are yourself lost or destroyed?
+ LUKE 9:25

It is no longer I who live, but Christ lives in me. So I live in this earthly body
by trusting in the Son of God, who loved me and gave himself for me.
+ GALATIANS 2:20

Trust in the LORD with all your heart; do not depend on
your own understanding. Seek his will in all you do, and
he will show you which path to take.
+ PROVERBS 3:5-6

IF YOU HAVE any experience with a toddler, you know the difficulty of getting one to surrender. Toddlers often stubbornly demand their own way, wanting control over what they eat, when they sleep, and what they wear. However, a loving mother knows what her children need to survive and thrive, and she knows that surrender and trust will make life go more smoothly for them, ultimately making them happier. How often do we act like toddlers in our relationship with God? We want life on our own terms. However, God promises that when we surrender and trust him with our lives, we will not be disappointed. When we fully surrender to God, we release our grip on our lives and instead cling to the one who truly knows what we need.

Prayer Prompts

Lord, it's difficult for me to release control over . . .
Your Word reminds me that in order to surrender, I must . . .

 # survival

How can I thrive in life instead of simply trying to survive?

꙰

*Study this Book of Instruction continually. Meditate on it day
and night so you will be sure to obey everything written in it.
Only then will you prosper and succeed in all you do.*
+ JOSHUA 1:8

*Commit yourselves wholeheartedly to these words of mine . . . so that as
long as the sky remains above the earth, you and your children may flourish
in the land the LORD swore to give your ancestors.*
+ DEUTERONOMY 11:18, 21

*The godly will flourish like palm trees and grow strong like the cedars
of Lebanon. For they are transplanted to the LORD's own house.
They flourish in the courts of our God. Even in old age they will still
produce fruit; they will remain vital and green.*
+ PSALM 92:12-14

DO YOU EVER FEEL like you're just surviving, barely holding on?
Are you in a pattern of responding to crises rather than living
proactively? That's survival mode. We can sustain it for a time, but not
forever. God desires his people to thrive—not in the absence of difficulty but in spite of it. When you doubt it is possible to really thrive
in life, look to God's Word for truth and encouragement. He promises
that the godly will flourish. When you decide to spend time with him,
even if the time is short, you are choosing to trust that God has everything in control. It is by his grace that we can experience goodness in
every season, even while in survival mode.

Prayer Prompts

*Lord, sometimes I doubt I can really thrive in life because . . .
Your Word promises that those who trust in you will . . .*

sympathy

Does God really sympathize with me in my time of need?

The LORD is like a father to his children, tender and compassionate to those who fear him. For he knows how weak we are; he remembers we are only dust.
+ PSALM 103:13-14

When he saw the crowds, he had compassion on them because they were confused and helpless, like sheep without a shepherd.
+ MATTHEW 9:36

This High Priest of ours understands our weaknesses, for he faced all of the same testings we do, yet he did not sin.
+ HEBREWS 4:15

N O TROUBLE comes to you without the watchful eye of your heavenly Father seeing it and sympathizing with you. No temptation, hurt, or pain comes into your life that doesn't touch the sympathetic heart of Jesus. Jesus endured temptation (Matthew 4:1). He felt the sting of betrayal (Isaiah 53:3). He experienced the deep sadness that comes with loss (John 11:35-36). He felt alone (Matthew 26:40). He even experienced pain and death (Matthew 27:26-50). The Lord sees you and understands how you feel. Open your heart to him and experience his presence, knowing that he is able to sympathize with whatever you are going through.

Prayer Prompts

Lord, I need to know you can sympathize with me about . . .
Your Word assures me that you know how I feel when it says . . .

tears

Is God with me when I feel so alone in my sadness? Does he see my tears?

— ❧ —

In my distress I cried out to the LORD; yes, I prayed to my God for help.
He heard me from his sanctuary; my cry to him reached his ears.
+ PSALM 18:6

You keep track of all my sorrows. You have collected all my tears in
your bottle. You have recorded each one in your book.
+ PSALM 56:8

I am convinced that nothing can ever separate us from God's
love. Neither death nor life, neither angels nor demons, neither
our fears for today nor our worries about tomorrow—not
even the powers of hell can separate us from God's love.
+ ROMANS 8:38

DEEP SORROW has the power to isolate us, making us feel cut off from others and even God. However, God promises that even if we don't have another soul to cry with, he sees our tears and hears our prayers. Whether or not we are aware of it, God is always with us, even in our darkest moments. Our tears are precious to him. Not only does he see every tear we cry, he also saves our tears. Perhaps this is because he knows they represent the loss of something that was important to us, and what is important to us is also important to him. The next time you are tempted to believe you are alone in your grief, whisper God's name as a way to remember that he is with you. Your soul can find the rest and healing it longs for by staying close to him.

Prayer Prompts

Lord, the last time I cried alone was over . . .
In my darkest moments, I know you are with me because your Word says . . .

temptation

How does awareness of my weaknesses make me able to resist temptation?

Guard your heart above all else, for it determines the course of your life.
+ PROVERBS 4:23

We are familiar with [Satan's] evil schemes.
+ 2 CORINTHIANS 2:11

"Why are you sleeping?" he asked them. "Get up and pray, so that you will not give in to temptation."
+ LUKE 22:46

Stay alert! Watch out for your great enemy, the devil. He prowls around like a roaring lion, looking for someone to devour.
+ 1 PETER 5:8

MANY PEOPLE sleepwalk through life, oblivious to the continual spiritual battle over their souls. However, God's Word urges us to open our eyes, stay alert, and be awake to Satan's temptations. Do we know which sins most tempt us? Are we aware of when we are most vulnerable to Satan's attacks? If we get to know our weaknesses well enough, we can avoid situations where we are most vulnerable to sin. This will help us stand firm in our commitment to God *before* temptation comes knocking on the door of our hearts. But we also need to ask for help from the Holy Spirit and godly friends. Ask the Lord to help you be proactive in your battle for those places in your heart most vulnerable to the enemy's attacks.

Prayer Prompts

Lord, I am most tempted to sin when . . .
Your Word encourages me to stand firm in godliness by . . .

❀ tenderness

How can I develop a tender heart toward someone who has caused me pain?

———————— ❧ ————————

Lord, don't hold back your tender mercies from me.
Let your unfailing love and faithfulness always protect me.
+ PSALM 40:11

Is there any encouragement from belonging to Christ? Any comfort from his love?
Any fellowship together in the Spirit? Are your hearts tender and compassionate?
Then make me truly happy by agreeing wholeheartedly with each other, loving
one another, and working together with one mind and purpose.
+ PHILIPPIANS 2:1-2

The Lord is like a father to his children, tender and
compassionate to those who fear him.
+ PSALM 103:13

WOMEN ARE OFTEN thought to be the more nurturing gender, but that doesn't mean tenderness always comes naturally to us—especially when we are faced with the difficult task of reacting to those who have caused us pain. However, a tender heart begins with prayer. Sit with God and think about how he has shown you tenderness and compassion. When you realize the depth of God's care for you, you are better able to care for others. It may take time for your heart to change toward someone who has hurt you, but prayerfully put yourself in her position. What hardships has she faced in life? How might her own unmet needs impact the way she interacts with you? As you consider this person, ask God to change the stubbornness and hardness in your heart into kindness, compassion, and tenderness.

Prayer Prompts
Lord, my heart feels hardened toward this person: . . .
When tenderness feels impossible, your Word reminds me . . .

testing

Does God test the quality of my faith? How?

Remember how the LORD your God led you through the wilderness for these forty years, humbling you and testing you to prove your character, and to find out whether or not you would obey his commands.

+ DEUTERONOMY 8:2

[God said,] "Jeremiah, I have made you a tester of metals, that you may determine the quality of my people."

+ JEREMIAH 6:27

Dear brothers and sisters, when troubles of any kind come your way, consider it an opportunity for great joy. For you know that when your faith is tested, your endurance has a chance to grow. So let it grow, for when your endurance is fully developed, you will be perfect and complete, needing nothing.

+ JAMES 1:2-4

TESTING AND TEMPTATION are two different things. Satan uses temptation to lead us away from God and into sin. God uses testing to purify his people and move them toward maturity. Even though testing can be painful, it brings many benefits. On the other side of testing we'll find a more committed faith, a deeper wisdom, and a more intimate relationship with God. When your faith is being tested, thank God because that means he is preparing you to accomplish great things for him in the future.

Prayer Prompts

Lord, I wonder if you are testing my faith through . . .
When testing makes me feel discouraged, your Word reminds me that . . .

🍂 thankfulness

How do I develop a more thankful heart?

———————— ⚭ ————————

Thank God! He gives us victory over sin and death through our Lord Jesus Christ.
✛ 1 CORINTHIANS 15:57

*Since everything God created is good, we should not
reject any of it but receive it with thanks.*
✛ 1 TIMOTHY 4:4

*It is good to give thanks to the LORD, . . . to proclaim your
unfailing love in the morning, your faithfulness in the evening.*
✛ PSALM 92:1-2

*Be thankful in all circumstances,
for this is God's will for you who belong to Christ Jesus.*
✛ 1 THESSALONIANS 5:18

WE LIVE IN A WORLD filled with less-than-perfect days and unpredictable circumstances. We experience ups and downs and never know what's around the corner. However, choosing to be thankful has the power to lift us above our circumstances, change our perspective, and shape the way we see God and the world. Thankfulness keeps us connected to God, no matter what life has in store. If it's difficult for you to find things to be thankful for, make a mental list of God's blessings in your life—what he has done for you and what he offers to all people. Don't wait to feel thankful before giving thanks; giving thanks will lead you to feel more thankful. Gratitude has the power to transform your heart so you see all of life as a gift to enjoy instead of a burden to bear.

Prayer Prompts

Lord, I am thankful for . . .
Your Word also reminds me to thank you for . . .

thoughtfulness

I have trouble just keeping up with my own life. How can I become more thoughtful of others?

———————— �֎ ————————

Be humble, thinking of others as better than yourselves. Don't look out only for your own interests, but take an interest in others, too.
+ PHILIPPIANS 2:3-4

Let's not get tired of doing what is good. At just the right time we will reap a harvest of blessing if we don't give up. Therefore, whenever we have the opportunity, we should do good to everyone—especially to those in the family of faith.
+ GALATIANS 6:9-10

IT IS SO EASY to home in on our agenda each day and miss important moments around us. How do we change our focus so that we are more "others-minded"? Being thoughtful is about growing more considerate and being attentive to others' feelings and needs. Thoughtfulness, like listening, is a form of love. God's Word calls us to love others by looking for opportunities to do good for them. Sometimes thoughtfulness is as simple as a kind word, an insightful question, or even giving someone the benefit of the doubt. Other times, thoughtfulness requires us to meet a larger need. Either way, we must look for opportunities to love others instead of waiting for opportunities to present themselves to us. Today, ask God to help you notice the needs around you and then take the time to show love in a tangible way.

Prayer Prompts

Lord, one thoughtful way I can love someone in my life today is by . . .
Your Word reminds me of these blessings I receive when I practice thoughtfulness toward others: . . .

# thoughts

How do my thoughts affect my actions?

❧

It is what comes from inside that defiles you. For from within, out of a person's heart, come evil thoughts, sexual immorality, theft, murder, adultery, greed, wickedness, deceit, lustful desires, envy, slander, pride, and foolishness. All these vile things come from within; they are what defile you.
✦ MARK 7:20-23

Fix your thoughts on what is true, and honorable, and right, and pure, and lovely, and admirable. Think about things that are excellent and worthy of praise. . . . Then the God of peace will be with you.
✦ PHILIPPIANS 4:8-9

You will keep in perfect peace all who trust in you, all whose thoughts are fixed on you!
✦ ISAIAH 26:3

OUR THOUGHTS hold great power because they guide our emotions and influence our actions. When we allow our minds to rabbit-trail down paths of unhealthy and sinful thoughts, we suddenly find ourselves far away from the kinds of attitudes that God desires for us. But when we choose to think about things that are true, good, and honoring to God, we find it easier to love God and others. God's Word promises that when our thoughts are fixed on him, we will experience peace—and peace brings joy, contentment, and satisfaction. Sometimes we must fix and then re-fix our thoughts on him. But over time, with discipline and practice, our thoughts will naturally bend toward godliness instead of selfishness, which will transform our actions from the inside out.

Prayer Prompts

Lord, these untrue or sinful thoughts often come to mind: . . .
Your Word reminds me that I should think about . . .

time 🍃

I want to spend more time with God, but I'm too busy. How can I better manage my time?

———————— ❧ ————————

Teach us to realize the brevity of life, so that we may grow in wisdom.
+ PSALM 90:12

I rise early, before the sun is up; I cry out for help and put my hope in your words.
+ PSALM 119:147

IT IS EASY to fill our days, both with things that matter and things that don't. If we feel like we don't have time to spend with God, we might need a shift in perspective. Every person is given the same twenty-four hours in a day. The issue is really what we do with the time we have been given. Yes, we must work, sleep, take care of children, and uphold our responsibilities. And yet, spending time with God often feels less important than many other things in life. What if we viewed time with God not as an option but as a necessity? When we take time to sit with God in silence, to prayerfully read his Word and listen for his voice, it changes the way we live. We are able to see clearly which tasks are important and which ones we should let go. We are better able to love others because we have taken time to experience God's love for us. When something causes you to talk yourself out of spending time with God, remember that nothing is more important than being with your Creator.

Prayer Prompts

Lord, it's hard for me to find time with you because . . .
Your Word tells me that when I am with you, I will experience . . .

🍂 tiredness

What can I do when I'm tired but I have to keep going?

❧

I am your God. I will strengthen you and help you.
I will hold you up with my victorious right hand.
✝ ISAIAH 41:10

Jesus said, "Come to me, all of you who are weary
and carry heavy burdens, and I will give you rest."
✝ MATTHEW 11:28

He gives power to the weak and strength to the powerless. Even youths will
become weak and tired, and young men will fall in exhaustion. But those
who trust in the LORD will find new strength. They will soar high on wings
like eagles. They will run and not grow weary. They will walk and not faint.
✝ ISAIAH 40:29-31

FATIGUE IS A SIGN that our bodies and souls are in need of attention. Being overly tired keeps us from thinking clearly and operating at our best. We can use our weariness as a reminder that we need to rely on God's strength. When we come to him in praise, he refreshes our hearts. When we come to him in prayer, he refreshes our souls. When we come to him in solitude, he refreshes our bodies. When we come to him through his Word, he refreshes our minds. When we come to him with gratitude, he refreshes our perspective. Whenever you feel burned and unable to press on, lean into God in praise, in prayer, in solitude, through his Word, or in gratitude. He understands your limitations and is waiting to give you the strength you need to get through today.

Prayer Prompts
Lord, I am feeling exhausted because . . .
Your Word promises that when I come to you for rest, you will . . .

tithing

I know I should tithe, but I have so many other expenses. How important is tithing to God?

———— ❧ ————

You must set aside a tithe of your crops—
one-tenth of all the crops you harvest each year.
+ DEUTERONOMY 14:22

I can testify that they gave not only what they could afford,
but far more. And they did it of their own free will.
+ 2 CORINTHIANS 8:3

You must each decide in your heart how much to give.
And don't give reluctantly or in response to pressure.
"For God loves a person who gives cheerfully."
+ 2 CORINTHIANS 9:7

THE OLD TESTAMENT emphasizes the command to tithe (give one-tenth of our income to God's work), but the New Testament doesn't use the word "tithe" except in reference to the Old Testament command. Instead, the New Testament emphasizes generosity. Generosity goes beyond tithing and is meant to encourage God's people to give sacrificially. For some this may mean giving less than one-tenth of our income, but for most it means giving much more than that! Our giving is a means of supporting the work of God in our local church and around the world. When you give God the first part of your income rather than what is left over, you demonstrate that he is your top priority and that you are grateful for the blessings he has given you. Instead of asking, *How much of my money do I need to give to God?* ask yourself, *How much of God's money do I keep?*

Prayer Prompts

Lord, this is how I feel about tithing: . . .
Your Word encourages me to grow in my generosity because . . .

🍁 traditions

How do spiritual traditions energize my faith?

─────────── ❧ ───────────

This is a day to remember. Each year, from generation to generation,
*you must celebrate it as a special festival to the L*ORD*.*
+ EXODUS 12:14

Watch out! Be careful never to forget what you yourself have seen. Do not let
these memories escape from your mind as long as you live! And be sure to
pass them on to your children and grandchildren. . . . Then they will learn to
fear me as long as they live, and they will teach their children to fear me also.
+ DEUTERONOMY 4:9-10

Your faithfulness extends to every generation,
as enduring as the earth you created.
+ PSALM 119:90

TRADITIONS with spiritual significance can have a profound impact on our faith because they promote togetherness and revive our memories of God's faithfulness. It is easy to forget past times when God has answered a prayer or provided for us. But setting up traditions keeps the memories fresh in our minds and gives us strength and hope that God will keep doing in the future what he did for us in the past. The greatest inheritance we can provide for succeeding generations is a legacy of traditions that remind them of God's blessings and warnings. What spiritual blessings would you like to keep alive for future generations, whether your own children or other younger people around you? How can you create a tradition around this special memory? Ask God to help your family and friends come together regularly to celebrate what he has done for you.

Prayer Prompts

Lord, I want future generations to know about the time you . . .
Your Word encourages me to incorporate traditions into my faith because . . .

tragedy

How does God help me in times of tragedy?

————— ❧ —————

Lord, you know the hopes of the helpless.
Surely you will hear their cries and comfort them.
+ PSALM 10:17

It is impossible for God to lie. Therefore, we who have fled to him for
refuge can have great confidence as we hold to the hope that lies before us.
This hope is a strong and trustworthy anchor for our souls.
+ HEBREWS 6:18-19

I am counting on the Lord; yes, . . . I have put my hope in his word.
+ PSALM 130:5

I am trusting you, O Lord, saying, "You are my God!"
My future is in your hands. . . . How great is the goodness
you have stored up for those who fear you.
+ PSALM 31:14-15, 19

WHEN TRAGIC CIRCUMSTANCES come our way, only one
thing will always keep us going: hope. We hope that life will
not always be this difficult, that our circumstances will improve, that
we will receive comfort for our hurting hearts. God's Word is the
best source of hope; it's full of promises that give us the strength and
encouragement we need to keep going. God promises his unfailing
love, his constant presence, his comfort, and a glorious future with
him. Whatever tragedy has struck your life, trust that God sees you,
hears your cries, and promises hope for your future.

Prayer Prompts

Lord, this tragedy has broken my heart: . . .
Even so, I will hold on to this hope from your Word: . . .

🍃 transitions

How can I find security and peace during a major life transition?

— ❧ —

LORD, you remain the same forever!
Your throne continues from generation to generation.
+ LAMENTATIONS 5:19

I am the LORD, and I do not change.
+ MALACHI 3:6

Jesus Christ is the same yesterday, today, and forever. So do not be attracted by strange, new ideas. Your strength comes from God's grace.
+ HEBREWS 13:8-9

Heaven and earth will disappear, but my words will never disappear.
+ MARK 13:31

This is my command—be strong and courageous! Do not be afraid or discouraged. For the LORD your God is with you wherever you go.
+ JOSHUA 1:9

WE ALL LONG to live in a world we can control, where circumstances are predictable. But change is one of the great constants of life, and God often uses major transitions to do some of his best work in us. Transitions force us to let go of the familiar and rely on God's presence and promises. Instead of trusting in our ability to adapt to new circumstances, we can trust in God's promise to be with us always. Will you choose to trust him as you enter into new seasons and difficult transitions? Be strong and courageous in the face of change, because God promises to be with you wherever you go.

Prayer Prompts

Lord, I am struggling to adjust to this difficult transition: . . .
Nevertheless, I will hold on to this encouragement from your Word: . . .

trials 🍃

How can I allow trials to strengthen
my faith instead of damaging it?

---- ✍ ----

*These trials will show that your faith is genuine. It is being tested as
fire tests and purifies gold—though your faith is far more precious
than mere gold. So when your faith remains strong through many
trials, it will bring you much praise and glory and honor on the
day when Jesus Christ is revealed to the whole world.*

+ 1 PETER 1:7

*We know that God causes everything to work together for the good of
those who love God and are called according to his purpose for them.*

+ ROMANS 8:28

TRIALS HAVE A WAY of flipping our faith upside down. They
challenge our core beliefs about God, raising big life questions
like "Is God really good?" "Does he hear my prayers?" "Why does
he let bad things happen?" "Does he care?" How can we allow great
adversity to strengthen our faith instead of destroying it? Perhaps the
best way to respond is by meditating on God's promises in his Word.
They remind us who God is and how he has kept his promises to his
people over the ages. You may not understand why God has called
you to walk through a particular crisis, but he promises to work all
of it into something good. Remember that you will have to endure
these trials for only a little while, and then there will be an eternity of
wonderful joy ahead.

Prayer Prompts
Lord, a current trial that is straining my faith is . . .
I know I can emerge from this trial stronger because your Word says . . .

 # trouble

After I've prayed about the trouble I'm facing, then what?

❧

Do what is right and good in the LORD's sight, so all will go well with you.
+ DEUTERONOMY 6:18

The LORD has told you what is good, and this is what he requires of you: to do what is right, to love mercy, and to walk humbly with your God.
+ MICAH 6:8

Rejoice in our confident hope. Be patient in trouble, and keep on praying.
+ ROMANS 12:12

We also pray that you will be strengthened with all his glorious power so you will have all the endurance and patience you need.
+ COLOSSIANS 1:11

SOMETIMES WE PRAY to be rescued from a certain problem and God quickly answers. But more often, even after we pray, we must face the difficulty before us. When we are in a troubling time, we can walk forward boldly while standing firm in obedience. God's Word has told us what to do in difficult seasons: Do what is good and right, keep telling others about God's faithfulness, rejoice in the hope we have as believers, be patient throughout the trial, and never stop praying. God promises to give us the strength, endurance, and patience to make it through to the other side of the difficulties. When you are faithful and obedient, despite the trouble, you are becoming the kind of person God can use to impact your family, your community, and even the world.

Prayer Prompts

Lord, I want you to deliver me from these troubles: . . .
Even if you don't, your Word gives me guidance and encouragement that . . .

trusting God 🍃

I know I can trust God for my eternal future, but why is it so hard for me to trust him with today and tomorrow?

— ❧ —

The LORD is good, a strong refuge when trouble comes.
He is close to those who trust in him.
+ NAHUM 1:7

Trust in the LORD always, for the LORD GOD is the eternal Rock.
+ ISAIAH 26:4

Commit everything you do to the LORD. Trust him, and he will help you.
+ PSALM 37:5

O LORD of Heaven's Armies, what joy for those who trust in you.
+ PSALM 84:12

JESUS TELLS HIS FOLLOWERS not to be anxious, yet so many of us spend our lives fretting over circumstances we cannot control. Trusting God begins when we choose to believe he is loving and good, and that he only wants good things for us. When we dwell on problems, give in to worry, or try to control the future, we are choosing not to trust that God is looking out for our best interests. Trusting God is not only a moment-by-moment decision but also a lifelong discipline. Whenever you notice anxious thoughts starting to form about tomorrow, stop and tell God your worries and fears. Fill your thoughts with his Word and choose to believe that he has everything under control. He promises great things, both for right now and for your eternal future.

Prayer Prompts
Lord, tomorrow has me worried about . . .
Your Word promises that those who trust you . . .

🍂 trustworthiness

How can I become more trustworthy?

───────── ❧ ─────────

*I know, my God, that you examine our hearts
and rejoice when you find integrity there.*
+ 1 CHRONICLES 29:17

*A gossip goes around telling secrets,
but those who are trustworthy can keep a confidence.*
+ PROVERBS 11:13

*Trustworthy messengers refresh like snow in summer.
They revive the spirit of their employer.*
+ PROVERBS 25:13

*Teach me your ways, O LORD, that I may live according to your truth!
Grant me purity of heart, so that I may honor you.*
+ PSALM 86:11

PEOPLE WHO CONSISTENTLY tell the truth are trustworthy
and can be counted on to do what they promise. Do you long
to be known as trustworthy? If so, there is one perfect role model
you can follow—the one who created truth and set the principles
of moral law in motion. Truth is not just a character trait of God; it
is the essence of who he is. Therefore, God cannot lie or go back on
a promise he's made. As his followers, we need to echo his example.
When we are women of our word, those around us will notice our
integrity and be drawn to the Lord. If you struggle in this area, ask
God to transform your heart and teach you how to become trustworthy like him in every way.

Prayer Prompts

Lord, sometimes it is hard for me to be trustworthy in this area: . . .
Your Word declares your trustworthiness this way: . . .

341

turning to God

What can I do when I feel helpless?

———— ✧ ————

Asa cried out to the LORD his God, "O LORD, no one but
you can help the powerless against the mighty! Help us,
O LORD our God, for we trust in you alone."
+ 2 CHRONICLES 14:11

The LORD is my strength and shield. I trust him with all my heart.
He helps me, and my heart is filled with joy. I burst out in songs of thanksgiving.
+ PSALM 28:7

I look up to the mountains—does my help come from there?
My help comes from the LORD, who made heaven and earth!
+ PSALM 121:1-2

Don't worry about anything; instead, pray about everything.
+ PHILIPPIANS 4:6

WHEN WE FEEL LIKE there is nothing we can do, we are in the perfect place to learn that there is only one thing left to do—turn to God and pray. Sometimes we exhaust all our options before we remember to talk to God, but that's where we should start. Pray that God would help you look at the situation from his perspective. Pray that he would show you how you have blinded yourself to the many ways in which he is already helping you. If you insist on trying to get yourself out of trouble, you will never see what God can do. When you turn to God, trusting him to help you, you open the lifeline to the one who loves doing the impossible!

Prayer Prompts

Lord, I feel helpless in this situation: . . .
Your Word reminds me that I have this hope because . . .

# uncomfortable situations

Why is it good to put myself in uncomfortable situations?

———————————— ❧ ————————————

Jesus . . . watched the rich people dropping their gifts in the collection box. Then a poor widow came by and dropped in two small coins. "I tell you the truth," Jesus said, "this poor widow has given more than all the rest of them. For they have given a tiny part of their surplus, but she, poor as she is, has given everything she has."
+ LUKE 21:1-4

When the teachers of religious law who were Pharisees saw [Jesus] eating with tax collectors and other sinners, they asked his disciples, "Why does he eat with such scum?" When Jesus heard this, he told them, "Healthy people don't need a doctor—sick people do. I have come to call not those who think they are righteous, but those who know they are sinners."
+ MARK 2:16-17

JESUS OFTEN put himself in situations many would find uncomfortable. He ate with despised sinners and had conversations with immoral women. He even praised those who, like the poor widow, made themselves uncomfortable in order to help others. The truth is, the Christian life was never meant to be comfortable. We are called to take risks in the name of Jesus, in order to bless others and point them to him. Perhaps that means beginning a friendship with someone who is different from you. Maybe it's giving more than you budgeted for. Each time you step into the discomfort, you learn to trust God a little bit more—perhaps because you *need* to trust him. What risk might God be calling you to take?

Prayer Prompts

Lord, I want to trust you with this uncomfortable situation: . . .
Your Word encourages me to step out of my comfort zone and . . .

unforgivable sin

Is there any sin God will not forgive?

———— ❧ ————

Every sin and blasphemy can be forgiven—except blasphemy
against the Holy Spirit, which will never be forgiven.
+ MATTHEW 12:31

The king will do as he pleases, exalting himself
and claiming to be greater than every god,
even blaspheming the God of gods.
+ DANIEL 11:36

JESUS PROMISES to forgive all our sins, and yet the Bible says
blasphemy against the Holy Spirit cannot be forgiven. Why is
this the only unforgivable sin? When we reject the Holy Spirit, we
reject the only one who can bring us to God so that our sins can be
forgiven. And without forgiveness of sins, there is no salvation and
eternal life. It's not that God won't forgive us; it's that if we blaspheme
the Holy Spirit, we won't put ourselves in a position to be forgiven.
If we repent of our sins, God offers forgiveness for *all* of them. We
have only to ask. Blasphemy against the Holy Spirit is refusing to ask.
The thought of an unforgivable sin can often make Christians feel
uneasy. However, if you have accepted Jesus as your personal Savior,
then be assured that you are completely forgiven.

Prayer Prompts

Lord, when I think about all you have forgiven me for, I feel . . .
When I feel afraid of not being forgiven, your Word reminds me . . .

 # unhappiness

Why am I often discontent when I have so much?

❧

Don't love money; be satisfied with what you have.
For God has said, "I will never fail you. I will never abandon you."
+ HEBREWS 13:5

True godliness with contentment is itself great wealth. After all, we brought
nothing with us when we came into the world, and we can't take anything with
us when we leave it. So if we have enough food and clothing, let us be content.
+ 1 TIMOTHY 6:6-8

Even though the fig trees have no blossoms, and there are no grapes
on the vines; even though the olive crop fails, and the fields lie empty
and barren; even though the flocks die in the fields, and the cattle
barns are empty, yet I will rejoice in the LORD! I will be joyful in the
God of my salvation! The Sovereign LORD is my strength! He makes
me as surefooted as a deer, able to tread upon the heights.
+ HABAKKUK 3:17-19

UNHAPPINESS SNEAKS into our lives for a variety of reasons. Sometimes present troubles overshadow the ways God has blessed us in the past. Conversely, sometimes dwelling in the past causes us to miss out on the blessings of today. Being unhappy or discontent can also come when we confuse wants with needs or when we compare ourselves and our possessions with others. In any case, choosing unhappiness robs us of the joys in life and in our relationships. To live a happy life and protect yourself from discontentment, keep your focus on God's blessings, discipline your mind to find the good in every situation, and be thankful.

Prayer Prompts

Lord, sometimes I am tempted to believe that I would be happy if only I had . . .
Your Word encourages me to be content with what I have because . . .

unity

How can I find unity with others who are so different from me?

— ❧ —

Make every effort to keep yourselves united in the Spirit, binding yourselves together with peace.
+ EPHESIANS 4:3

You are all children of God through faith in Christ Jesus. And all who have been united with Christ in baptism have put on Christ, like putting on new clothes. There is no longer Jew or Gentile, slave or free, male and female. For you are all one in Christ Jesus.
+ GALATIANS 3:26-28

Just as our bodies have many parts and each part has a special function, so it is with Christ's body. We are many parts of one body, and we all belong to each other.
+ ROMANS 12:4-5

UNITY IS NOT about everyone agreeing. It's about learning how to take different opinions and direct them all toward a shared purpose and goal. God creates everyone differently; therefore we should expect differences of opinion. However, differences can be positive, such as the various parts making up Christ's body. Unity usually becomes difficult to achieve when we're already convinced that our opinion is the best. This mind-set keeps us from listening to new ideas that might actually inform our opinions for the better. Ask God to help you be open to others' opinions so that you don't miss out on the rich blessing of diversity.

Prayer Prompts

Lord, I find it difficult to feel unity with . . .
Your Word says unity in diversity is important because . . .

🍁 unplugging

What is the spiritual danger of constantly being connected to technology?

— ❦ —

Jesus often withdrew to the wilderness for prayer.
+ LUKE 5:16

Now, dear brothers and sisters, one final thing. Fix your thoughts on what is true, and honorable, and right, and pure, and lovely, and admirable. Think about things that are excellent and worthy of praise.
+ PHILIPPIANS 4:8

Be careful how you live. Don't live like fools, but like those who are wise. Make the most of every opportunity in these evil days.
+ EPHESIANS 5:15-16

JESUS OFTEN WITHDREW from crowds and busyness in order to be with his Father. If Jesus thought it essential to unplug, metaphorically speaking, how much more intentional ought we to be about unplugging in an age of mass communication and technology? We live with constant interruptions, and as a result, we have become distracted. We're poor listeners, and we've lost our ability to connect deeply with others. Take time to assess your technology use and the way it impacts your relationships. How can you detach from routine distractions, especially technology, in order to be fully present with God and others? Unplugging takes effort and intentionality, but is important for spiritual growth. God understands you may feel uncomfortable letting go of being "connected." But trust that the most important use of your time is to be connected to him—your ultimate source of power.

Prayer Prompts

Lord, when I think about unplugging from technology, I feel . . .
Your Word says that staying connected to you is most important because . . .

values 🌿

How can I maintain godly values in today's world?

— �֍ —

*No one can serve two masters. For you will hate one and love
the other; you will be devoted to one and despise the other.
You cannot serve God and be enslaved to money.*
+ MATTHEW 6:24

Wherever your treasure is, there the desires of your heart will also be.
+ LUKE 12:34

Guard your heart above all else, for it determines the course of your life.
+ PROVERBS 4:23

EVERYONE HAS VALUES, good or bad, and our actions show what
they are. John Ortberg states, "We will always take the most care
of that which we value most deeply." Check your heart by asking yourself, *How do I spend most of my free time? Where do I spend my
money? What is consuming my thoughts? What is the first thing
I think of when I wake up or the last thing I think about before I
go to bed?* Your answers to these questions will show what you value
most. God knows the world is vying for your attention, and that is why
he calls you to guard the affections of your heart so closely. If you find
your values slowly shifting away, ask God to reorient your heart back
to him. Move closer to God by spending a little more time with him
today, choosing to obey him down to the smallest decisions. Strive to
love and serve others. Over time, you will notice your values change to
better reflect the character of God.

Prayer Prompts

Lord, these worldly values are consuming my thoughts today: . . .
Your Word encourages me to value above all else . . .

vanity

How can I recognize vanity in my own life?

❧

Charm is deceptive, and beauty does not last;
but a woman who fears the LORD will be greatly praised.
+ PROVERBS 31:30

People judge by outward appearance, but the LORD looks at the heart.
+ 1 SAMUEL 16:7

Don't be concerned about the outward beauty of fancy hairstyles,
expensive jewelry, or beautiful clothes. You should clothe yourselves
instead with the beauty that comes from within, the unfading beauty
of a gentle and quiet spirit, which is so precious to God.
+ 1 PETER 3:3-4

WE LIVE IN A CULTURE that places great importance on
beauty and outward appearance. We post photos on social
media in the hope that others will view us as flawless, fashionable
women who have it all together. But God sees through our appearance and deep into our hearts. He knows that behind every woman's
façade and apparent vanity is a little girl who feels insecure and
lonely and longs to be genuinely known and loved. Do you relate to
any of these feelings? What might it feel like to live in the truth that
the one who created you loves you fully and unconditionally? God
is able to heal every insecurity and satisfy every longing. Start by
talking to him about where you notice vanity in your life. Ask him
to show you what your heart truly longs for when you strive to be
beautiful. And trust that he is able to make you into a praiseworthy
woman—not because of how you look but because of who you are.

Prayer Prompts

Lord, these are a few ways I notice vanity in my life: . . .
When I feel insecure, your Word reminds me that . . .

victory 🍂

What are some victories I can achieve day by day?

———————————— ❧ ————————————

Study this Book of Instruction continually. Meditate on it
day and night so you will be sure to obey everything written in it.
Only then will you prosper and succeed in all you do.
+ JOSHUA 1:8

Abraham never wavered in believing God's promise.
In fact, his faith grew stronger, and in this he brought glory to God.
+ ROMANS 4:20

I have discovered this principle of life—that when I want to do what is right,
I inevitably do what is wrong. . . . Oh, what a miserable person I am!
Who will free me from this life that is dominated by sin and death?
Thank God! The answer is in Jesus Christ our Lord.
+ ROMANS 7:21, 24-25

Victory comes from you, O LORD.
+ PSALM 3:8

W E OFTEN BELIEVE that to be victorious, we must do something big. But the truth is, victory begins by obeying God in the little things: what we say, what we look at, how we react to others, what we think about, and whether or not we tell the truth. It takes discipline to obey God each day as we face many small battles and temptations. The more little battles we win, the stronger our faith will be. But it is only through Christ's power that anyone can have victory over sin, evil, and death. So take it one day at a time. Today's victory is all you need for today. Remember that God is a mighty warrior who will never stop fighting for those he loves.

Prayer Prompts

Lord, with your help, today I long to achieve victory over . . .
Your Word reminds me that my victory comes from . . .

 # vision

How can I align my vision with God's plan for me? Why is it important for me to seek God's vision for the future?

—— ❧ ——

"My thoughts are nothing like your thoughts," says the LORD. "And my ways are far beyond anything you could imagine. For just as the heavens are higher than the earth, so my ways are higher than your ways and my thoughts higher than your thoughts."
+ ISAIAH 55:8-9

Jesus replied, . . . "Those who walk in the darkness cannot see where they are going. Put your trust in the light while there is still time; then you will become children of the light."
+ JOHN 12:35-36

The most important commandment is this: . . . "You must love the LORD your God with all your heart, all your soul, all your mind, and all your strength."
+ MARK 12:29-30

IT HAS BEEN SAID that "vision is a picture of the future that produces a passion in the present." Lack of vision is like trying to see underwater without a mask—everything is blurry, nothing makes sense, and we can feel impossibly lost. If we want to see our life's direction more clearly, we need a goal to know where we are headed. Think about the kind of person God wants you to be ten, twenty, or thirty years from now. What character traits do you want to possess? How can you take steps toward God's vision for your future today? Ask him to give you an eternal perspective as you envision your future, and trust him to help you navigate toward it with purpose and clarity.

Prayer Prompts

Lord, when I think about my future, I envision . . .
Your Word gives me this vision for my future: . . .

voice of God 🍃

How can I know if I am really hearing God's voice?

— ❧ —

Be careful how you live. Don't live like fools, but like those who are wise.
Make the most of every opportunity in these evil days. Don't act thoughtlessly,
but understand what the Lord wants you to do.
+ EPHESIANS 5:15-17

Don't copy the behavior and customs of this world, but let God transform
you into a new person by changing the way you think. Then you will learn
to know God's will for you, which is good and pleasing and perfect.
+ ROMANS 12:2

My sheep listen to my voice; I know them, and they follow me.
+ JOHN 10:27

When the Father sends the Advocate as my representative—
that is, the Holy Spirit—he will teach you everything and
will remind you of everything I have told you.
+ JOHN 14:26

IT TAKES TIME to recognize God's voice. There are no shortcuts to this. We become familiar with God's voice only through spending time with him. When we need guidance, we can open God's Word and talk to him about what is going on in our lives. We can ask him what he wants us to do, and then we need to be still and listen! We may feel as though nothing is happening during the silence, but we can trust that his Holy Spirit is working. Over time, God will transform us into new people who can read the Word through new eyes and hear his voice with new ears. Remember, God loves spending time with you and delights in your effort to know his voice better.

Prayer Prompts

Lord, I want to hear you speak to me about . . .
Your Word assures me you will speak this way: . . .

🌿 vulnerability

How can being vulnerable help me experience God?

— ❧ —

*Search me, O God, and know my heart; test me and know my
anxious thoughts. Point out anything in me that offends you,
and lead me along the path of everlasting life.*
+ PSALM 139:23-24

You spread out our sins before you—our secret sins—and you see them all.
+ PSALM 90:8

Confess your sins to each other and pray for each other.
+ JAMES 5:16

*There is no condemnation for those who belong to Christ Jesus.
And because you belong to him, the power of the life-giving Spirit
has freed you from the power of sin that leads to death.*
+ ROMANS 8:1-2

VULNERABILITY is being completely transparent with another person. It means revealing your real self: your deepest fears, hurts, sins, or doubts. Every human being has a need for that kind of intimacy, but often our fears of rejection hold us back. We naturally resist being vulnerable with God about our sins, especially the ones we don't want to give up. However, it is only through being vulnerable that we find true healing, restoration, renewal, and forgiveness. When you open your heart to God, admit your sin, and ask for forgiveness, your relationship with God is deepened. His mercy frees you from the burdens of your sin and releases you from a life of regret and guilt. You have nothing to fear and nothing to hide because God has promised there is no condemnation for those who belong to him.

Prayer Prompts

Lord, it is hard for me to talk with you about . . .
Your Word encourages me toward vulnerability because . . .

waiting

What does waiting well look like?

———— ❧ ————

Be still in the presence of the LORD, and wait patiently for him to act.
+ PSALM 37:7

As for me, I look to the LORD for help.
I wait confidently for God to save me, and my God will certainly hear me.
+ MICAH 7:7

Those who trust in the LORD will find new strength.
They will soar high on wings like eagles. They will run
and not grow weary. They will walk and not faint.
+ ISAIAH 40:31

The LORD must wait for you to come to him so he can show
you his love and compassion. For the LORD is a faithful God.
Blessed are those who wait for his help.
+ ISAIAH 30:18

WAITING is about being still and watching, allowing God to unfold matters in his timing. We desire quick fixes for our problems, but often God works differently. Sometimes he doesn't answer our prayer right away because real growth develops in the waiting and the watching. When we wait, we are continually confronted with the choice to either despair or trust. The Bible promises that those who choose to trust during times of waiting will be blessed with strength, hope, and confidence. What prayer are you still waiting for God to answer? Read his Word and be encouraged. He is doing great things in your heart as you wait for him to act.

Prayer Prompts

Lord, I am still waiting for . . .
Your Word encourages me to wait well by . . .

 # weakness

Why is God allowing me to go through a season of weakness?

—— ❧ ——

God blesses those who are poor and realize their need for him,
for the Kingdom of Heaven is theirs.
+ MATTHEW 5:3

The LORD is my strength and shield. I trust him with all my heart. He helps
me, and my heart is filled with joy. I burst out in songs of thanksgiving.
+ PSALM 28:7

I take pleasure in my weaknesses, and in the insults, hardships, persecutions,
and troubles that I suffer for Christ. For when I am weak, then I am strong.
+ 2 CORINTHIANS 12:10

HAVE YOU EVER wondered why God's Word says that the poor are indeed blessed? Perhaps it is because poverty—or any kind of weakness—forces us to depend on him. Sometimes God leads us into a season of weakness so that his power can be greatly displayed. He may put us in a situation where we will witness how he does the impossible. If we focus on trying to get ourselves out of trouble, we will never see what he can do. The struggle happens when we doubt he really can help us. One way to trust him with your future is to rec-ollect how he has helped you in the past. Pour out your heart to God, ask him for help, and trust that he will do it! God will either provide a way out of your situation or give you the perseverance to stay strong. Wait quietly and patiently for God to work. You'll discover that he always comes through.

Prayer Prompts

Lord, I am in a position where I need to trust you with . . .
Your Word assures me that . . .

wealth

Is it okay to be a wealthy Christian?

———————— ❦ ————————

When someone has been given much, much will be required in return; and
when someone has been entrusted with much, even more will be required.
+ LUKE 12:48

God will generously provide all you need. Then you will always have
everything you need and plenty left over to share with others.
+ 2 CORINTHIANS 9:8

The master was full of praise. "Well done, my good and faithful
servant. You have been faithful in handling this small amount,
so now I will give you many more responsibilities."
+ MATTHEW 25:21

Honor the Lord with your wealth and
with the best part of everything you produce.
+ PROVERBS 3:9

THE BIBLE MENTIONS many wealthy people who loved God (such as Abraham, David, Joseph of Arimathea, and Lydia) while saying nothing negative about the *amount* of wealth they had. Scripture doesn't focus on how much money we have, but rather on what we do with it. Those who have been given much wealth in this world have greater responsibility and higher standards for sharing with others and taking care of the poor. Jesus made one thing clear: Wherever our money goes, our hearts will follow after it. So work hard and succeed without guilt, but make sure to work just as hard at finding ways to please God with your money. Keep an eternal perspective so your master will say, "Well done, my good and faithful servant."

Prayer Prompts

Lord, you have entrusted me with . . .
Your Word tells me I am to be a good steward by . . .

# welcoming

How can I welcome others into my home and make it a place where they want to be?

— ❧ —

As soon as Laban heard that his nephew Jacob had arrived, he ran out to meet him. He embraced and kissed him and brought him home.
+ GENESIS 29:13

Do to others whatever you would like them to do to you.
+ MATTHEW 7:12

Cheerfully share your home with those who need a meal or a place to stay. God has given each of you a gift from his great variety of spiritual gifts. Use them well to serve one another.
+ 1 PETER 4:9-10

The LORD . . . blesses the home of the upright.
+ PROVERBS 3:33

THE WELCOME MATS by our front doors are more than a symbol of entry; they are a transition from outside to inside, from stranger to friend. When people enter our homes, we should do all we can to make them feel welcome and wanted. We can greet them warmly and focus on their needs. Are they hungry or thirsty? Do they need a listening ear or a sympathetic heart? Maybe they've come for encouragement or friendship. Our decorating, menu, and level of tidiness are not as important as our presence with our guests. Good hospitality is a foretaste of the ultimate hospitality: God warmly welcoming us into his heavenly home. Your hospitality may be the way in which another person comes to understand and accept God's invitation to join him in his eternal home—heaven.

Prayer Prompts

Lord, I pray for the people who will come into my home this week: . . .
Your Word reminds me how to love them when they arrive: . . .

wickedness 🍃

How should I respond when I see wicked people prospering?

———————— ❧ ————————

I tried to understand why the wicked prosper. But what a difficult task it is! Then I went into your sanctuary, O God, and I finally understood the destiny of the wicked. . . . In an instant they are destroyed. . . . But as for me, how good it is to be near God!
+ PSALM 73:16-17, 19, 28

The LORD watches over the path of the godly, but the path of the wicked leads to destruction.
+ PSALM 1:6

The eyes of the LORD watch over those who do right; his ears are open to their cries for help. But the LORD turns his face against those who do evil; he will erase their memory from the earth.
+ PSALM 34:15-16

The LORD has told you what is good, and this is what he requires of you: to do what is right, to love mercy, and to walk humbly with your God.
+ MICAH 6:8

WHY DO THE RIGHTEOUS sometimes suffer while those who consistently do wrong prosper? As difficult as this is to understand, the Lord isn't silent. He tells us the ultimate destiny of the wicked: He will turn his face against them and erase them from memory. In contrast, God promises to be faithful to the godly. When you find yourself discouraged by seeing those who do wrong succeed in this world, turn your focus back to God. He holds their fate in his hands. For now, do what is right, love mercy, and walk humbly with your God.

Prayer Prompts

*Lord, when I see people prosper even though they don't follow you, I feel . . .
Your Word assures me that . . .*

 # will of God

How can I discover God's will for my life?

❧

Seek his will in all you do, and he will show you which path to take.
+ PROVERBS 3:6

The LORD leads with unfailing love and faithfulness all who keep his covenant and obey his demands.
+ PSALM 25:10

My child, listen to what I say. . . . Then you will understand what is right, just, and fair, and you will find the right way to go.
+ PROVERBS 2:1, 9

ANYONE WHO BELIEVES in God has probably asked, "What is God's will for my life?" Sometimes "God's will" seems so vague; however, God has already revealed his general will for all believers in his Word. The Bible has dozens of clear commands for us to follow: worship God only, love our neighbors and our enemies, tell the truth, do not covet, do not steal, be sexually pure, remain faithful, teach our children spiritual truths, don't gossip, don't use God's name disrespectfully, read his Word regularly, don't let money control us, let the Holy Spirit control our lives. In addition to God's general will, he also created each person for a specific purpose, and he calls us to certain tasks. It is usually through steady obedience to his general will that we find specific direction for our lives. At the end of your life, it won't matter what job you had or where you lived. The only thing that will truly matter is whether you have been faithful to God and lived a full life of loving him and others.

Prayer Prompts

Lord, one way I can better follow your general will for my life is by . . .
If I follow your commands, your Word promises me that . . .

wisdom 🌿

How can I learn to be wise?

—————— ✂ ——————

Fear of the LORD is the foundation of true wisdom.
All who obey his commandments will grow in wisdom.
+ PSALM 111:10

If you need wisdom, ask our generous God, and he will give it to you.
+ JAMES 1:5

Your laws please me; they give me wise advice.
+ PSALM 119:24

Anyone who listens to my teaching and follows it is wise,
like a person who builds a house on solid rock.
+ MATTHEW 7:24

Come and listen to my counsel.
I'll share my heart with you and make you wise.
+ PROVERBS 1:23

As WOMEN, we all have areas in our lives that we long to know how to handle wisely. Maybe we need wisdom in a situation at work, we need help with a certain relationship, or we want to know how to raise godly children. God promises he is faithful to give wisdom to those who ask. When you go to God with your issue, ask yourself this: *Am I in his Word regularly? Do I take time to listen to him when I pray? Am I actively fighting against sin in my life?* If you can answer yes to these questions, you are on the path to wisdom. Spend time with God, reflect on his Word, and allow him to teach you his ways.

Prayer Prompts

Lord, I need wisdom on how to handle this situation: . . .
Your Word encourages me to gain wisdom by . . .

witnessing

How do I witness to others when I don't have a very exciting testimony?

❧

Has the Lord redeemed you? Then speak out!
Tell others he has redeemed you from your enemies.
+ PSALM 107:2

[Jesus] told them, "Go into all the world and
preach the Good News to everyone."
+ MARK 16:15

How beautiful are the feet of messengers who bring good news!
+ ROMANS 10:15

God has not given us a spirit of fear and timidity, but of power, love, and
self-discipline. So never be ashamed to tell others about our Lord.
+ 2 TIMOTHY 1:7-8

Those who are wise will shine as bright as the sky, and those who lead
many to righteousness will shine like the stars forever.
+ DANIEL 12:3

TO WITNESS SIMPLY MEANS to tell others about something we have experienced. Our stories of how we met and grew to love Jesus are the greatest stories we could ever tell. And the best way Satan can keep others from hearing about Jesus is by convincing believers their stories aren't worth telling. Take time to think about the wonderful things God has done in your life. Did he rescue you from something? Give you an incredible gift? Put someone in your life at just the right time? Allow you to feel his loving presence? Ask God to help you learn how to better articulate your own story, and grow in courage to tell it.

Prayer Prompts

Lord, I feel like my story is . . .
Your Word encourages me to witness because . . .

women 🍂

What can I learn about Jesus from the way he interacted with women?

——————— ❦ ———————

Jesus began a tour of the nearby towns and villages, preaching and announcing the Good News about the Kingdom of God. He took his twelve disciples with him, along with some women who had been cured of evil spirits and diseases. Among them were Mary Magdalene, from whom he had cast out seven demons; Joanna, the wife of Chuza, Herod's business manager; Susanna; and many others who were contributing from their own resources to support Jesus and his disciples.
+ LUKE 8:1-3

Jesus stood up again and said to the woman, "Where are your accusers? Didn't even one of them condemn you?" "No, Lord," she said. And Jesus said, "Neither do I. Go and sin no more."
+ JOHN 8:10-11

IN FIRST-CENTURY JEWISH CULTURE, women were treated as second-class citizens. They were not permitted to be educated or to take part in public worship. The Bible is careful to emphasize that Jesus ministered to women in all levels of society, as seen from the list of women in Luke 8. The mention of Joanna, the wife of King Herod's business manager, reminds us that Jesus' influence reached far and wide, high and low. When the disciples deserted Jesus at his crucifixion, the women remained with him and ministered to him. Jesus valued women in every way. If you ever feel that being female excludes you from playing a major role in God's plan, remember these women from God's Word.

Prayer Prompts

Lord, sometimes I fear that being a woman hinders me from . . .
Your Word shows that you love, care for, and include women by . . .

 # words

How powerful are the words I speak?

——————— ❧ ———————

Let everything you say be good and helpful, so
that your words will be an encouragement to those who hear them.
+ EPHESIANS 4:29

Take control of what I say, O LORD, and guard my lips.
+ PSALM 141:3

If you claim to be religious but don't control your tongue,
you are fooling yourself, and your religion is worthless.
+ JAMES 1:26

I tell you this, you must give an account on judgment day for every idle
word you speak. The words you say will either acquit you or condemn you.
+ MATTHEW 12:36-37

OUR WORDS ARE GIFTS we can give to God and others. Even though our tongues are small, they hold incredible power. They can be used to praise God and bless others, but if they are not controlled, they can set our whole lives on fire (James 3:5-6). If we have a tendency to complain, gossip, use profanity, or criticize others, then perhaps God desires to help us change how we use our words. We can change our speech by becoming aware of what comes out of our mouths and then, with the power of the Holy Spirit, changing destructive words into those that are gracious, thankful, encouraging, loving, truthful, and a blessing to others. What kind of impact do you want your words to have on others? If your mouth continually causes you to make mistakes, remember God's grace. Learning to bless others with our words takes a lifetime, and it's something we continually need God's help with.

Prayer Prompts

Lord, please help me change this part of my speech: . . .
Your Word says my words are important because . . .

work

How can I glorify God in a job that feels unfulfilling?

———— ❧ ————

Whatever you do, do it all for the glory of God.
+ 1 CORINTHIANS 10:31

Never be lazy, but work hard and serve the Lord enthusiastically.
+ ROMANS 12:11

Work willingly at whatever you do, as though you were working for the Lord rather than for people. Remember that the Lord will give you an inheritance as your reward.
+ COLOSSIANS 3:23-24

God is not unjust. He will not forget how hard you have worked for him and how you have shown your love to him by caring for other believers.
+ HEBREWS 6:10

WORK IS GOD'S DESIGN for our lives, and how we do it matters to God. However, we all go through seasons when our work feels dull, frustrating, and even meaningless. Whether we work in the corporate world or at home, what we do has value to God. He searches for those who work with perseverance, courage, and enthusiasm. If your work feels unfulfilling, ask God to change your attitude as you reflect on his promises. Look for opportunities each day to serve God and others. God promises that when you work with this perspective, he will reward you. Take heart in the truth that nothing you do for the Lord is ever meaningless.

Prayer Prompts

Lord, this is how I feel about my work: . . .
Your Word encourages me to have a perspective of . . .

 worry

What can help when worry overwhelms me?

———— ✦ ————

[Jesus said,] "Here on earth you will have many trials and sorrows.
But take heart, because I have overcome the world."
+ JOHN 16:33

The LORD keeps watch over you as you come and go, both now and forever.
+ PSALM 121:8

Don't worry about these things, saying, "What will we eat? What will
we drink? What will we wear?" These things dominate the thoughts of
unbelievers, but your heavenly Father already knows all your needs.
Seek the Kingdom of God above all else, and live righteously, and
he will give you everything you need.
+ MATTHEW 6:31-33

He will feed his flock like a shepherd. He will carry
the lambs in his arms, holding them close to his heart.
He will gently lead the mother sheep with their young.
+ ISAIAH 40:11

WORRYING DOESN'T make a problem go away, nor does it prepare us to deal with it. The only thing worry does is consume us—our time, energy, faith, and trust in God. What worries weigh on your heart today? If Jesus were right beside you, what do you think he would say about your worries? When we feel consumed by worry, we can make a conscious effort to turn those thoughts into prayer. God assures us in his Word that he will care for us, lead us, and give us everything we need. Tell him what burdens you today and then release it into his control.

Prayer Prompts

Lord, some worries on my heart today are . . .
Your Word reminds me there is no need to worry because . . .

worship

Why is worshiping God important?

————— ❧ —————

Oh, how great are God's riches and wisdom and knowledge! How impossible it is for us to understand his decisions and his ways! For who can know the LORD's thoughts? Who knows enough to give him advice? And who has given him so much that he needs to pay it back? For everything comes from him and exists by his power and is intended for his glory. All glory to him forever! Amen.

+ ROMANS 11:33-36

Come, let us worship and bow down. Let us kneel before the LORD our maker, for he is our God. We are the people he watches over, the flock under his care.

+ PSALM 95:6-7

You are worthy, O Lord our God, to receive glory and honor and power. For you created all things, and they exist because you created what you pleased.

+ REVELATION 4:11

HAVE YOU EVER experienced incredible joy yet still felt like there was something missing? Maybe it was a beautiful sunset, your child's first belly laugh, or the wedding of a close friend. All of these events call for a response from us. Our joy in something is made complete only when we give praise and glory to the one who gave it to us. This is worship. Dallas Willard writes in *The Spirit of the Disciplines*, "In worship we engage ourselves with, dwell upon, and express the greatness, beauty, and goodness of God." We can do this anytime and anywhere. Take time to reflect on God's beauty in the world and his goodness in your life, and respond to him with worship.

Prayer Prompts

Lord, one way I recognize your beauty and goodness in my life is . . .
Your Word gives me these words to worship you: . . .

❧ worthiness

How am I worthy to be a follower of God?

———————————— ❧ ————————————

There is no condemnation for those who belong to Christ Jesus. And because you belong to him, the power of the life-giving Spirit has freed you from the power of sin that leads to death. The law of Moses was unable to save us because of the weakness of our sinful nature. So God did what the law could not do. He sent his own Son in a body like the bodies we sinners have. And in that body God declared an end to sin's control over us by giving his Son as a sacrifice for our sins.
+ ROMANS 8:1-3

MOST OF US STRUGGLE to see ourselves with twenty-twenty vision. Either we fail to see our faults, or we fail to see our value. God loves us for who we are, not for what we do. God loved us before we made our first mistakes, before we uttered our first words, and even before we took our first breaths. His love for us is an eternal thread woven throughout our lives and fortified through the life, death, and resurrection of Jesus. It's easy to get so caught up in the experience of serving God that we lose sight of the greatest privilege of all—knowing God and being known by him. Our names are registered as citizens of heaven, which means we belong, without question, to the eternal Kingdom of God. Nothing we do on earth can compare with that privilege or joy. Don't get caught in the trap of basing your identity or self-worth on your performance. Rejoice that God's unconditional love makes you worthy.

Prayer Prompts

Lord, sometimes I believe you'll love me more if . . .
Your Word says I am already loved because . . .